SOUTHEAST ASIA
1945

AUSTRALIA AND THE VIETNAM WAR

PETER EDWARDS is the Official Historian and general editor of the nine-volume *Official History of Australia's Involvement in Southeast Asian Conflicts 1948–1975*. He is also the author of the volumes dealing with politics, strategy and diplomacy, *Crises and Commitments* (1992) and *A Nation at War* (1997). His other books and monographs include *Robert Marsden Hope and Australian Public Policy* (2011), *Arthur Tange: Last of the Mandarins* (2006), *Permanent Friends? Historical Reflections on the Australian-American Alliance* (2005), and *Prime Ministers and Diplomats* (1983). Currently an Adjunct Professor at the Alfred Deakin Research Institute of Deakin University, he is a Member of the Order of Australia, a Fellow of the Australian Institute of International Affairs, and a former Trustee of the Shrine of Remembrance in Melbourne.

AUSTRALIA AND THE VIETNAM WAR

PETER EDWARDS

A NewSouth book

Published by
NewSouth Publishing
University of New South Wales Press Ltd
University of New South Wales
Sydney NSW 2052
AUSTRALIA
newsouthpublishing.com

© Australian War Memorial
First published 2014

10 9 8 7 6 5 4 3 2 1

This book is copyright. Apart from any fair dealing for the purpose of private study, research, criticism or review, as permitted under the Copyright Act, no part of this book may be reproduced by any process without written permission. Inquiries should be addressed to the publisher.

National Library of Australia Cataloguing-in-Publication entry
Title: Australia and the Vietnam War/Peter Edwards.
ISBN: 9781742232744 (hardback)
ISBN: 9781742241678 (ePub/Kindle)
ISBN: 9781742246697 (ePDF)
Notes: Includes index and bibliography.
Subjects: Vietnam War, 1961–1975.
 Vietnam War, 1961–1975 – Participation, Australian.
 Vietnam War, 1961–1975 – Australia.
Dewey Number: 959.7043394

Design Di Quick
Cover images FRONT A section of soldiers from C Company, 2RAR /NZ (ANZAC), taking part in the battalion's final operation in Phuoc Tuy province in May 1971 before returning to Australia later in the month. Carrying the section's M60 machine gun is Private Ray Beattie (left) of St Kilda, Victoria. (John Alfred Ford, 1971; AWM FOD/71/0258A/VN)
BACK Soldiers of 7th Battalion, Royal Australian Regiment (7RAR), watching a Chinook helicopter lift off after dropping them in the landing zone for the start of Operation Santa Fe in Phuoc Tuy province. (Michael Coleridge, 1967; AWM COL/67/1048/VN)
Printer Everbest, China

All reasonable efforts were taken to obtain permission to use copyright material reproduced in this book, but in some cases copyright could not be traced. The author welcomes information in this regard.

This book is printed on paper using fibre supplied from plantation or sustainably managed forests.

CONTENTS

PREFACE *xi*

ABBREVIATIONS *xvii*

CHRONOLOGY *xxi*

1 DECOLONISATION AND THE COLD WAR IN SOUTHEAST ASIA 1945–50 *1*

The decolonisation of Southeast Asia *2*
The Cold War *16*

2 AUSTRALIA AND SOUTHEAST ASIA 1945–53 *20*

The Chifley government's foreign and defence policies *22*
The Chifley government, the Indonesian Revolution and the Malayan Emergency *26*
The Menzies government and Australian conservatism *29*
Menzies and Spender *31*
The Menzies government and Indochina *32*
The Menzies government and the Malayan Emergency *35*
The RAAF in Malaya *37*
Australia and the Korean War *38*
Australia and the First Indochina War *41*

3 AUSTRALIA AND SOUTHEAST ASIA 1954-60 *45*

The 'united action' crisis *46*
The Geneva Conference *48*
The creation of SEATO *50*
The Strategic Reserve and the commitment of troops to Malaya 1955 *52*
Australian troops and the Emergency 1955–60 *55*
Australia and Vietnam 1955–60 *59*
Australia, Indonesia and West New Guinea *63*

4 THE CRISES OF THE EARLY 1960s *67*

The Laos crises 1959–61 *68*
Commitments to Thailand and Vietnam 1962 *73*
Confrontation 1963 *80*
Defence review 1963 *84*
The commitment to the defence of Malaysia *87*
The end of Diem, November 1963 *91*
Two conflicts, two allies *95*

5 COMMITMENTS TO CONFRONTATION AND VIETNAM 1965 *101*

The two crises deepen *102*
The commitment of a battalion to Confrontation *109*
The commitment of a battalion to Vietnam *112*
The announcement and parliamentary reaction *116*
Reactions at home and abroad *121*
Operations in Confrontation *125*
1RAR at Bien Hoa *127*
The Malaysia–Singapore split and the commitment of a battalion group *130*
The Indonesian coup and its impact on Australian policy *131*

6 THE TASK FORCE AND THE ELECTION 1966 *134*

A new Prime Minister   *134*
Operations in Borneo   *138*
The long election campaign   *140*
The establishment of the task force in Phuoc Tuy   *144*
The battle of Long Tan   *150*
Relations with allies and enemies   *152*
'All the way with LBJ'   *156*
The commitment confirmed and increased   *158*

7 ESCALATION OF THE COMMITMENT, ESCALATION OF CONTROVERSY 1967   *162*

The escalation of dissent   *162*
The war of attrition   *166*
British withdrawal, American pressure   *170*
The new task force commander   *171*
The minefield   *173*
The third battalion   *178*
ANZAC in Vietnam   *180*
The task force and its third commander   *181*
The commitment of three services   *182*
Death of a Prime Minister   *185*

8 THE TURNING-POINT 1968–69   *187*

The revolutions of 1968   *187*
The Tet offensive and its impact   *189*
A missed opportunity?   *191*
Another new Prime Minister   *192*
Gorton on foreign and defence policies   *195*
Australian protest   *199*
The task force 1968–69   *202*
RAN and RAAF commitments 1968–69   *213*
The 1969 election   *214*

9 SOCIAL DISSENT, POLITICAL DIVISION AND MILITARY WITHDRAWAL 1969-72 *218*

The first Australian withdrawal   *220*
The first Moratorium   *222*
Task force operations 1969–70   *225*
The second withdrawal, the civic action crisis and a new Prime Minister   *229*
The Pentagon Papers   *232*
Operating under a withdrawal 1971–72   *238*
Increasing the advisory role 1971–72   *240*
The withdrawal of RAN and RAAF forces   *241*
The Easter offensive   *242*

10 THE WHITLAM GOVERNMENT AND THE END OF THE VIETNAM WAR 1972-75   *245*

The suspension of conscription, the withdrawal of the AATTV   *246*
The 'Christmas bombing' and the near rupture in Australia–US relations   *248*
Recognition of the Democratic Republic of Vietnam   *252*
From 'forward defence' to 'the self-reliant defence of Australia'   *253*
The fall of Saigon 1975   *255*

11 LESSONS, LEGACIES AND LEGENDS   *261*

Defence and strategic policy   *263*
Dominoes   *268*
Operational methods   *274*
Conscription   *275*
The veterans' experience   *277*
Some final reflections   *284*

APPENDICES

1 Australian Army deployment in Vietnam 1962–73   *289*
2 Australian chain of command and battalion deployment in Vietnam 1962–73   *290*
3 Persons named   *291*

NOTES   *299*

FURTHER READING   *309*

INDEX   *322*

PREFACE

In January 1965 the Australian government decided to send an infantry battalion to Borneo to help Britain and its Commonwealth partners to secure Malaysia's borders from Indonesian incursions. Three months later the government announced that it would send another battalion overseas, this time to help another powerful ally, the United States, to protect another Southeast Asian country, the Republic of Vietnam (commonly known as South Vietnam), against the threat posed by insurgents supported by the communist Democratic Republic of Vietnam (North Vietnam). The commitment to Borneo ended within two years, during which time the threat to the integrity and security of Malaysia was successfully overcome; it cost little blood or treasure; it was met by deploying service personnel, almost all of whom had enlisted voluntarily; it had bipartisan support in Parliament; its wisdom was seldom challenged; its operations were largely conducted in secret; and, although it had been a major concern for policy-makers, the media and the general public in the early 1960s, it was quickly forgotten by most Australians. By contrast, the commitment to Vietnam lasted more than seven years (or ten, if one starts with the commitment of a team of advisers in 1962), making it Australia's longest overseas conflict in the 20th century and the largest and most costly other than the two world wars; it did not prevent the downfall of the Republic of Vietnam ten years later; it was maintained partly by deploying conscripts, chosen by a highly controversial, selective ballot of men too young to vote; its wisdom and morality were challenged by an increasing number of Australians, provoking deep divisions in Australian society and politics; it was linked to bitter, worldwide controversies that remained prominent for decades; and for years afterwards it was identified with strategic, diplomatic, military, political and social failure and ineptitude.

This book seeks to explain how and why Australia became involved in the Vietnam War (more accurately but less commonly known as the Second Indochina War); how Australian forces fought the war; how the war affected Australian society and politics; and how 'Vietnam' and 'the Vietnam era' left enduring legacies on Australian politics, society, strategy and diplomacy. It says much about Australia's alliance with the United States in a conflict widely seen as a 'hot war' within the global Cold War. But it also shows that Australia's commitment to the Vietnam War was in many ways different from that of the United States. The strategic concerns, diplomatic style and operational methods of a global superpower located in the northern hemisphere were markedly different from those of a middle-sized regional power, adjacent to Southeast Asia. This book puts the Australian commitment in the context of Australia's relations with Southeast Asia in the decades after the end of the Second World War, with special reference to Australia's involvement in two other conflicts in the region, the Malayan Emergency of 1948–60 and the Indonesian Confrontation of 1963–66. It explains why Australia's Southeast Asian conflicts in the third quarter of the 20th century have been described both as 'wars of diplomacy' (referring particularly to alliance diplomacy) and as 'wars of decolonisation'.

This book is not part of the *Official History of Australia's Involvement in Southeast Asian Conflicts 1948–1975*, but it relies heavily on the information and arguments found in the nine volumes of that series of which, as Official Historian, I was general editor and author of the two volumes dealing with politics, strategy and diplomacy. While I draw most heavily from those two volumes and the three by Ian McNeill and Ashley Ekins on the Australian Army in Vietnam, I have also made substantial use of the information and insights provided by the authors of the other four volumes: Peter Dennis and Jeffrey Grey on Australian operations in the Malayan Emergency and the Indonesian Confrontation; Brendan O'Keefe on medical aspects of the three conflicts, with an essay by FB Smith on the Agent Orange debate; Chris Coulthard-Clark on the Royal Australian Air Force in Vietnam; and Jeffrey Grey on the Royal Australian Navy throughout the whole period. Readers familiar with the tradition of Australian official war histories might regard this as the counterpart for the Southeast Asian conflicts to CEW Bean's *Anzac to Amiens* or Gavin Long's *The Six Years War*. That is to say, it is a relatively short history of Australia's involvement in a conflict (in this case, several conflicts), written by the Official Historian who was responsible for a multi-volume history of that involvement.

While this book draws heavily on the *Official History*, it aims to meet some contemporary requirements. Seven of the nine volumes of the *Official History* were published in the 1990s. While they have stood up well to the scrutiny of commentators and scholars in subsequent years, it is clearly appropriate to draw on more recent publications and commentaries. Moreover, this book is written primarily for a 21st-century readership, for whom the Vietnam era is remote and whose awareness of military affairs is framed by Australia's involvement in more recent conflicts, particularly in Iraq, Afghanistan and East Timor. It addresses some of the principal questions that readers with no personal knowledge of the Vietnam era now ask: Why was there a war in Vietnam? How and why did Australia come to be involved? What was the domino theory and did it have any validity? Was Australia simply paying a premium for the strategic insurance provided by the Australian–American alliance? Was Australia really 'all the way' with the United States in its commitment to the Vietnam War? What was the nature of the Australian military involvement, including the relationships between the Australians and their American, New Zealand and South Vietnamese allies, and between regulars and national servicemen? Which elements of the three services were involved and how well did they perform operationally? Why did many Australians protest against conscription and the war? What have been some of the enduring legacies of the commitment and the lessons that Australians have drawn from the experience?

This is no more than a concise introduction to a long and complex subject. Many of the topics discussed, and others related to them, have been treated at much greater length elsewhere. A bibliographic note indicates where, both in the volumes of the *Official History* and in other publications, readers may find more information and detailed discussion of some of the themes of this book, and of topics for which there is insufficient space here, including the individual experiences of soldiers and other participants in the conflicts and controversies it discusses. The focus here is on the decisions by political and military leaders, which led to tens of thousands of Australians finding themselves in a bloody conflict in Southeast Asia, and to suggest a perspective that 21st-century Australians might find useful in contemplating the lessons of a controversial war fought some 50 years ago.

Anything associated with the Vietnam War is likely to abound in paradoxes and contradictions. This book is both an individual product and the result of a great team effort; its preparation has been both extremely long and relatively brief. For many years, especially since the publication of *A Nation at War* in 1997, I have been encouraged to write a shorter history of Australia's experience of the Vietnam War, linking it with the Malayan Emergency and the Indonesian Confrontation. I thought it appropriate to wait until after the publication of the ninth volume of the *Official History*, in 2012. On the advice of the then Director of the Australian War Memorial, Steve Gower, the Memorial's Council commissioned me to write this book. I am grateful to them for their support, which continues and extends the work of the Memorial in supporting the tradition of Australian official war histories, for which governments of all political persuasions have granted unrestricted access to official records and an assurance of publication without political or official censorship. It is a tradition of which all Australian governments, and the Australian people, should be proud. I hope and believe that the team I was honoured to lead has lived up to the privileges and responsibilities of preparing an Australian official war history: this book is presented in the hope that it will bring the fruits of all our labours to a wider range of readers.

While the themes selected and the views expressed in this work are my own responsibility, this book relies heavily on the dedicated work, over many years, of the team of historians and researchers who contributed their considerable skill to the *Official History*. Those historians and researchers, especially the authors Ian McNeill, Ashley Ekins, Peter Dennis, Jeffrey Grey, Chris Coulthard-Clark, Brendan O'Keefe and FB Smith, would undoubtedly wish to acknowledge the contribution of the many others who are listed in the preface to each volume – researchers, archivists, librarians, officials, professional colleagues, families, friends and not least the veterans of the various conflicts. To single out any at this time would be invidious. I can only state with all possible emphasis that whatever merit there may be in this book should be attributed to the skill and dedication of all those who worked on the *Official History* as members of the Official History Unit of the Australian War Memorial and those who gave us their support and assistance in many and varied ways.

For support and assistance in the preparation of this book, I wish to express my gratitude to the Council of the Australian War Memorial, especially successive chairmen General Peter Cosgrove and Rear Admiral Ken Doolan; to successive Directors Steve Gower and Brendan Nelson; to the Memorial staff, especially Linda Ferguson and Ashley Ekins, Anne Bennie, Ron Schroer, Stuart Bennington, Craig Berelle, Kate Dethridge, Alison Wishart, Matthew Cramp, Robert Nichols, Andrew McDonald and Christina Zissis; and to Phillipa McGuinness, Karen Penning and Di Quick at NewSouth Publishing. The manuscript of the book has been read by Richard Chauvel, Phillip Deery, Ashley Ekins, Ashley Hay, Michael O'Brien and Robert O'Neill, all of whom have offered helpful comments. Responsibility for any remaining errors of fact or interpretation is mine alone. My greatest debt, as always, is to my wife, Jacky Abbott, for her support and toleration of the preoccupations of a recidivist historian.

Peter Edwards

ABBREVIATIONS

AATTV	Australian Army Training Team Vietnam
ABC	Australian Broadcasting Commission
ACP	Australian Communist Party
ACTU	Australian Council of Trade Unions
AFV	Australian Force Vietnam
AIF	Australian Imperial Force
ALP	Australian Labor Party
ANZAM	Anglo–New Zealand–Australia–Malaya (a defence agreement between UK, Australia and New Zealand governing forces in the Malayan area)
ANZUS	Australia New Zealand United States Security treaty
APC	armoured personnel carrier
ARVN	Army of the Republic of Vietnam
ASIO	Australian Security Intelligence Organisation
CCOSC	Chairman of the Chiefs of Staff Committee (Australia)
CDNSA	Committee in Defiance of the National Service Act
CGS	Chief of the General Staff (Australia)

CIA	Central Intelligence Agency (US)
COMAFV	Commander Australian Force Vietnam
COMUSMACV	Commander of the United States Military Assistance Command Vietnam
CPA	Communist Party of Australia
CT	communist terrorist
DLP	Democratic Labor Party
DRV	Democratic Republic of Vietnam (commonly known as North Vietnam)
FAD	Foreign Affairs and Defence (committee of the Australian Cabinet)
FANK	Forces Armées Nationales Khmer
FFV	Field Force Vietnam
FPDA	Five Power Defence Agreement
FSB	fire support base
HQ	headquarters
JWTC	Jungle Warfare Training Centre
MATT	Mobile Advisory Training Team
MCP	Malayan Communist Party
MHR	Member of the House of Representatives (Australian Parliament)
MRLA	Malayan Races Liberation Army
NATO	North Atlantic Treaty Organization
NCO	non-commissioned officer
NLF	National Liberation Front (National Front for the Liberation of South Vietnam)
NVA	North Vietnamese Army (the common name for the People's Army of Vietnam)
PAP	People's Action Party (Singapore)
PAVN	People's Army of Vietnam (commonly known as the North Vietnamese Army)
PF	Popular Force
PKI	Partai Kommunis Indonesia (Communist Party of Indonesia)
PLAF	People's Liberation Armed Forces

PRG	Provisional Revolutionary Government [of South Vietnam]
PTSD	post-traumatic stress disorder
RAAF	Royal Australian Air Force
RAF	Royal Air Force (UK)
RAR	Royal Australian Regiment (1RAR is 1st Battalion, Royal Australian Regiment, 2RAR is 2nd Battalion, Royal Australian Regiment, and so on)
RAN	Royal Australian Navy
RANHFV	Royal Australian Navy Helicopter Flight Vietnam
RF	Regional Force
RSL	Returned Services League (formerly the Returned Soldiers', Sailors' and Airmen's Imperial League of Australia, today the Returned and Services League)
RTFV	RAAF Transport Flight Vietnam
RVN	Republic of Vietnam (commonly known as South Vietnam)
SAS	Special Air Service
SEAC	South-East Asia Command
SEATO	South-East Asia Treaty Organization
SOS	Save Our Sons
TAOR	tactical area of responsibility
TPI	totally and permanently incapacitated
UMNO	United Malays National Organisation
USMACV	United States Military Assistance Command Vietnam
VCI	Viet Cong infrastructure
VVAA	Vietnam Veterans' Association of Australia
VVFA	Vietnam Veterans' Federation of Australia
YCAC	Youth Campaign Against Conscription

CHRONOLOGY

1945

17 AUGUST
Sukarno and Hatta proclaim the independence of Indonesia.

2 SEPTEMBER
Japanese surrender ends the Second World War.

2 SEPTEMBER
Ho Chi Minh proclaims the independence of the Democratic Republic of Vietnam.

1946

NOVEMBER–DECEMBER
First Indochina War begins.

1948

FEBRUARY
Communist conference in Calcutta, followed by insurgencies in several countries in Southeast Asia.

AUGUST
Beginning of the Malayan Emergency.

1949

4 APRIL
Formation of the North Atlantic Treaty Organization (NATO).

10 DECEMBER
Liberal–Country party coalition wins election in Australia, with RG Menzies as Prime Minister.

27 DECEMBER
Netherlands formally transfers sovereignty to independent government of Indonesia, including all of former Netherlands East Indies except West New Guinea.

1950

14 JANUARY
Democratic Republic of Vietnam recognised by Soviet Union and China.

8 FEBRUARY
Australia recognises the French-sponsored State of Vietnam under Bao Dai.

17 AUGUST
President Sukarno proclaims unitary Republic of Indonesia.

1951

1 SEPTEMBER
ANZUS treaty signed.

1953

MARCH
French Minister Letourneau visits Australia.

1954

7 MAY
Surrender of French forces at Dien Bien Phu, on the eve of the opening of the Indochina session of the Geneva Conference.

JULY
Ngo Dinh Diem becomes Prime Minister of State of Vietnam under Bao Dai.

JULY
Geneva Accords establish temporary partition of Vietnam at 17th parallel.

SEPTEMBER
Formation of the South-East Asia Treaty Organization (SEATO) by United States, United Kingdom, France, Thailand, Pakistan, the Philippines, Australia and New Zealand.

1955

OCTOBER
Ngo Dinh Diem deposes Bao Dai and proclaims Republic of Vietnam with himself as President.

1957

SEPTEMBER
Ngo Dinh Diem visits Australia.

1959

JANUARY
Communist party in Hanoi authorises armed action by communists in South Vietnam.

1960

JULY
Malayan Emergency declared over.

DECEMBER
Hanoi leadership establishes the National Front for the Liberation of South Vietnam (NLF).

1962

MAY
Meeting of ANZUS Council of Ministers, after which Australian government announces the deployment to Vietnam of the Australian Army Training Team Vietnam (AATTV), comprising 30 officers and senior NCOs, and an RAAF squadron of Sabre fighters to Thailand.

JULY
Geneva Agreement on Laos.

1963

JANUARY
Indonesian government declares policy of *konfrontasi* or Confrontation against proposed federation of Malaysia.

16 SEPTEMBER
Federation of Malaysia formed.

1–2 NOVEMBER
Assassination of President Diem and Ngo Dinh Nhu.

23 NOVEMBER
Assassination of President John F Kennedy.

1964

JUNE
Australian government announces increase in AATTV to 80 advisers.

2–4 AUGUST
Gulf of Tonkin incident, followed by US congressional resolution.

AUGUST
Australia provides six Caribou transport aircraft in RAAF Transport Flight Vietnam (RTFV).

10 NOVEMBER
Australian government introduces defence measures including selective conscription for 20-year-old males under the National Service Act.

1965

JANUARY
Australian government commits an infantry battalion and an SAS squadron to Confrontation in Borneo (decision announced in Feb). AATTV increased to 100 advisers.

30 MARCH–1 APRIL
Military staff talks between US, Australian and NZ representatives in Honolulu.

29 APRIL
Prime Minister Menzies announces commitment of an infantry battalion to Vietnam.

MAY
1RAR and support elements, totalling about 1100 men, arrive at Bien Hoa air base, to serve with a US brigade.

9 AUGUST
Separation of Singapore and Malaysia.

SEPTEMBER
Additional elements (artillery, engineers, army aviation and logistics) arrive at Bien Hoa, raising commitment to a battalion group of about 1400 men.

30 SEPTEMBER–1 OCTOBER
Coup and counter-coup in Jakarta. In following months President Sukarno gradually removed from power, to be succeeded by army regime headed by General, later President, Suharto. Killing and imprisonment of hundreds of thousands of real or alleged communists destroys PKI.

1966

26 JANUARY
Harold Holt succeeds Menzies as Prime Minister.

8 MARCH
Australian government announces its commitment to be raised to a task force of two infantry battalions with combat and logistic support; total of about 4500 men, including 500 conscripts.

APRIL–JUNE
Australian task force arrives in Vietnam and establishes base at Nui Dat in Phuoc Tuy province. Logistic support group established at Vung Tau.

JUNE
1RAR completes tour and returns to Australia.

JUNE
RAAF sends squadron of Iroquois helicopters to support task force.

11 AUGUST
Indonesia and Malaysia formally end Confrontation

18 AUGUST
Battle of Long Tan.

OCTOBER
President LB Johnson becomes first incumbent US President to visit Australia.

NOVEMBER
Holt government wins record majority in election fought on Vietnam and conscription.

22 DECEMBER
Australian government announces further increases in the commitment to Vietnam, including elements from all three armed services.

1967

MARCH–MAY
Australian task force constructs barrier minefield near Dat Do in Phuoc Tuy province.

JULY
Presidential advisers Clark Clifford and Maxwell Taylor visit Australia and other US allies, seeking further troop commitments.

JULY
Defense Secretary Robert McNamara commissions study of US policy on Vietnam, later known as 'the Pentagon Papers'.

JULY
UK announces withdrawal of forces 'east of Suez'.

17 OCTOBER
Australian government announces the commitment of a third infantry battalion, a tank squadron, a joint RAAF/RAN helicopter squadron, and other elements, bringing total commitment to more than 8000 personnel. Australia informs US that no further additions possible.

17 DECEMBER
Harold Holt missing, presumed drowned.

21 DECEMBER
Memorial service for Holt attended by President Johnson, Prince Charles, British Prime Minister Harold Wilson, RVN President Thieu and other dignitaries.

1968

10 JANUARY
John Gorton sworn in as Prime Minister.

JANUARY
UK announces acceleration of the withdrawal of forces 'east of Suez'.

15-25 JANUARY
Gough Whitlam, Leader of the Opposition, visits Vietnam.

30-31 JANUARY
Start of Tet offensive throughout South Vietnam.

2 FEBRUARY
Prime Minister Gorton announces that Australia will make no further additions to commitment in Vietnam.

FEBRUARY
Australian task force involved in major operations near Bien Hoa/Long Binh bases and in Phuoc Tuy.

16 MARCH
US Army company involved in brutal killing of hundreds of Vietnam civilians at My Lai. Incident does not become public until Nov 1969.

31 MARCH
President Johnson orders halt to most bombing of North Vietnam and announces that he will not seek re-election.

5 MAY-4 JUNE
Second communist offensive ('mini-Tet'). Australian battalions supported by tanks involved in major battles at Fire Support Bases Coral and Balmoral north of Saigon.

7-9 JUNE
Prime Minister Gorton visits troops in Vietnam.

5 NOVEMBER
Richard Nixon wins presidential election in US (takes office in January 1969).

1969

8 JUNE
President Nixon announces a policy of 'Vietnamisation' and the withdrawal of 25 000 US troops.

17 JULY
Task force begins final operation to clear the Dat Do minefield; finally declared cleared on 31 May 1970.

2 SEPTEMBER
Ho Chi Minh dies in Hanoi, aged 79.

OCTOBER–NOVEMBER
Large anti-war demonstrations in US, including first 'Moratorium'.

16 NOVEMBER
First public revelations of the My Lai massacre.

1970

22 APRIL
Prime Minister Gorton announces that one battalion will not be replaced at the end of its tour in November, reducing the task force to two battalions.

30 APRIL
50 000 ARVN and 30 000 US troops attack communist sanctuaries in Cambodia. Widespread protests in US, especially on university campuses.

8 MAY
First Moratorium protests in Australia: 120 000 march in Australian cities in protest against Australian involvement in Vietnam War.

31 AUGUST
AATTV increased to more than 200, its highest strength, in late 1970 and early 1971.

18 SEPTEMBER
Second Moratorium protest in Australian cities.

OCTOBER–NOVEMBER
Australian task force reduced from three to two battalions.

1971

FEBRUARY
AATTV opens Jungle Warfare Training Centre at Nui Dat: moved in October to Van Kiep near Ba Ria; closed in December.

10 MARCH
William McMahon succeeds Gorton as Prime Minister. (1908–1988)

30 MARCH
Prime Minister McMahon announces graduated withdrawal of 1000 personnel from all services over three months.

30 JUNE
Third and last Moratorium protest in Australia.

JULY
Publication of Pentagon Papers in US.

18 AUGUST
Prime Minister McMahon announces that nearly all combat troops will be withdrawn by Christmas, logistic forces soon afterwards; AATTV to remain.

8 DECEMBER
Last major withdrawal of combat troops from Vietnam.

1972

FEBRUARY–MARCH
Withdrawal of most remaining army and RAAF forces, leaving headquarters group and small contingent of soldiers, mostly in AATTV, in non-combat roles. HMAS *Sydney* undertakes the last of its 23 voyages between Australia and South Vietnam.

30 MARCH
North Vietnamese forces begin Easter Offensive. Finally repulsed by September, with aid of US air support.

APRIL–MAY
President Nixon authorises bombing of Hanoi–Haiphong area and mining of North Vietnamese ports.

7 NOVEMBER
President Nixon re-elected.

2 DECEMBER
Labor government elected in Australia, with Gough Whitlam as Prime Minister. In subsequent days conscription suspended, imprisoned draft resisters released, last troops ordered out of Vietnam.

18 DECEMBER
Last Australian troops (headquarters group and AATTV) withdraw, leaving a platoon to guard embassy in Saigon.

18–29 DECEMBER
Following breakdown of peace talks, 'Christmas bombing' of Hanoi and Haiphong ordered by President Nixon.

1973

11 JANUARY
Governor-General Sir Paul Hasluck proclaims cessation of hostilities in Vietnam by Australian forces. *(1905–1993)*

27 JANUARY
Peace treaty signed by representatives of US, RVN, DRV and PRG.

26 FEBRUARY
Prime Minister Whitlam announces establishment of diplomatic relations with DRV; diplomatic relations with RVN maintained, PRG not recognised.

MAY–JUNE
The last Australian soldiers, the platoon guarding the embassy in Saigon, leave Vietnam.

JULY
Australian Embassy in Hanoi opened under *chargé d'affaires*.

1974

9 AUGUST
Richard Nixon resigns as US President, succeeded by Gerald Ford.

1975

JANUARY–APRIL
PAVN 'Ho Chi Minh offensive' sweeps through South Vietnam.

25 APRIL
Australian Embassy in Saigon closed.

30 APRIL
RVN surrenders to PAVN troops, ending the Second Indochina War.

6 MAY
Australian government extends recognition to the new regime in South Vietnam.

11 NOVEMBER
Whitlam government dismissed by the Governor-General, Sir John Kerr.

— ONE —

DECOLONISATION AND THE COLD WAR IN SOUTHEAST ASIA 1945-50

The atomic bombs dropped on Hiroshima and Nagasaki in August 1945 brought the Second World War to an end, but did not begin a period of peace and political stability. During the next ten years, many parts of the world were riven with tensions and conflicts, amid a widespread fear of a third global war, in which atomic bombs or even more devastating weapons might be used. Southeast Asia was one of the most bitterly contested regions, but well-informed observers and even participants found it difficult to understand the complex forces involved. With the advantages of historical perspective, we can see the cauldron of Southeast Asian politics in the late 1940s and early 1950s as a complex interaction between long-standing local rivalries and two of the great historical processes of the post-1945 world – the decolonisation of the European empires, and the Cold War between the communist 'East' and the non-communist 'West', led respectively by the Soviet Union and the United States, together with their respective friends, allies and satellites.

THE DECOLONISATION OF SOUTHEAST ASIA

In the late 1940s and early 1950s the only certainty about the future of Southeast Asia was that it would be very different from its past.¹ At the outbreak of the Second World War the region was dominated by the European empires, which had extended their dominance over much of Africa and Asia starting in the 16th century, with a marked expansion in the 19th. By 1939 the Netherlands controlled most of the chain of islands from Sumatra in the west to the western half of New Guinea in the east; France governed the mainland territories collectively known as Indochina; Britain's vast empire included Burma and a number of colonies and protectorates on the Malayan peninsula and its offshore islands, and on the western and northern coasts of Borneo; the United States governed the Philippines, a territory it had acquired from its victory over Spain in 1898; and Portugal had a tiny colony on the eastern half of the island of Timor. Only Thailand remained independent but, bordered by British territories on one side and French on the other, it generally deferred to both European powers.

After their victory over Germany, Italy and Japan in 1945, the British, French and Dutch authorities expected to reassert their pre-war control over their respective territories. Their desire to return was driven by much the same motives as those that had been behind their original acquisition, sometimes summarised as ['gold, God and glory'] – that is, to gain access to valuable resources, to spread Christianity, and to acquire the prestige that accompanied imperial status. In particular, the European governments, economically exhausted by years of depression and war, wanted to regain strategically valuable resources such as oil, rubber, tin and rice. The French and the Dutch especially sought reassurance that, after their humiliation at the hands of Nazi Germany and Japan, they could now return to the top table of world powers. They were shocked to discover the strength of the resistance that they encountered from nationalist movements seeking independence. The ease and speed with which the Japanese established control over Southeast Asia in 1941–42 had destroyed the aura of European invincibility. The fall of Singapore in February 1942 had had a huge symbolic effect in the Dutch and French territories as well as the British. When Japan in turn was defeated in 1945, the European powers encountered a great variety of political forces, all seeking to grasp the opportunity of the new post-war era to claim 'national liberation' or 'independence'.

During the 1920s and 1930s, when the European colonial powers had appeared to be firmly in control of their respective possessions, important developments had been taking place in the nationalist movements. The intelligentsia and political activists across the region recognised that their traditional structures had been defeated by the European powers. They now thought, discussed and wrote not only about their desire for independence but also about the nature of the post-colonial governments they hoped to form. In many and varied ways, they became familiar with European political concepts, such as democracy, self-determination, liberalism, socialism and communism. In a great historical irony, they determined to turn these European ideas against their European rulers and apply them to the independent national governments they intended to create.

While the desire to be rid of colonial rule was widespread in Southeast Asia, the groups who asserted claims to independence and national liberation were many and diverse. The differing nature of colonial rule in British, French and Dutch territories, and within each of those empires, affected the nature of the anti-colonial movements. All colonies were governed primarily in the interests of the metropolitan powers, but the levels of political repression, economic exploitation and concern for the interests and welfare of the colonial subjects varied greatly. The use of

✳ ['direct' or 'indirect' rule] – that is, whether the colonial powers exercised their control through their own colonial administrations or through compliant local authorities – differed in different territories. Some large and disparate areas, incorporating numerous traditional states or polities, were governed as one territory, while others with a sense of national identity were divided into smaller units. The size and influence of racial and ethnic groups, including both indigenous populations and immigrant communities, most notably the Chinese, varied greatly. Religious and philosophical identifications, including Islam, Buddhism, Hinduism, Christianity and Confucianism, reinforced some ethnic or racial divisions and cut across others. Some groups worked with the colonial powers and hoped to achieve independence in an amicable transfer of power; others had fought their colonial masters with every weapon available to them. During the war some groups had collaborated with the Japanese, seeing this as a way to strengthen their claims to post-war independence; others, particularly those of Chinese ethnic origin, had taken up arms against the Japanese, who treated their Chinese subjects with particular brutality.

Consequently, the aims and methods of those fighting for independence were diverse, often conflicting, and extremely difficult for external observers to comprehend. Some groups wanted the borders of the new independent countries to reflect those drawn up by the European colonialists; others fought for separatist causes based on ethnic, regional or religious identities. Some were communist, at a time when communist movements around the world not only expected at least ideological and diplomatic, if not economic or military, support from like-minded governments and movements but also proclaimed their allegiance to the Soviet Union and its leader, Joseph Stalin, who had emerged with enhanced prestige and power from the world war. In Vietnam at least, some Trotskyites proclaimed their support for an ideology that was even more revolutionary than that of the Stalinists. Other nationalist groups were willing to ally themselves with communists in 'national fronts' to gain independence, in the hope of sharing power in the post-colonial regime, while others again were suspicious of, or openly hostile to, the communists, for a variety of religious, political, social and economic reasons. It was obvious to all that the future of the region would be greatly affected by the outcome of the titanic civil war in China between the Nationalists, led by Jiang Jieshi (Chiang Kai-shek) and the communists, led by Mao Zedong (Mao Tse-tung), which would bring the communists to power in October 1949.

Two Southeast Asian countries became independent soon after the war's end. In 1946 the United States lived up to the promise it had given in the 1930s, to grant independence to the Philippines. Britain granted independence to Burma (Myanmar) in 1948, soon after India and Pakistan and just before Ceylon (Sri Lanka). Although Burma has generally been regarded as part of Southeast rather than South Asia, the story of its decolonisation has more in common with that of its western than of its eastern neighbours. Portugal's return to its tiny colony on Timor attracted little attention. The parts of Southeast Asia of most concern to the external world, especially Australia, in the years after 1945 were those parts of the former British, French and Dutch empires that are known today as Malaysia, Indonesia, Vietnam, Laos and Cambodia, together with Thailand.

THE INDONESIAN REVOLUTION

From the late 16th to the early 20th century, the Dutch expanded their interests in the islands they called the East Indies, often in competition with the Portuguese and British. In the 17th and 18th centuries, the Dutch East India Company dominated trade in spices and other cash crops. After 1800, when the company was dissolved, the Dutch territories became colonies. Despite strong resistance from several islands and regions, including Aceh, Bali and Lombok, the Dutch gradually expanded their possessions. In 1886 the Dutch, Germans and British determined their respective spheres of influence on the island of New Guinea, with the Dutch claiming the western half, the Germans taking the northeastern quarter and the British the southeastern quarter, but the Dutch did not establish a strong presence in West New Guinea until well into the 20th century. The predominant view in the independence movement was to seek a single Indonesia, incorporating all of the Netherlands East Indies, even though there had been no such polity before the arrival of the Dutch. Nevertheless, the territory of the future Indonesia and the nature of its government were contested, as many islands and regions retained a strong sense of local identity and some nationalists thought West New Guinea should be excluded.

On 17 August 1945, two days after Japan had announced its surrender and before the official documents were signed, the leader of the nationalist movement in the Netherlands East Indies, Sukarno, and his closest associate, Mohammad Hatta, proclaimed the independence of Indonesia. The Dutch entered negotiations with the nationalists, but they sought to establish a federation of semi-autonomous units in a 'United States of Indonesia', which the nationalists regarded as an attempt to preserve an indirect form of Dutch influence. Two agreements, in 1946 and 1948, broke down over fundamental issues and the Dutch twice used military force in what were euphemistically called 'police actions'. The Dutch attempted to use Sukarno's and Hatta's war-time collaboration with the Japanese to denigrate their nationalist credentials, without success. The Dutch also played on the resentment in the 'outer islands' towards domination by Java, but again without success. The nationalist army could not match the weapons of the Dutch, but their skilful use of guerrilla tactics gained widespread popular respect.

Sukarno, a complex and charismatic figure, brought together many groups in the nationalist coalition under a vaguely worded program of *panca sila*, or five principles, which could be translated as belief in God, nationalism, humanitarianism, social justice and democracy. The leaders of the movement were predominantly secular, non-communist nationalists. In 1948 elements of the Indonesian communist party, the Partai Kommunis Indonesia (PKI), based at Madiun in central Java, attempted to take over the revolutionary movement to direct it towards their own political ends. Troops of the nationalist army, led by Colonel AH Nasution, crushed this attempted coup. The army emerged from this internal conflict with great prestige and a deep antipathy towards the Indonesian communists.

The secular, republican nationalists were also challenged by Darul Islam, a fundamentalist Islamic movement that sought to establish Indonesia as an Islamic state under sharia law. This group failed to take over the nationalist movement, but retained considerable strength in some areas, especially west Java, Aceh (in northern Sumatra) and southern Sulawesi, and took militant action against the nationalists for years after independence.

Despite these challenges, when the Dutch finally granted independence to Indonesia in 1949, after four years of revolutionary struggle, it was to a secular democratic republic. President Sukarno and his government would continue to face challenges from the communists, from Islamic fundamentalists, and from regional separatists in the outer islands, but their secular, non-communist nationalism was in effective control. Although the Dutch had transferred sovereignty to a federated Republic of the United States of Indonesia, by August 1950 Sukarno was able to proclaim a unitary state, the Republic of Indonesia. In one respect, the nationalists' victory was less than complete. The western half of the island of New Guinea (later known as Irian Jaya and today as the provinces of Papua and West Papua) remained in Dutch hands, the only part of the old Netherlands East Indies not to be incorporated into the independent Indonesia.

THE VIETNAMESE REVOLUTION

The state of Nam Viet, based on the Red River delta in what is now northern Vietnam, struggled for independence from the Chinese empire for about 1000 years before attaining that goal in 939CE. Its major city, Hanoi, was founded in 1010. Thereafter Vietnamese history was characterised by several enduring themes. Despite a political culture that was more deeply influenced by Chinese standards and concepts than any other in Southeast Asia, the Vietnamese fiercely protected their independence against domination by China. The Vietnamese steadily expanded their control southwards from the Red River delta, obliterating the kingdom of Champa, which had controlled much of what is now central Vietnam, by the 16th century and reaching the Mekong delta by the mid-18th century. While the ideal of a united Vietnamese state persisted, so did regional tensions and loyalties. [For most of the 18th century, Vietnam was divided between two rival families, the Trinh in the north and the Nguyen in the south.] Not until 1802 did a southerner impose unity on the country, taking the throne as Emperor Gia Long and establishing the last Vietnamese dynasty, which survived (at least in name) until 1955. The imperial capital was established at Hue in central Vietnam.

The French moved forcibly into Indochina in the mid-19th century, completing their conquest by 1883. Thereafter the French governed Indochina as five entities. Cochinchina (now southern Vietnam) was ruled directly as a colony, while Annam (central Vietnam) and Tonkin (northern Vietnam) were designated as protectorates, with the emperor as the nominal ruler. The tiny and fragile kingdom of Laos and the larger kingdom of Cambodia, heir to the once powerful Khmer kingdom at Angkor, were also ruled as protectorates.

The French came for imperial prestige and to spread Catholic Christianity: they stayed principally for economic gain. Rice, coffee, rubber and coal became major sources of income. The French imposed harsh labour conditions, a rapacious tax system, and monopolies on essentials such as salt. The ruling elite was predominantly French, but a small Vietnamese class of large landowners was created, especially in the south, where cash crops for export displaced the subsistence farms of the peasants. Many rural Vietnamese were unemployed or were compelled to work in the harsh conditions of the mines, plantations and construction projects. The indigenous middle class was small and weak. Some Vietnamese received a French education, but this served principally to create an intelligentsia who wanted the much-vaunted political and cultural values of metropolitan France applied to the colonies: they saw little evidence of liberty, equality or fraternity in Indochina. Discontent and opposition to the colonial system were widespread at all levels of society, especially in the northern provinces, but the French vigorously repressed all nationalist or anti-colonial movements, whether moderate or radical in nature, even those willing to collaborate with the colonial authorities. This repression served only to deepen the discontent and to favour the dominance within the anti-colonial movement of those best equipped by organisation and doctrine to operate in secret: the communists. The Moscow-line communists acted ruthlessly against the Trotskyites as well as less revolutionary nationalists to ensure their own leadership of the nationalist movement.

Unlike the leaders of most nationalist movements, Ho Chi Minh spent most of his formative years outside his native land. Born Nguyen Sinh Cung in 1890 in a northern province of Vietnam, he lived abroad from 1911 to 1941. The Marxist and Leninist ideas he encountered in London and Paris, especially Lenin's theory of imperialism, struck him as highly relevant to Vietnam under French rule. He became a founding member of the French Communist Party in 1920; studied in Moscow at the School for the Toilers of the East, a training ground for Asian revolutionaries; and worked at the headquarters of the Communist International (Comintern). A professional revolutionary, he worked under a number of aliases, adopting the name Ho Chi Minh ('the bringer of enlightenment') in the 1940s. In 1929 and 1930 he helped to unite three communist factions to form the Indochinese Communist Party (ICP) in Hong Kong, where he narrowly escaped imprisonment by the British. As the name suggests, the ICP sought to establish communist regimes across all of French Indochina, but its political and military activities in Laos and Cambodia as well as Vietnam were largely dominated by Vietnamese.

After the fall of France in 1940 the colonial authorities in Indochina, who were aligned with the collaborationist Vichy regime, allowed the Japanese to take effective control. Ho returned to Vietnam in 1941. During the wartime years the communist leadership was hard hit, especially in the south. At this time Ho and his close associates Truong Chinh, Pham Van Dong and Vo Nguyen Giap emerged as the leaders of the Vietnamese communists, with their greatest strength and support in and around the Red River delta. Under Ho's leadership the communists emphasised their aspirations for independence and played down their dedication to class struggle. With some non-communist nationalist groups they formed the Viet Nam Doc Lap Dong Minh, or Vietnam Independence League, generally known as the Viet Minh. While some other nationalist groups worked with the Japanese, the Viet Minh gained popular support by seizing and distributing rice from Japanese grain stores during a famine created largely by Japanese policies. The Viet Minh also formed the nucleus of what became the People's Army of Vietnam (PAVN), creating guerrilla forces from 1941 and main forces from 1944. The military impact of their anti-Japanese efforts was minimal, and they devoted considerable time and effort to crushing rival Vietnamese groups, but they laid the foundations of a ruthlessly effective military force.

In March 1945 the Japanese suddenly disarmed the Vichy French regime and established a client government of Vietnam. During the chaos of the next six months, as the likelihood of Japan's defeat became increasingly clear, the Viet Minh, under Ho's leadership, used their military and political skills to establish pre-eminence in the independence movement. On 2 September, the day the Japanese signed the surrender, Ho proclaimed to a huge crowd in Hanoi the independence of the Democratic Republic of Vietnam (DRV), including the territories that the French had called Tonkin, Annam and Cochinchina. The Indochinese Communist Party announced its own dissolution in November 1945, although it is clear that the DRV government and the Viet Minh continued to be led by Ho and his communist associates, who also exerted strong influence on the communist movements in Laos and Cambodia. In 1951 separate communist parties were formed in Vietnam, Laos and Cambodia. The Vietnam Workers' Party, by far the most powerful of these, ensured that the political and military actions of the Lao and Cambodian parties continued generally to serve Hanoi's interests, until the rise of the Khmer Rouge in Cambodia in the 1970s.

The French proved even more determined than the Dutch to return to their former colonial possessions. Even the French communists gave little support to the DRV. In late 1946 negotiations broke down, the French took military action and the DRV leadership withdrew to the mountains of northern Vietnam to begin a guerrilla war. The First Indochina War had begun.

From the outset it was clear that the outcome of this conflict would be greatly influenced by the attitude of the United States. During the war, Ho had formed a close relationship with officers of the Office of Strategic Services, a predecessor of the Central Intelligence Agency (CIA), and he appealed several times to the Americans for support. His 1945 declaration of independence borrowed extensively from Thomas Jefferson's 1776 declaration, in an obvious plea for sympathy. President Harry Truman was caught between the traditional American antipathy towards French colonialism and his need to strengthen the French government against the communist threat in Europe. The official American position in 1945–46 was that the United States would not oppose the restoration of French sovereignty in Indochina, but would not support its reimposition by force. In fact, it began giving indirect support to the French, initially on a modest scale.

For decades afterwards, the Americans and their allies would debate whether Ho Chi Minh was a 'genuine' nationalist or a communist. The debate was based on the assumption that any communist would make his own country's national interests subordinate to those of the international movement led by Joseph Stalin in the Soviet Union. Given the way that most communist parties throughout the world declared their allegiance to Stalin and acted accordingly, it was an understandable belief. In Ho's case, however, it was a false distinction. Ho was both a dedicated Marxist-Leninist and a dedicated Vietnamese nationalist. He had decided that Vietnam's best path to independence was through cooperation with the international communist movement, and that an independent Vietnam should be governed according to Marxist-Leninist principles. He sought and gained support from communist allies, but he was also determined to defend Vietnamese independence against any external power, irrespective of ideology. He inherited a traditional concept of Vietnam, which ran from the mountains north of the Red River delta to the Mekong delta in the south, but governed from Hanoi, not the former imperial capital of Hue in the centre, and certainly not Saigon in the south. Moreover, like many Vietnamese leaders in earlier times, Ho and his colleagues would expect to exercise a significant degree of hegemony, or 'brotherly leadership', over like-minded regimes in Laos and Cambodia.

THE MALAYAN EMERGENCY

The British territories in Southeast Asia, on and around the Malayan peninsula and on the island of Borneo, had been acquired in piecemeal fashion, often in rivalry with the Portuguese and the Dutch. In 1824 the

British and Dutch agreed on a border between their respective spheres of influence on the Malayan peninsula and in Sumatra. Although the peoples on either side of this border have many ethnic and cultural traits in common, this remains the modern border between Indonesia and Malaysia. On peninsular Malaya the British governed largely through the traditional Malay rulers or sultans: it was often said that 'the British adviser ruled and the Malay ruler advised'. Under British rule large numbers of Chinese and Indian immigrants were brought to the Malay states, mostly as indentured labour for the rubber plantations and tin mines. Between 1880 and 1957 Malaya's population increased five-fold, from 1.5 million to 7.75 million, largely through the influx of Chinese and Indian immigrant labourers. Other Chinese and Indians prospered in business. In the 1930s it seemed that an acceptable balance had been achieved, with the Malays being granted some privileges and the Chinese prospering commercially. But tensions always remained between Malays and Chinese, while law and practice created a large community of landless Chinese squatters, mostly on the fringes of towns and villages. Although only a minority of the Chinese minority, the squatters were numerous enough to prove a fertile ground for a communist movement, which looked to the Chinese Communist Party for inspiration.

Three islands off the Malayan peninsula, Singapore, Malacca and Penang, were known as the Straits Settlements and separately administered. Singapore, acquired by the British in 1819, gained a reputation as a vigorous commercial entrepôt with a Chinese-dominated population. Three other British territories were located on the island of Borneo, the majority of which was part of the Netherlands East Indies. Sabah, Sarawak and Brunei had very different histories and systems of administration from peninsular Malaya and from each other. Sarawak had been governed by a British family, the Brookes, known as 'the white rajahs'; Sabah (formerly known as North Borneo) by the British North Borneo Company; and Brunei by its Sultan under a British protectorate.

In 1945 Sabah and Sarawak became British crown colonies, while the protectorate over Brunei was renewed.

In 1947 and 1948 the Labour government in Britain granted independence to its South Asian empire, including Burma as well as India, Pakistan and Ceylon, but it wished to retain Malaya. Tin and rubber were among the few commodities for which Britain, economically exhausted by the war, received a substantial income in American dollars. Britain's return to Malaya after 1945 was not opposed by as strong a nationalist movement as those in the Netherlands East Indies or Vietnam, but neither was it welcomed. The local population was divided on political, economic and racial grounds. The British had difficulty in shaping constitutional arrangements, amid conflicting demands between equal rights for all Malayans (including the Chinese and Indians) and special privileges for the Malays. By 1947 the Chinese passed the Malays as the largest ethnic group in Malaya and Singapore together, with the heavy Chinese preponderance in Singapore outweighing the Malay majority on the peninsula.

In 1946 the British created the Malayan Union, which gave equal rights to all citizens of all races. Intense dissatisfaction by the Malays led to the formation of a Malay nationalist party, the United Malays National Organisation (UMNO), and in 1948 the adoption of a new constitution, the Federation of Malaya, which gave much greater authority to the Malays, especially the Sultans and traditional hierarchies. Both the Malayan Union and the Federation of Malaya included Malacca and Penang but excluded Singapore, in order to maintain a Malay majority of the population, but Britain's policies and administration in Malaya in the late 1940s had created considerable distrust on all sides.

During the war the Malayan Communist Party (MCP) had formed the Malayan Races Liberation Army (MRLA). Despite its name the MRLA was, like the MCP, overwhelmingly Chinese. While it did engage in some guerrilla activity against the Japanese, alongside British units, it looked mainly to establish a communist regime in post-war Malaya. It was far weaker than, for example, the Vietnamese communists, with its support coming almost entirely from the landless Chinese squatters. Malays of all levels of society generally supported UMNO, which worked towards an independent, Malay-led government. As Muslims, the Malays were opposed to communism, especially when aligned with China. The MCP also suffered major setbacks during and after the war, which were only explained when its members discovered in 1947 that their Secretary-General since 1939, Lai Tek, had been a secret agent for both the Japanese and the British, betraying many of their leaders and finally absconding with most of the party's funds.

In 1948 the Malayan Communist Party, with a more militant leadership headed by the 23-year-old Chin Peng, took up arms against the British. The colonial authorities were obliged to declare a state of emergency, giving the name to what became a 12-year conflict. Although their resources were limited, the communists – known initially as 'bandits', then as 'communist terrorists' or 'CTs' – held the initiative for some time, using weapons and guerrilla tactics developed during the war. Despite the severe economic, military and political pressures confronting Britain both at home and across its global empire, the British government had to devote precious resources, including national servicemen as well as regular troops, in an effort to quell the communist insurgency along the Malayan peninsula.

In the late 1940s, therefore, the British, the French and the Dutch all faced major challenges when they attempted to return to their colonies in Southeast Asia, but the nature, the strength and the composition of the independence movements that they faced differed greatly.

THE COLD WAR

The turmoil in Southeast Asia was not the principal focus of the world's attention in the late 1940s. These were the years in which the Cold War took the shape that would last more than four decades. The American vision of the post-war international order, based on democracy, capitalism and international trade, clashed with that of the Soviet Union, based on state planning, [autarky,] and political and economic repression. During and immediately after the war, the Soviet Union incorporated some previously independent countries, including the Baltic states of Latvia, Lithuania and Estonia, into its own territory, and established tight control over much of eastern and central Europe. The defeated Germany was effectively divided into a democratic West and a communist East, as was its former capital. West Berlin was a virtual island within the communist East Germany. A coup in 1948, when the combination of ruthless political tactics and the threat of military force placed the formerly democratic Czechoslovakia under the control of Soviet-aligned communists, had a profound impact on opinion in Western countries. The danger of Soviet control stretching further across Europe was taken very seriously. In both France and Italy, the communist parties were very strong, while their rivals were divided and often ineffective. In this atmosphere, leaders of several western European countries, most prominently the Labour government in Britain, appealed to the United States for support. Their fear was not of American imperialism but of a reversion to isolationism.

By the end of the 1940s, a combination of domestic and international pressures had led the United States to undertake a policy of containment of the Soviet Union and its influence around the world. Not only had the North Atlantic Treaty Organization (NATO) been formed, but Washington also declared that it would support free peoples anywhere around the world in the struggle against communism. The major focus of the Cold War in the late 1940s and early 1950s was Germany, especially Berlin, where the Western powers mounted an airlift in 1948–49 to defeat a Soviet attempt to strangle the allied enclave. But the whole future of Europe, and the balance of world power, seemed to be at stake. The Western powers, which had joined with the Soviet Union to defeat the Nazi and fascist form of totalitarianism, now faced a major challenge from another form, Soviet-led communism.

Given the importance of the issues at stake, it was hardly surprising that the Western powers, principally the United States and its allies including Britain, France and the Netherlands, looked at developments throughout the world through the prism of the Cold War. In 1948 communist-led insurgencies broke out across much of South and Southeast Asia, including Malaya, the Netherlands East Indies, India, Burma and the Philippines. The insurgents were rebelling against not only colonial regimes but also newly independent governments and even nationalist movements led by non-communist groups. Earlier that year a number of Asian communist parties gathered for a conference in Calcutta. Western governments believed that the Soviet leaders had used this gathering to encourage, if not to instruct, communists throughout Asia to take up arms, in order to distract European governments from their political and military actions to counter communism in Europe. Ever since then, scholars have debated whether the sudden rash of insurgencies in 1948 was inspired by Moscow or was due to local circumstances. Both may well have contributed. The Soviet leaders had good reason to encourage insurgencies in the Asian colonies of European powers, while the various communist movements probably decided to take up armed struggle only if they believed that the local conditions were favourable. Whatever the inspiration for the 1948 insurgencies may have been, it was natural that, in the late 1940s and early 1950s, many in the West regarded communist-led insurgencies in Asia as separate but related theatres in a global conflict between the communist and non-communist worlds.

The British and other European governments pressed their belief that the anti-colonial rebellions were masterminded by the Soviet leaders in Moscow, in part because of their need for American support. The United States had emerged from the Second World War with unmatched military and economic strength, while its European allies, including Britain, France and the Netherlands, were economically exhausted and, in many cases, politically fragile. Proud of its own origins as a group of colonies that had fought a revolutionary war to win independence from Britain, the United States had traditionally been unsympathetic to European colonialism. Before, during and immediately after the Second World War, the United States, especially during the administration of President Franklin D. Roosevelt (1933–45), urged Britain, France and other European powers to move quickly towards granting independence to their colonies, not least in Southeast Asia. When the Allies formed Southeast Asia Command (SEAC) in the latter years of the war and placed it under Admiral Lord Louis Mountbatten, a close relative of the British royal family, some Americans jested that SEAC stood for 'Save England's Asian Colonies', an aim for which they had little sympathy. In the last years of the war and the early years of peace, the desire of the Europeans, not least the British under Winston Churchill, to reclaim their imperial possessions conflicted with the American pressure to grant independence as quickly as possible. [Roosevelt had a particular distaste for French colonialism in Indochina and North Africa.]

As the lines of the Cold War were drawn in the late 1940s, the United States had to decide whether its longstanding antipathy towards European colonialism was outweighed by the need to support Western governments against the global threat of communism. The Americans were pleased that Britain granted independence to 'the jewel in the imperial crown', India (partitioned into India and Pakistan), in 1947 and Ceylon and Burma in 1948. While Britain was more reluctant to part with Malaya, it was coming round to accepting independence. As will be seen below, the United States exerted its considerable diplomatic pressure to help remove the Dutch from the Netherlands East Indies. The nationalist army's suppression of the communist rebellion at Madiun made it impossible for the Dutch to claim that they were fighting a communist rebellion. The French determination to reassert their control in Indochina posed a more difficult dilemma for Washington. Under Roosevelt's successors, both the Democrat Harry S Truman (1945–53) and the Republican Dwight D Eisenhower (1953–61), American administrations felt compelled to swallow their anti-colonialist principles and to support the French in the name of fighting international communism. The American support did not include armed forces but took the form of increasingly large financial contributions. It would prove the first step towards an extremely costly commitment.

AUSTRALIA AND SOUTHEAST ASIA 1945-53

After the trials of two world wars and the Great Depression, Australians after 1945 sought nothing more ardently than security.[1] In the turmoil of the post-war world, the greatest threat to security, both at home and abroad, appeared to be communism. In the global balance, the ruthless expansion of Soviet power and influence in Europe and the increasing likelihood of a communist victory in the Chinese civil war were the dominant concerns for Australians, as for the rest of the Western world. At home the Communist Party of Australia had changed its name to the Australian Communist Party (ACP) in 1944, supposedly to demonstrate that it was concerned more with Australian than Soviet policies and conditions, but in fact its policies continued to be aligned with those of Moscow, from which it received financial support. By 1945 the ACP had 23 000 members, had gained a seat in the Queensland Parliament, and controlled some municipal councils, but its greatest strength lay in the trade unions. Communists and their allies had effective control of unions in several vital industries, notably on the waterfront, and by 1945 were widely believed to dominate the Australian Council of

Trade Unions (ACTU) and the trades and labour councils in several states. A wave of strikes in 1946–47 demonstrated the communists' industrial power.

The reaction against communist control of the union movement began before the war had ended. A group of Roman Catholics led by a young lay activist, BA Santamaria, formed the Catholic Social Studies Movement, which used its journal, *News Weekly*, and some communist-style political techniques to encourage Catholic workers to influence union politics and policies to accord with Catholic teachings. From 1945 the Labor Party itself formed 'industrial groups' of anti-communist unionists. The 'groupers' and 'the Movement' worked closely together until they were regarded as virtually synonymous, extending their influence first in the unions and then in the organisation of the Labor Party, especially in Victoria. In the late 1940s many Labor traditionalists welcomed the work of the Movement and the predominantly Catholic groupers in countering the communists.

Within the unions and the Labor Party, questions of defence and foreign policy were generally seen through the prism of the intense struggle between the communists and the groupers. The Labor government, led by JB 'Ben' Chifley as Prime Minister, tried to maintain a distinction between its hostility to Australian communism and its government-to-government relations with the Soviet Union, but this was made increasingly difficult as the Australian communists professed their allegiance to Stalin. Industrial militancy, largely communist-inspired, reached a climax with a coalminers' strike in 1949, which was broken when Chifley sent troops into the mines. In the same year the leader of the ACP, Lance Sharkey, was imprisoned for sedition after he said that, if Soviet troops came to Australia in pursuit of aggressors, they would be welcomed by the Australian working class just as they had been welcomed by the people of Europe they had liberated.

THE CHIFLEY GOVERNMENT'S FOREIGN AND DEFENCE POLICIES

The most prominent figure in shaping Australian foreign policy in the late 1940s was Dr HV Evatt. After stepping down from the High Court to enter politics, Evatt was Minister for External Affairs in the Curtin and Chifley governments from 1941 to 1949. Evatt had a largely free hand in making foreign policy, an area in which few other Labor parliamentarians had a substantial interest. Evatt played a prominent role in drafting the Charter of the United Nations Organisation in 1945, after which he showed such a degree of faith in quasi-legal processes to resolve international disputes that some said the United Nations was 'the church of his religion'. His strong advocacy of the rights of small and medium powers, including opposition to the veto power granted to the permanent members of the Security Council (the United States, the Soviet Union, the United Kingdom, France and China) antagonised all five, but especially Britain, which expected support from members of the British Empire and Commonwealth. Evatt, who was also Attorney-General, delegated considerable authority to Dr JW Burton, whom he appointed as Secretary of the Department of External Affairs at the age of 32 in 1947. Burton was a liberal internationalist, regarded by many of his colleagues as a secular crusader for radical causes including the nationalist independence movements in Asia. He emphasised the role of social and economic reform in reducing the appeal of communism and removing the conflicts that could lead to war. Burton blamed the United States at least as much as the Soviet Union for the outbreak of the Cold War.

Chifley, who was Treasurer as well as Prime Minister, delegated foreign policy largely to Evatt and Burton, but he took a close interest in some areas. He had a particular sympathy for the post-war plight of Britain and for its Labour government. He welcomed the grant of independence to India and was instinctively opposed to colonialism and the exploitation of colonial workers. Initially Chifley had some reservations about Britain's relations with the Soviet Union, but by the end of the decade he had come to sympathise with Britain's staunch opposition to Soviet communism.

The Minister for Defence from 1946 to 1949, John Dedman, was heavily preoccupied with his other portfolio as Minister for Post-War Reconstruction, leaving considerable scope in the field of strategic policy for the Secretary of the Defence Department, Sir Frederick Shedden, and the Chiefs of Staff of the three armed services. Shedden, who had been the department's head since 1937 and Secretary of the War Cabinet throughout the war, modelled himself on Sir Maurice Hankey, the influential secretary to both the Cabinet and the Committee of Imperial Defence in London. Despite the resentment felt in some quarters about Britain's wartime record, not least over Singapore, Shedden continued to push Australian defence policy towards a close alignment with Britain and the Commonwealth. This approach was shared by the service chiefs, who thought it unwise to place any reliance on the United Nations or to give special emphasis to the problems of the Pacific – two of Evatt's favourite themes. Defence policy, in their view, had to be global and based on the British Commonwealth. The government's five-year defence program of 1947, announced by Dedman but probably shaped largely by Shedden and the service chiefs, emphasised the importance of British Commonwealth cooperation and gave a larger share of defence expenditure to the navy than to the army or air force, because the British Commonwealth 'remains a maritime Empire, dependent on sea power for its existence'.[2] The chiefs also regarded nationalist movements, especially but not solely those aligned with communism, as threats to Australian security. Throughout the late 1940s tensions between the Defence and External Affairs Departments over the Cold War and the role of independence movements in Asia were exacerbated by the personal hostility between the experienced Shedden and the youthful Burton.

After a Soviet official in Canada defected in 1945, American intelligence agencies became increasingly aware of the extent of Soviet espionage in Western countries. In Australia suspicion fell principally on scientists in the Council for Scientific and Industrial Research (the forerunner of the Commonwealth Scientific and Industrial Research Organisation) and diplomats in the Department of External Affairs. In 1948 the United States cut off the flow of classified material to Australia, just at the time when intelligence agencies in the United States, British, Canadian, Australian and New Zealand governments were establishing enduring arrangements to share information. With these concerns in mind, the Chifley government established the Australian Security Intelligence Organisation (ASIO) in 1949. It would subsequently be confirmed that two diplomats in the department were leaking classified material to the Soviet Union, using the ACP as the channel. Burton resisted the creation of ASIO and the increasingly close links between the Australian, British and American defence and intelligence agencies, while Shedden, who liked to reminisce about his wartime relationship with American and British leaders, did all he could to encourage them.

Another significant development in this turbulent post-war period passed with much less attention. Australia's military traditions, not least the Anzac legend, had been built on the great citizen armies of the two world wars, the Australian Imperial Force (AIF) of 1914–18 and the Second AIF of 1939–45, created by hundreds of thousands of voluntary recruits who served for the duration of the war. The small and under-resourced permanent army served only as a cadre to these great citizen armies. In 1948 the government decided to establish, for the first time, a substantial regular army. The principal combat force, the infantry, would be formed from the three battalions of volunteers then serving as the Australian component of the British Commonwealth Occupation Force in post-war Japan. These three battalions became the 1st, 2nd and 3rd Battalions, Royal Australian Regiment (1RAR, 2RAR and 3RAR).

From this time onwards, the Australian Army would see the citizen forces as supporting the regulars, rather than the reverse. While other elements of all three armed services would be involved, the principal focus of Australian military involvement in overseas conflicts, both politically and militarily, would be the commitment of one or more battalions of the Royal Australian Regiment.[3]

In the first half of the 20th century, few Australians dissented from the official view that Australia should adhere closely to the principle that the British Empire spoke with one voice in international affairs. Until the 1940s, Australian leaders saw their principal role in world affairs as seeking to influence the authorities in London, so that the British Empire's foreign policy took adequate notice of Australian national interests. In the late 1940s, amid the widespread fear of a third world war against the Soviet Union, few non-communists challenged the prevailing view that the West must stand firm against Moscow and its allies. Those who did were often linked to what communists called 'fraternals' and their opponents called 'fronts' – organisations created and inspired by communists in order to develop support for the Soviet Union. In 1949 Australian communists joined with a small number of Christians and intellectuals to form the Australian Peace Council, effectively the Australian branch of the World Peace Council, created to mobilise support for the Soviet Union in response to the formation of NATO. The Christians and intellectuals were concerned that Western opposition to communism might lead to a third world war, possibly involving nuclear weapons. At the time, however, and for years afterwards it was easy to see the non-communists associated with the Peace Council who criticised Western policies as acting essentially in Stalin's interests. Their public support was limited. A much greater concern for most Australians was whether the United States, Britain and other Western countries were both able and willing to stand up to the threat of expansionist communism, around the world and especially in Southeast Asia.

While there was little tradition of dissent over foreign policy or engagement in overseas conflicts, Australians had long differed sharply over compulsory military service abroad. In the early years of Federation, there was broad support for compulsory military training for young males within Australia, but overseas service was associated with the interests of the Empire rather than the nation. This principle of compulsory service at home but only voluntary recruits overseas was laid down in the Defence Act of 1903: it explained why the large volunteer army raised for the 1914–18 war was called the Australian Imperial Force (AIF). When Prime Minister WM Hughes sought to introduce conscription in 1916 and 1917, to replace the heavy losses suffered by the AIF on the Western Front, he precipitated the most divisive and bitter controversy in Australian politics in the early decades of the century. In the Second World War, John Curtin created deep tensions in his own government and party when he tried to permit Australian conscripts to serve overseas, alongside the draftees of the US Army. The result was an awkward compromise, in which the conscripts of the militia could serve only in the islands north of Australia and south of the Equator, including the legendary battles on the Kokoda Track. For years afterwards, many on the Labor side retained a deep and visceral opposition to conscription for military service overseas. Among them was a dissident member of Curtin's Cabinet – Arthur Calwell.

THE CHIFLEY GOVERNMENT, THE INDONESIAN REVOLUTION AND THE MALAYAN EMERGENCY

The first real test for Australian policy towards Southeast Asia in the late 1940s came with the Indonesian Revolution. During its wartime exile in Australia, the Dutch colonial government won few friends in the Labor

Party, and the Chifley government had little sympathy for its attempt to return after the war. Soon after the declaration of independence in August 1945, the Australian government indicated its support for the nationalists by referring the incipient conflict to the United Nations. The Australian government's sympathy for the nationalists went beyond what either the British or the Americans thought appropriate, but Australian waterside workers maintained pressure on the government by imposing bans on ships carrying munitions and supplies to the Dutch. In 1947, after the first Dutch 'police action', the United Nations established a Good Offices Committee of three nations, one to be nominated by each of the contending parties and the third to be chosen by the first two. The Indonesian nationalists nominated Australia, the Dutch nominated Belgium, and Australia and Belgium nominated the United States. The Australian diplomats on the Good Offices Committee played a vital role in the subsequent complex negotiations, which were interrupted by military action, until the Netherlands finally transferred sovereignty to an independent government in December 1949. The Americans initially feared that opposing Dutch aspirations to return to their colonial possessions might strengthen the communists in the Netherlands, in a similar manner to their policy concerning French Indochina, but later, especially after the nationalists crushed the communist rebellion at Madiun, they worked to ease the Dutch out. Australian diplomacy helped to resolve the impasse over the inclusion of Dutch-held West New Guinea in the new republic's territory by gaining agreement that this should be left for future negotiation. The combination of Chifley's sympathy for colonial workers, Evatt's wish to resolve international conflicts through the United Nations, Burton's strong support for Asian independence movements, and vigorously independent diplomacy had had a positive outcome, which earned enduring respect and friendship from the new Indonesian government.

This success coloured the approach of the Chifley government to British requests for assistance when the colonial authorities declared the state of emergency in Malaya in 1948. Australians had many reasons to take a particular interest in the outcome of this insurgency. They had fresh and vivid memories of the impact of the Japanese conquest of Malaya and Singapore in 1942, placing thousands of Australians into harsh captivity and apparently exposing Australia itself to the risk of invasion. Australians had substantial interests in the Malayan tin-mining and rubber industries, but when some members of the public and the press urged the Australian government to support the British colonial authorities in combating the communist insurgents, they received an unsympathetic response. The Australian diplomats in the area found it difficult to persuade the Chifley government that Malaya was very different from Indonesia, in that the insurgents were drawn only from the Chinese community and were essentially loyal to the Chinese Communist Party. The diplomats were also impressed by the British intelligence assessments that the Malayan insurgency had been prompted by Moscow through the Calcutta conference. There was a distinctly Australian aspect to this argument, for the insurgency had broken out shortly after the Australian communist leader, Lance Sharkey, had visited Singapore on his way home from Calcutta. He was thought to have been the messenger who conveyed the message to the MCP to take up arms, in the interests of the global communist movement.

By contrast, Chifley believed that the insurgency arose essentially from the exploitation of local workers by European capitalists: the working conditions in the tin mines and on the rubber plantations gave ample grounds for such a view. Evatt was more susceptible to persuasion by the British authorities that this was indeed a communist, rather than a broadly based nationalist, rebellion. Burton's sympathy for nationalist movements was taken to extreme lengths: at one point he advanced the theory that the inspiration came from a band of Chinese Nationalists, the opponents of the Chinese communists to whom the Malayan Communist Party owed allegiance. The outcome was that the Chifley government, notwithstanding its broad sympathy and support for the Attlee Labour government in Britain, provided only minimal support for the British authorities in Malaya. Australia sent some small arms and 'walkie-talkie' radio sets, but Chifley ensured that there would be no direct request from Britain for troops, letting it be known that he would reject any such request. Under this Labor government, no Australian troops would be sent to Malaya.

THE MENZIES GOVERNMENT AND AUSTRALIAN CONSERVATISM

The general election of December 1949, a major turning-point in Australian politics, saw the Chifley Labor government defeated by a coalition of the Liberal and Country parties, with Robert Menzies as Prime Minister. From April 1939 to October 1941, Menzies had led the country as prime minister in the early years of the Second World War, before falling from power at the hands of his own side of politics. He was then widely discredited, but in 1944 and 1945 he had played a central role in the creation of the Liberal Party from various non-Labor parties, factions and groups. The 1949 victory was therefore a personal triumph for Menzies. The election was fought largely on domestic issues, with the Menzies-led coalition advocating free-market economic policies to replace the Labor Party's attempt to nationalise the banks and continue wartime rationing, but the coalition's victory also had implications for foreign policy. Menzies' admiration for Britain and his opposition to communism, both in Australia and globally, were widely advertised. Much of Australian politics for the next two years revolved around his unsuccessful attempt to make the ACP illegal.

While this proposal was defeated and his hold on office was often tenuous for some years, Menzies succeeded in identifying himself with the strong popular instinct to seek post-war political and economic security through a return to conservative values and institutions. The mainstream Christian denominations experienced a strong revival in the 1950s and generally exercised their influence on social and political issues in a conservative manner. The principal newspapers in the state capitals, the major source of news for most Australians, were similarly supportive of the conservative parties. Their influence was extended in the late 1950s when newspaper organisations were given a leading role in establishing the new medium of television. The vigorous post-war immigration from Europe included substantial numbers of 'new Australians' from the Baltic countries and other parts of eastern and central Europe who associated communism and socialism with the expansionist, oppressive and murderous regimes in the Soviet Union and its satellites. In post-war Australia, the armed services were held in high esteem and the principal ex-service organisation, the Returned Soldiers', Sailors' and Airmen's Imperial League of Australia (generally known as the RSL), advocated conservative positions on defence policy as well as supporting generous repatriation benefits.

With these pillars of support, a strongly anti-communist stance in foreign affairs strengthened the political position of the Liberal and Country parties and divided the Labor Party. The commentators and intellectuals on the non-communist left who argued that the insurgencies in Southeast Asia should be seen as worthy nationalist movements, rather than communist advances in the Cold War, faced an uphill battle in public debate, as they were often identified with the Peace Council and other communist fronts. Menzies and other conservatives instead saw the post-1945 dismantling of the European colonial empires as a threat to Australian security, particularly if they brought communist movements to power. After the experience of the Japanese southward thrust in 1941 and 1942, many Australians perceived East and Southeast Asia as a source of potential threats: after 1949, the idea of communist China as a powerful and populous threat from the north resonated with earlier fears of Japan. In this climate, the emphasis on the conservative side of politics shifted slowly, from an initial support for the return of the colonial powers to an effort to ensure that the newly independent, post-colonial governments would be sympathetic to the West.

MENZIES AND SPENDER

For a short time after the election, Menzies seemed to hanker after the old ideal of a single foreign policy for the entire British Empire. In 1950 he made the last serious suggestion that Britain, Australia and the other Dominions should coordinate a 'common Empire foreign policy' on major international questions. This was anachronistic and impossible, but in subsequent years, when he frequently spoke of himself as 'British to the bootstraps', he was thinking of the pre-1939 imperial club dominated by the old, white Dominions. He found it difficult to reconcile himself to the changes in the Commonwealth as British colonies in Asia, Africa and the Caribbean gained their independence in the 1950s and 1960s. While recognising the importance to Australia of relations with countries like Japan and Indonesia, he seldom visited them and was manifestly uncomfortable when he did. The development of relations with Asian countries was left largely to the Minister and Department of External Affairs, while Menzies concentrated his attention heavily on links with London and Washington.

The first Minister for External Affairs in the new government was PC (from 1952, Sir Percy) Spender. In just 16 months as Minister for External Affairs, from December 1949 to April 1951, Spender laid down many of the foundations of Australian foreign policy for the next generation. To ensure Australian security, Spender sought the closest possible security relationship with the United States and a focus on financial and technical aid to Southeast Asia, to promote material welfare and political stability there as 'the best defence against … Communist imperialism'.⁴ The focus on Southeast Asia continued the outlook that had developed in External Affairs under Evatt and Burton, but the strong opposition to 'Soviet imperialism' and any expansion of Chinese communist influence, and the emphasis on security relationships with the United States rather than with Britain, were distinctly new. During his brief term, Spender established the principal themes of Australian foreign policy in a major parliamentary speech; he played an important role in the Commonwealth conference that inaugurated the Colombo Plan for financial and technical assistance to Asian countries; and he negotiated the Australia–New Zealand–United States (ANZUS) security treaty.

THE MENZIES GOVERNMENT AND INDOCHINA

The Menzies government's first major policy decision on Southeast Asia came within weeks of the election. In 1949 the French government, accepting that the war against the Viet Minh could not be won solely by military means, tried to create a non-communist alternative to the DRV. Under the Elysée Agreement, the French recognised the independence of Vietnam, Laos and Cambodia as 'Associated States' in the French Union. The emperor, Bao Dai, who had abdicated in 1945, was reinstated as head of state of Vietnam. Even Bao Dai was dissatisfied with the highly restricted degree of 'independence' provided under the agreement, but France sought international recognition of Vietnam's new status. Governments in the United States, Britain and

Australia and their advisers faced a profound dilemma. Bao Dai was seen as an unreliable playboy, more at home on the French Riviera than in Vietnam, while Ho Chi Minh was known to be highly respected by a large proportion of the Vietnamese population. The Americans were especially disappointed at the highly limited degree of independence granted to the Bao Dai government, repeatedly urging the French to concede more. While Ho Chi Minh was a Moscow-trained communist, American and Australian officials were well aware that he was widely regarded as a genuine nationalist, not only in Vietnam but also throughout Southeast Asia. The fragility of the Bao Dai regime and the popular support for Ho and the DRV were well known, but the French and others in Western capitals argued that international recognition of the new State of Vietnam would strengthen its position. Only this, they said, could prevent a communist victory over most of Indochina which would in turn create a threat to Malaya, Thailand, Burma and Indonesia.

Even those Americans who accepted that the United States had global interests and responsibilities usually placed Southeast Asia below other parts of the world, such as Europe, the Middle East, East Asia, and North, Central and South America. By the end of 1949, the Truman administration was coming reluctantly to the conclusion that, in order to contain Chinese communism, to promote Japanese economic recovery, and to support Britain and France in Europe, Southeast Asia must be treated as a major arena for confrontation with international communism. In January 1950 Ho announced that the DRV was the only legitimate government of Vietnam and called for international recognition. The Soviet Union and the new government of the People's Republic of China responded promptly. The American Secretary of State, Dean Acheson, under intense criticism from conservative Republicans for having 'lost' China and for the State Department's alleged sympathy for communism, cited the Chinese and Soviet actions as proof that Ho was a communist, not a nationalist, and recommended that the United States recognise

Bao Dai. Soon afterwards, the Americans began providing substantial military and economic aid to the French-sponsored governments in Indochina. Military intervention was far from anyone's thoughts, but the United States had undertaken a major commitment to the security of Indochina.

At the Commonwealth Conference in Colombo in January 1950, Spender encountered strong pressure from the British representatives, particularly Ernest Bevin and Malcolm MacDonald, to support the French and to recognise the Bao Dai regime. Bevin, a former trade union leader now Foreign Secretary in the Attlee Labour government, was a major architect of the Western response to the Soviet threat, including the formation of NATO. He consistently argued that the Soviet Union was pursuing its global ambitions 'by all means short of war' and, now that it was meeting firm resistance in Europe, was inspiring insurgencies in Southeast Asia and elsewhere in the world, such as those in Indochina and Malaya, in order to distract Western governments. MacDonald, Britain's senior diplomatic representative in the region with the title of Commissioner-General for Southeast Asia, emphasised the local roots of the various insurgencies and the need to raise economic standards in the European colonies to counter the attractions of communism. He argued that a communist victory in any one part of Southeast Asia would jeopardise the security of its neighbours, saying that a victory for Ho and the Viet Minh in Vietnam would expose Thailand and in turn Malaya, for which he had direct responsibility.

While conscious of the weakness of the Bao Dai regime and the popular support for Ho and the DRV, Spender decided that, on balance, recognition 'could not do positive harm' and agreed to recommend it to his government. In early February, the government announced that it had recognised the State of Vietnam, immediately after similar announcements by both Britain and the United States. In his major speech on foreign policy, Spender defended the decision. He recognised the widespread view that the Viet Minh sought only an independent Vietnam and would resist domination by the Soviet Union or China, but noted that Ho had 'received his political training in Moscow'. If the Viet Minh governed all of Vietnam, he said, it would establish 'a regime scarcely distinguishable from other Communist satellite governments'.[5] The Menzies government had decided to accept the opinion of the British Labour government and the Democratic administration in Washington that Indochina had to be seen primarily as a theatre in the Cold War rather than as an exercise in decolonisation. It was an important step towards a commitment in Indochina, but the decision aroused little attention or criticism in Australia.

THE MENZIES GOVERNMENT AND THE MALAYAN EMERGENCY

Australians paid much closer attention to another incipient conflict in Southeast Asia. In early 1950 a series of articles in the Melbourne *Herald* by Denis Warner and the newspaper magnate Sir Keith Murdoch urged Australia to contribute troops or air force squadrons to support the British authorities in Malaya, where the insurgents were 'the advance guard of the Red revolution that plans to seize all Asia in its tyrannical grasp'.[6] Sympathetic comments by Eric Harrison, a minister in the Menzies government, provoked a debate, in which communists and some Labor spokesmen denounced the idea of Australian military involvement in colourful terms. Australian communists argued that Australian capitalists, including ministers in the Menzies government, only sought to defend their financial interests against 'Malayan democracy'. Several major newspapers campaigned for active involvement; only the left-leaning Melbourne *Argus* was critical. Burton, still Secretary of the Department of External Affairs, argued that any action would be seen as colonialism by India, Pakistan, Ceylon and the Philippines. After tentative feelers had been put out, the British explicitly requested three forms of support from the Royal Australian Air Force (RAAF): a transport squadron of Dakotas; a squadron of Lincoln bombers; and assistance with servicing aircraft.

Notwithstanding his widely advertised sympathy for Britain and his consciousness of Malaya's importance to Australian security, Menzies was markedly cautious in his response. He and his ministers were dubious about Britain's ability to handle the situation; they doubted whether a jungle insurgency could be effectively countered by 'orthodox military operations' by troops and bombers; and they feared the impact of a 'militaristic' decision on opinion both in Australia and in the region. After considerable discussion, the government agreed first to send the squadron of RAAF Dakotas, politically the least sensitive form of military commitment. It also agreed to provide aircraft servicing, which subsequently proved impossible to implement for technical reasons. For some time it reserved its decision on the Lincoln bombers, uncertain about both their military value and the political reaction. These doubts were overcome by the unexpected outbreak of the war in Korea on 25 June. The government announced that conflicts in Korea, Indochina and Malaya all formed 'part of the global pattern of imperialistic Communist aggression', and it was therefore appropriate to react to the outbreak of the Korean War by sending a flight of Lincoln bombers to Malaya.[7]

The government's caution about any military commitment to Malaya prompted the decision to send a military mission of eight officers from all three services to investigate all aspects of the British conduct of the campaign. This reflected a degree of confidence in political and military circles that Australia had developed considerable expertise in fighting in Southeast Asian jungles, particularly during the campaigns in New Guinea in the Second World War, and might pass on some benefits from this expertise to the British. The military mission supported the view that the Malayan insurgency should be seen as part of the Cold War, and its outcome would be related to success or failure in the other Asian theatres of the Cold War, especially French Indochina. It generally supported the British conduct of the campaign, but shared the doubts of Menzies and his ministers that bombing jungle areas was of great military value.

THE RAAF IN MALAYA[8]

After the debate over the commitment to Malaya in 1950, few Australians took much interest in the RAAF's involvement in what became known as the Emergency. At the request of the British, the strength of the squadron of Lincoln bombers was raised from six to eight aircraft in 1951. On the other hand, commitments in Korea and elsewhere required the RAAF to reduce the squadron of Dakota transport aircraft from eight to four, and then to withdraw it altogether in 1952. Australian governments constantly sought opportunities to place Australians in leadership roles in joint Commonwealth positions, military as well as diplomatic. For two years, from 1953 to 1955, an RAAF officer, Air Vice Marshal Frederick Scherger, was Air Officer Commanding in Malaya, in command of all RAF and RAAF units.

The Dakotas of No. 38 (Transport) Squadron were posted to the British Far Eastern Air Forces, requiring them to fly courier and supply services to Ceylon, Borneo, the Philippines, Indochina, Hong Kong and Japan. In Malaya, the Dakotas were employed principally in dropping supplies to ground forces operating deep in the jungle, as well as casualty evacuation, leaflet drops, reconnaissance, target marking, troop carrying and, on one occasion, dropping paratroops. While far from glamorous, the squadron's work was considerable and the aircrew and groundcrew were justified in thinking that their work was 'vital and ... done well'.⁹

By contrast, continuing controversy surrounded the usefulness of bombing in counter-insurgency operations. While many in RAF Bomber Command thought that bombers were better used in Cold War operations elsewhere, the British authorities in Malaya were pleased to employ the Lincoln medium bombers of No. 1 (Bomber) Squadron. Firm evidence of casualties inflicted on the guerrillas of the MRLA was hard to obtain, but the British commanders insisted that continual harassment of their jungle bases and supply lines by bombing, for which the Lincolns were well suited, served both to damage the enemy's morale and to improve the morale of the civilian population. The ground forces expressed greater appreciation when the emphasis of the air campaign shifted from saturation bombing to carefully targeted strafing and rocket attacks on the camps of the communist guerrillas. The Lincoln bombers remained in Malaya until the end of 1958.

AUSTRALIA AND THE KOREAN WAR

The link between the outbreak of the Korean War and the despatch of Lincoln bombers to Malaya was not the only point at which Australia's commitment to Korea shaped Australian involvement in Southeast Asia. Australia fought in Korea from 1950 to 1953 as part of a 16-nation coalition, sanctioned by the United Nations Security Council, to which the United States contributed by far the greatest strength as well as the military leadership. Australia committed forces from all three armed services, each fighting alongside allied services rather than in direct support of their compatriots. The RAAF's No. 77 Fighter Squadron fought alongside its US Air Force counterparts. The Royal Australian Navy (RAN) kept two warships in Korean waters, engaged in blockade and ship-to-shore bombardment. The principal Australian fighting was done by first one, then two battalions of the Royal Australian Regiment. These battalions joined with counterparts in the British 27th Infantry Brigade to form the 27th Commonwealth Brigade. After Australia raised its commitment to two battalions, Australian officers were given command of the Commonwealth brigade.

The Korean War was a long and costly campaign that ended in an armistice rather than a peace treaty. It re-established the *status quo ante bellum* of a communist north and a non-communist south, rather than marking a victory of the 'free world' over the international communist movement. Nevertheless, Korea established itself in many Australian minds as a model for post-1945 commitments. In the ensuing years, Australian governments would prefer their overseas commitments to be part of a large coalition, authorised by the United Nations, which included both the United States and Britain, as well as other friendly countries, with the United States providing the essential military power but with Australian ground forces integrated more closely with British and other Commonwealth allies. The presence or absence of these elements would greatly influence the willingness of Australian governments to commit forces overseas.

At the same time, the Korean War experience reinforced the ambiguous attitude that Australian political and military leaders had towards the American military. They respected the enormous military power of the United States, but sometimes questioned the discretion and wisdom with which that power was exercised. During the Korean War, while Australians admired the brilliance of some of the strategies employed by the commander of US and UN forces, General Douglas MacArthur, they also shared the deep concerns of the British over MacArthur's threat to use nuclear weapons and his thrust to the Yalu River, which led to the intervention by the Chinese. A recurring theme, seldom expressed except in highly classified documents or private conversations, was the fear that the United States might over-react in a crisis, for example in the Taiwan Straits, turning a minor international incident into a major, potentially nuclear, war between the United States and China. Menzies and his colleagues believed that, while Britain might be much less powerful than in former times, it still had greater judgment in the exercise of power. This underlay the Australian preference to act militarily in a multilateral framework, preferably including Britain as well as the United States, so that a MacArthur-like military leader might be constrained by a group of coalition allies.

The Korean War was expensive in money as well as lives, and the boom in wool prices that it created, while welcome to Australia's wool producers, had a severely inflationary impact on the national economy. To bring the budget under control, the Menzies government introduced a cap on defence expenditure of £200 million, and kept it at that figure as the economy grew in subsequent years so that it formed a decreasing proportion of gross national product. Australian budgets gave priority to 'national development' – major infrastructure projects designed to strengthen the economy in the medium and long term. This constraint and the consequent limit on the size and capabilities of the armed services required the government to place an even greater emphasis on Australia's alliances to ensure its security. Menzies and his colleagues were only too conscious that Australia's 'great and powerful friends' were located on the other side of the globe and had more important interests in regions of the world closer to their homes. The fear that drove Australian policy was that Britain, the United States or both might withdraw from Southeast Asia, leaving Australia exposed to threats from the north. Australia could not defend itself: consequently, Australia's meagre forces would not be deployed independently, but only in conjunction with those of either the United Kingdom, or the United States, or preferably both.

Combined with political and diplomatic support, Australia's necessarily small military commitments would be deployed in such a way as to encourage Britain and the United States to remain committed, with their far greater forces, to the security of Southeast Asia. In return for the vocal political and diplomatic support, and such military support as could be provided, Australian governments sought the greatest possible degree of access to high-level planning in London and Washington, seeking to influence British and American policies in ways that reflected Australian national interests.

This was the origin of the strategic posture known as ['forward defence'] that would shape Australian foreign and defence policies for the next generation. Under this posture, Australia's forces would be deployed only in Southeast Asia, rather than the regions surrounding the principal Britain–Australia routes through the Mediterranean, the Suez Canal and the Red Sea, where so much of Australia's military tradition had been established. They would be deployed only in coalitions led by either or both of its great allies, with those powers providing the greater part of the military strength as well as the necessary logistic and other support. In the view of the government and its advisers, a totally independent military posture was simply impossible, as it required a level of military expenditure beyond Australian resources.

AUSTRALIA AND THE FIRST INDOCHINA WAR[10]

When Spender's short but creative term as Minister for External Affairs ended, he was succeeded by [Richard Casey,] whose tenure of the portfolio would be the longest in the 20th century. Casey had long experience in international affairs. In the 1920s he had served as, in effect, the personal representative of Prime Minister SM Bruce in the Cabinet offices in Whitehall; in the 1930s he had been a Cabinet minister in Australia; in the 1940s he had been the head of Australia's first diplomatic mission in Washington, before being appointed by Winston Churchill as a minister

[*Baron Richard Casey (1890–1976)]

in the United Kingdom Cabinet resident in the Middle East, and then Governor of Bengal. The hallmarks of his term as Minister for External Affairs from 1951 to 1960 were a flair for personal diplomacy; a marked effort to ensure the close collaboration of Australia, Britain and the United States; and a strong interest in developing Australia's relations with Asia, especially Southeast Asia.

Casey's first overseas visit as Minister for External Affairs was, at his department's suggestion, to Asia, where he was struck by the importance of developments in Southeast Asia. He reported to Parliament on the importance of Indochina and Burma (which was also facing a communist insurgency) to the security of Southeast Asia. If Indochina or Burma were lost to the communists, he said, Thailand would be outflanked, rendering Malaya vulnerable even without direct military aggression. This in turn would imperil Indonesia and, then, Australia. Arguments along these lines, known as the 'domino theory' after a speech by President Eisenhower in 1954, were common in the early 1950s. The concept that one victory by an expansionist international movement could soon lead to another was readily accepted by many, reflecting the world's recent experience with Nazi Germany in the late 1930s and early 1940s, the Soviet Union in the late 1940s and, fresh in Australian minds, the Japanese southward thrust in 1941–42.

The domino theory was based on two ideas. The first was the military value to an insurgent movement in one country of a sympathetic government in a neighbouring country, both as a source or channel for supplies and as a location for sanctuaries. For example, the successes gained by Ho Chi Minh and his colleagues in the Viet Minh in their war against the French, especially in the northern provinces, owed much to the communist victory in China in October 1949. After that time, not only did the Chinese provide substantial material support to the Viet Minh (albeit only a fraction of what the Americans were providing to the French), but the communist army, the People's Army of Vietnam (PAVN), could also retreat to sanctuaries inside China whenever the pressure from the French became too severe.

The second pillar of the domino theory was a matter of morale and mood. Each communist victory lent credibility to the claim that the socialist revolution was the wave of the future, leading inevitably to worldwide success. In that sense, passionate communists and ardent anti-communists were equally vigorous advocates of the domino theory: the former hoped and the latter feared that one communist success would lead, almost inevitably, to another and then another. In material terms, communist insurgents in archipelagoes such as Indonesia or the Philippines, or a peninsula like Malaya, were at a relative disadvantage, because Western dominance in naval power restricted external supplies; but in the ideological dimension of the Cold War, communist movements around the world gained inspiration and motivation from any success.

After Casey's visit, the first of many to Asia, his department opened diplomatic missions in Saigon and Rangoon and upgraded the consulate in Bangkok to diplomatic status. The initial reluctance of the United States to support a French colonial war was by this time totally outweighed by its fear of communism in Europe, skilfully exploited by the French. The value of American aid rose from $10 million in 1951 to $1.1 billion in 1954, representing about 78 per cent of the cost of France's war effort.[11] At the same time, the French obstinately refused to accede to American advice. Bao Dai was regarded by the Americans as much as by the Vietnamese as an indolent playboy, and the French refused to give sufficient concessions to the State of Vietnam to give it credibility as an authentic expression of Vietnamese national aspirations, or to support the Vietnam National Army they had created so that it had some hope of matching the PAVN.

The Australian government was sympathetic to the French proposal that the Western powers with an interest in Southeast Asia – the United

Kingdom, the United States, France, Australia and New Zealand – establish what became known as the Five-Power Staff Agency to coordinate their political and military planning for the region. The English-speaking powers, however, suspected that France was more interested in defending its colonial interests than in a general Western campaign against communism, while the Americans were reluctant, after the human and financial costs of the Korean War, to become involved in another land war in Asia. All that emerged was a relatively weak military liaison group, lacking the powers for which the French had hoped or the access to the high-level planning of London, Washington and Paris to which the Australians aspired.

As the French position in Indochina deteriorated in the face of Viet Minh advances, Casey sought to demonstrate to Australia's allies and to the electorate that the fate of Indochina was important to Australian security. In 1953 he invited Jean Letourneau, the French minister responsible for relations with the Associated States (Vietnam, Laos and Cambodia), to visit Australia. The visit gave Letourneau the opportunity to assert that France was not fighting a colonial war but was 'shutting the door to Communism's advance in South-east Asia'.[12] The Australians promised diplomatic support to the French and indicated a willingness to provide technical aid. After lengthy discussions, Australia sent several shiploads of arms and other items to Indochina, where they arrived in May 1954, when the French and the PAVN were approaching the decisive battle of the First Indochina War. The Letourneau visit and the arms shipments had little military significance, but they demonstrated to Britain, the United States and the Australian public that the Australian government was prepared to give political, diplomatic, and a token degree of military support to the French position in Indochina.

THREE

AUSTRALIA AND SOUTHEAST ASIA 1954-60

By 1953–54 the PAVN had become a large and formidable force, highly motivated and proficient in both conventional and guerrilla warfare, receiving substantial material support from the Soviet Union and China, and able to use sanctuaries in China and supply lines through Laos. Moved by the war's enormous financial and human costs, together with increasing doubts over its strategic wisdom and moral justification, French public opinion was turning against the war in Indochina. As the likelihood of negotiated settlement grew, the French military aimed to strengthen their position by establishing a forward base at Dien Bien Phu, near the Laotian border, from which they aimed to strike decisive blows against the Viet Minh's supply lines. The base was totally dependent on air supply. The military leader of the PAVN, Vo Nguyen Giap, devised a system of trenches that surrounded the French base and penetrated into it. At the same time Soviet-supplied anti-aircraft guns and artillery pieces were manhandled into the surrounding hills. Outnumbered and outmanoeuvred by Giap and the PAVN, the French forces became trapped. In the early months of 1954 it became increasingly clear that

France, often described in newspaper headlines as one of the 'Big Four' (the other three being the United States, the Soviet Union and Britain), was facing an ignominious defeat at the hands of a revolutionary army.

THE 'UNITED ACTION' CRISIS[1]

At this time the major powers agreed that Indochina should be discussed at a conference they had already decided to convene in Geneva in May to discuss the post-armistice situation in Korea. In April the United States received desperate calls from the French for American intervention in Indochina in order to stave off a humiliating defeat. Diplomatic exchanges and public discussion raised the possible use not only of massive conventional forces but also of tactical nuclear weapons. Opinion in Washington was deeply divided. Some political and military leaders, including the Chairman of the Joint Chiefs of Staff, Admiral Arthur W Radford, favoured American intervention, but others, including the army's Chief of Staff, General Matthew Ridgway, were strongly opposed to involvement in another land war in Asia. President Eisenhower laid down a series of conditions to be filled before the United States would intervene, one of the most important of which was the active cooperation of Britain and other Commonwealth nations, including Australia. It was already becoming clear that the British government, led by Prime Minister Winston Churchill and Foreign Secretary Anthony Eden, was strongly opposed to military intervention, instead seeking a diplomatic solution at the Geneva Conference, which Britain and the Soviet Union would co-chair. In late March Eisenhower's Secretary of State, John Foster Dulles, who had earned a reputation as a combative opponent of communism, called for 'united action' in Indochina by a coalition of nations, in which they expected Australia to be prominent.

In the midst of a major world crisis, the Australian government was thus torn between the sharply opposed positions of its two great power allies, exacerbated by personal animosity between Dulles and Eden. In Australia a highly successful visit by the young Queen Elizabeth II had raised sentimental attachment to the monarchy and the connection with Britain to extraordinary levels, complicating the government's reaction to what was portrayed in the media as a choice between supporting Britain and supporting the United States. Casey and his departmental officials could see grave risks in any 'internationalisation' of Western military intervention, but ministers also feared that a failure to support the United States could lead to an American withdrawal from Southeast Asia, enabling the communists to take control of all of Vietnam, in turn threatening the security of the rest of Southeast Asia and eventually Australia. For much of April and May, Australia was engaged in intense diplomacy with both allies. Reluctant to offend either Britain or the United States, the government played for time by saying that it could not make a major commitment before the federal election, to be held on 29 May.

During this time a brief dispute prefigured many of the central issues of the global debate on Vietnam a decade later. An Anglican bishop, Dr EH Burgmann, two historians of Asia, JW Davidson and CP Fitzgerald, and the Australian historian Manning Clark published a statement arguing that the Viet Minh were not communists, subservient to the Soviet Union and China, but nationalists. Liberal parliamentarians, led by the vehemently anti-communist WC Wentworth and Senator John Gorton, responded by citing extensive evidence that Ho and his colleagues were avowed communists who had proclaimed that the revolution in Vietnam was part of the Soviet-led world revolution. Before this exchange, confined largely to the *Canberra Times* and backbench Members of Parliament, could have much effect in educating the Australian public on the complexities of Vietnamese nationalism and communism it was completely overshadowed by 'the Petrov affair'.

On 13 April Menzies announced that Vladimir Petrov, a Soviet intelligence agent working under diplomatic cover at the Soviet Embassy in Canberra, had defected. Within days the Soviet Union severed diplomatic relations with Australia, and the government announced that a Royal Commission would be held into Soviet espionage in Australia. Occurring in the already tense atmosphere of an extremely close election campaign, these events dominated Australian politics for months. The government was narrowly returned in the election, having gained less than 50 per cent of the two-party preferred vote.

Just before the election, the Department of External Affairs told its missions that the election had not been the principal reason Australia opposed the 'internationalisation' of military operations in Indochina. The military and political aims of any internationalisation were unclear; the Geneva Conference should be given a genuine opportunity to reach a settlement; and most Asian countries would oppose it, making United Nations backing impossible. Australia could not see what could be achieved without the introduction of American and other ground forces, which would risk Chinese intervention and thus a third world war. Australia therefore wanted to see an honourable settlement negotiated at Geneva. This was a clear statement of a policy that echoed that of neither major ally, but was clearly closer to the British position than to the American. The United States government expressed frustration and disappointment, but only in mild terms. By this time, the focus of all attention was on the Geneva Conference.

THE GENEVA CONFERENCE[2]

General Giap timed the PAVN's final assault on the French position at Dien Bien Phu for the greatest political effect, securing victory on the day before the Geneva Conference began its discussion of Indochina.

For the next three months the world's great powers negotiated the future of Indochina in the aftermath of the DRV's triumph over the French. Australia was an observer, not a full participant, but Casey was heavily involved in diplomatic discussions not only with senior representatives of the United States, Britain, France and other friendly powers but also with China's Zhou Enlai (despite the fact that Australia, like the United States but unlike Britain, did not recognise the communist government in Beijing) and India's Prime Minister Jawaharlal Nehru.

In late July the conference produced a Final Declaration and three ceasefire agreements, which came to be known collectively as the Geneva Accords. They provided for the partition of Vietnam into two zones, divided by a line roughly along the 17th parallel, with a demilitarised zone on either side of the line. The PAVN (which signed the ceasefire agreements for Laos and Cambodia as well as Vietnam) would withdraw its forces to the northern zone and the French their forces to the southern, before withdrawing from Vietnam altogether. People were to be allowed to 'regroup' to whichever zone they preferred. The establishment of foreign military bases and the introduction of military forces were prohibited in either zone, and neither was to constitute part of a military alliance. The division of Vietnam along the 17th parallel was stated to be temporary: elections to be held in both zones in 1956 would reunite Vietnam. An International Supervisory Commission, comprising India, Poland and Canada, was established to supervise the implementation of the Accords.

The provision for people to 'regroup' to either the northern or southern zone implied a more permanent division than the provision for elections in 1956 to reunite all of Vietnam. A number of unilateral declarations and statements created further ambiguities and discord. Although the Eisenhower administration knew that the preservation of Laos, Cambodia and the southern half of Vietnam under non-communist regimes was the best that the Western powers could achieve, it was reluctant to be publicly associated with any concession of territory to a communist administration. Consequently it distanced itself from the Accords, not formally endorsing them but allowing them to come into effect, while immediately starting to take steps to ensure that no further territory would be 'lost' to the communists. With France now removed from Indochina, the United States took on the role of seeking to preserve an anti-communist state in southern Vietnam, as well as non-communist governments in Laos and Cambodia. Despite its extreme fragility, Bao Dai's State of Vietnam claimed to be the rightful government of all Vietnam and refused to be bound by the Accords. The Viet Minh, for their part, felt that pressure from their communist allies, the Soviet Union and China, had denied the DRV half of the victory it had earned by its military success. During and after the Geneva Conference, both communist powers indicated that, while supporting the DRV's claim to all of Vietnam, they were prepared to accept a lasting partition, if that were the price of avoiding a major war with the United States. For Hanoi, however, this was a temporary setback to its longstanding ambitions: the DRV would undoubtedly seek to gain the control of all Vietnam that it had sought since 1945, as well as a leading role in Laos and Cambodia. The Geneva Accords, therefore, established an armistice that enabled France to withdraw from a long, costly and unsuccessful colonial war, but did not create a durable political settlement. The First Indochina War had ended, but the lines were already drawn for the next.

THE CREATION OF SEATO[3]

Many in the West feared that the State of Vietnam, south of the 17th parallel, was so fragile that it might succumb to its northern rival, the DRV, even before the elections scheduled for 1956, leading quickly to communist victories in Laos, Cambodia and possibly other Southeast

Asian 'dominoes'. The United States and other countries therefore moved promptly to establish a collective defence organisation, intended to be a Southeast Asian equivalent to NATO. A treaty in Manila in September 1954 created the South-East Asia Treaty Organization (SEATO), comprising the United States, Britain, France, Australia, New Zealand, Thailand, the Philippines and Pakistan. The terms of the Geneva Accords prevented the inclusion of South Vietnam, Laos and Cambodia as members of SEATO, but they were covered by a protocol to the Manila Treaty, which designated them as areas that fell within its scope. The United States made a unilateral declaration that its commitment was limited to opposing communist aggression, and Casey on behalf of Australia made an oral statement along similar lines. SEATO was clearly aimed at resisting communist expansion, seen to be emanating from China and North Vietnam.

In comparison with NATO, SEATO had obvious flaws. The commitment undertaken by each member was phrased in weaker terms than that in the North Atlantic Treaty; fewer Asian nations than Australia and others had hoped had joined, with Malaya and Indonesia among those that had not joined; Pakistan was clearly more concerned about its hostile relationship with India than with security in Southeast Asia; and France was extremely reluctant to return to the site of its humiliating defeat. Nevertheless, the new alliance had considerable appeal for the Australian government. The United States, with its unrivalled military strength, was committed to the security of Southeast Asia, in a multilateral environment that should reduce the risk of resort to nuclear weapons or other steps which might lead to a major war with China; Britain was committed to the security of all of Southeast Asia, not just Malaya and other British territories; France was, on the face of it, similarly committed; and the organisation at least included some Asian nations, including Thailand, which was prepared to stand firmly against communist expansion rather than to adopt its traditional stance of bending with the prevailing wind. The Military Planning Office established at the SEATO headquarters in Bangkok offered the prospect of Australia's longstanding goal – access to the high-level military planning of its allies, especially the United States. By the end of the decade the government had succeeded in having an Australian soldier, Major General John Wilton, appointed head of the Military Planning Office, in his last appointment before becoming Chief of the General Staff (CGS, the position now known as Chief of Army).[4] In the late 1950s and early 1960s SEATO was more prominent than ANZUS in Australia's political and military planning, and the government's public rhetoric underlined SEATO's importance.

THE STRATEGIC RESERVE AND THE COMMITMENT OF TROOPS TO MALAYA 1955[5]

In the early 1950s Australia's political and military leaders discussed with their British and New Zealand counterparts arrangements to collaborate in the defence of Southeast Asia. These discussions led to what was called ANZAM, a joint British–Australian–New Zealand command to integrate intelligence and defence planning for the Malayan area. (The acronym was sometimes said to stand for Anglo–New Zealand–Australia–Malaya agreement.) Although it received much less public attention than ANZUS or SEATO, the agreement to establish ANZAM in 1953 was crucial to the decision that, in the event of a major war, Australia would deploy all three services to Malaya, not to the Middle East. To give substance to these plans, the British Chiefs of Staff proposed the creation of a Far East Strategic Reserve, to which the three Commonwealth countries would each contribute forces. Unlike the United States, Britain wanted to have forces on the ground in Southeast

Asia – in military parlance, [forces-in-being] – both as a deterrent against major aggression by communist powers, including China and North Vietnam, and to be available for use in counter-terrorist actions. The Indochina crisis of 1954 brought these discussions to a head, and the creation of the Far East Strategic Reserve was announced in early 1955. Australia's contribution would be two RAN destroyers or frigates in Malayan waters, together with an annual visit by an aircraft carrier; a fighter wing, a bomber wing and an airfield construction squadron from the RAAF; and an infantry battalion with supporting arms. The army commitment was the most politically sensitive, as this would be the first time that Australian troops had been committed overseas other than for a major war.

The three Commonwealth nations hoped that the United States could be linked with their defence planning, but the Americans maintained their reluctance to make any commitments in advance, relying on the mobility and flexibility of their forces to respond to whatever situation might arise. They were also reluctant to give any impression that a 'white men's club' was seeking to direct affairs in Asia. Nevertheless, ['quadripartite planning'] between the United States, Britain, Australia and New Zealand became a holy grail for Australian policy-makers for the next decade.

The Menzies government took every opportunity to link the Far East Strategic Reserve with SEATO, claiming that it was 'an integral part of the defence effort within the structure of the Manila Treaty'.⁶ This was a sensitive issue in Malaya and Singapore, each of which was moving towards self-government. Although the party that was leading Malaya to independence, UMNO, was anti-communist, Malaya had not joined SEATO. The leaders of UMNO and the other emerging parties were reluctant to be associated with the Strategic Reserve if it were closely linked with SEATO operations. In Singapore, with a predominantly Chinese population, association with SEATO was even more sensitive. The British authorities in Malaya pressed Australia to state clearly that the troops and other elements committed to the Strategic Reserve would definitely be used in counter-terrorist operations in the Emergency. The government was willing to permit this, but did not want Australian forces to be involved in responding to either inter-communal strife in Malaya or left-wing riots in Singapore. After prolonged negotiations, the government allocated primary and secondary roles to the Australian forces. Their primary role was to deter and to counter 'further communist aggression in Southeast Asia'; their secondary role was to take part in operations against the CTs in Malaya, provided this did not detract from their primary role. To distance them from any involvement in internal stability, the Australian battalion was located, not in Singapore as first planned, but in Penang and Perak, in the northeast of the Malayan peninsula close to the Thai border.

The deployment of Australian troops to Malaya became a highly sensitive issue in Australian politics, because these discussions coincided with a deep and bitter split in the Australian Labor Party (ALP). Although in the late 1940s and early 1950s the mainstream of the party had welcomed the work of the groupers in countering the communists' aggressive political and military tactics, by 1954 many felt that the right-wing anti-communists were using a mirror-image of communist tactics to try to dominate the party's policies and leadership. The issue came to a head at the federal conference of the ALP in 1955, after which a substantial section of the party, mostly from Victoria and largely but not entirely Catholic, split to form the Australian Labor Party (Anti-Communist). In 1957 they took the name the Democratic Labor Party (DLP). A similar split in Queensland led to the formation of the Queensland Labor Party, which subsequently merged with the DLP.

A central element of the DLP's outlook was that the ALP was failing to support strong measures against communism in Southeast Asia as well as in Australia. The question of 'troops to Malaya' therefore took on great symbolic significance in the internecine warfare within the political and industrial wings of the labour movement. (For years afterwards, the slogan 'no troops to Malaya' could be seen painted on railway culverts in Melbourne.) In December 1955 Menzies called an early election to take advantage of the division in Labor ranks, and won comfortably, only 18 months after his narrow victory in 1954. From this time onwards, DLP preferences at elections would be highly important in keeping the Liberal–Country Party coalition in government, and the ALP on the opposition benches, until 1972. The electoral support came at a price, for the Liberal–Country Party coalition could not appear to moderate its anti-communist positions, at home or abroad, without jeopardising the crucial electoral support of the DLP. This basic electoral arithmetic underpinned the government's foreign policies for years to come.

[handwritten annotations: *quadripartite planning / UNITED *forces in being / ACTION *creation of SEATO]

AUSTRALIAN TROOPS AND THE EMERGENCY 1955–1960[7]

Australia's air force commitment to the Strategic Reserve initially took the form of the Lincolns of No. 1 (Bomber) Squadron, which had been serving since 1950. Around the time of their withdrawal in late 1958, they were replaced by the Canberra bombers of No. 2 Squadron and the Sabre fighters of No. 3 and No. 77 Squadrons. Stationed at Butterworth, the aircrew and groundcrew of these squadrons trained for their Strategic Reserve role and seldom took part in any Emergency operations. The RAN commitment of two destroyers or frigates, and an annual visit by an aircraft carrier, was largely symbolic, both as a contribution to deterrence in the region and in counter-terrorist operations in the Emergency. Unlike Confrontation and the Vietnam War in the 1960s, there was no requirement to maintain a blockade against the supply of arms to the terrorists from outside Malaya. On a few occasions, the RAN ships provided naval gunfire support to ground units ashore. The most significant role of the RAN in Malaya was a substantial contribution to the development of the Royal Malayan (from 1963, Malaysian) Navy, including the provision of officers who served as the Chief of Staff, the professional head of the service, from 1960 to 1967.

The most important Australian commitments both to the Emergency and to the Strategic Reserve were the infantry battalion and support units. A pattern of 'roulement' or rotation by the three battalions of the Royal Australian Regiment was established, based on two-year tours of duty. The 2nd Battalion, Royal Australian Regiment (2RAR), served from 1955 to 1957, succeeded by 3RAR from 1957 to 1959; 1RAR from 1959 to 1961; 2RAR on its second tour from 1961 to 1963; and 3RAR on its second tour from 1963 to 1965. Although it was often overshadowed by the more dramatic commitments of the 1960s, the commitment of an Australian infantry battalion to Malaysia continued until the early 1970s. The contribution of those battalions during conflicts in the 1960s is discussed in later chapters.

The operations undertaken by the RAR battalions in the Emergency, fulfilling their supposedly secondary role, largely comprised patrolling in small units in order to seek CTs in the jungle and to exert pressure on the remaining guerrillas in the last areas to be declared 'white', that is, free from Emergency conditions. The Australians learned much about jungle warfare and counter-insurgency, applying the lessons learned in Malaya in its training programs and doctrine at home, as the army directed its planning for future operations almost exclusively on Southeast Asia. In 1954 the army reopened the Jungle Warfare Training Centre at Canungra in Queensland, first established to prepare soldiers for the New Guinea campaigns in the 1939–45 war.

The Australians performed well in this type of warfare, and their contribution was welcome, but by the time Australian troops were committed to the Emergency it was already clear that the communists would be beaten. After the guerrillas' early successes, the British had gradually gained the upper hand. A number of measures contributed to this success, including the close coordination of civil, police and military authorities, the creation of 'New Villages' to separate the rural villagers from the insurgents, and the skilful use of intelligence gained by an effective Special Branch of the police. Of crucial importance was the promise by the British in 1954 that they would grant independence to Malaya in a form that would be congenial to the Malay majority while protecting the rights of Chinese and Indian minorities, even while Emergency conditions continued. The number of guerrillas in the MRLA had probably reached a peak of 8000 in 1951, but by 1955 was down to about 3000. On the government side, there had been up to 19 battalions of Commonwealth forces, including units from Britain, Malaya, East Africa and Fiji, as well as Australia and New Zealand. Consequently, the Australians were involved in 'a long, frustrating and occasionally bloody clean-up operation',[8] which was nonetheless important to the future of Malaya.

Malaya gained its independence, known as 'Merdeka' or freedom, in 1957. (The band of 2RAR, nearing the end of the battalion's first tour, played at the Merdeka celebrations.) The new independent government, led by Prime Minister Tunku Abdul Rahman, asked the Commonwealth forces to remain and to continue fighting the communist guerrillas. The warmth of the relationship between the Australian and Malayan governments was confirmed in visits by Tunku Abdul Rahman to Australia and by Menzies to Malaya in 1959. When the Emergency was officially declared over in 1960, the remainder of the MCP retired to the jungle across the Thai border, severely weakened but still a potential nuisance. As part of the Strategic Reserve the Australian battalion, and some other elements, remained in the region, engaged in Strategic Reserve exercises and available for use if requested by the Malayan government.

The success of the operations by Australia, in a British-led coalition of national forces, had considerable impact on Australian political and military leaders. The army's leaders were reinforced in their confidence that soldiers, especially the infantrymen of the Royal Australian Regiment, were skilled in the tactics of counter-insurgency operations in Southeast Asian jungles. Political leaders drew the lesson that, in the right circumstances, Western powers could intervene successfully in a former colony, at the request of the leaders of the post-colonial government, to help ensure that that government would be friendly to the West. Those who had asserted that such interventions would damage Australia's credibility among Asian nationalists had, it seemed, been proved to be wrong (or, in the case of peace movements, to be acting in the interests of communists). In the coming years, this gave at least some in high office confidence in the prospects of success of intervention by the United States and its allies in Indochina.

For decades afterwards, even into the 21st century, the Malayan Emergency was studied as a model of successful counter-insurgency.[9] Many political and military authorities in the Western world studied the techniques that had proved successful: the careful coordination of civil, police and military agencies; the importance of intelligence and of food denial; the emphasis on 'winning hearts and minds' rather than on killing large numbers of the enemy; the establishment of protected villages to separate the guerrillas from the rural population; the use of small-unit tactics, including skilled reconnaissance, patient ambushes and quiet patrols deep into the jungle to unsettle the enemy on his own territory. From an early stage in the Vietnam commitment, comparisons were made with Malaya and many turned to those with Malayan experience for advice. In fact, the relevance of Malaya to Vietnam was always arguable.[10] The MRLA comprised at most a few thousand guerrillas, while the PAVN comprised hundreds of thousands of highly skilled and motivated soldiers, well equipped to fight both conventional and guerrilla campaigns; the enemy in Malaya came from an easily identifiable minority, while it was impossible in Vietnam to tell who might be an enemy or potential enemy; as the colonial power, the British authorities had the ability to enforce coordination of the civil, police and military authorities, unlike the Americans in Vietnam; and the British in Malaya had a clear, positive goal of independence for a competent indigenous government with clear majority support, as well as a military strategy capable of realising that goal.

AUSTRALIA AND VIETNAM 1955-60[11]

Despite the Geneva Accords and the creation of SEATO and the Strategic Reserve, the State of Vietnam in the southern zone seemed so fragile in 1954 that many observers did not expect it to survive even to contest the elections scheduled for 1956, let along to succeed in them. Before the Geneva Conference ended, Bao Dai appointed Ngo Dinh Diem as Prime Minister. In a blatantly rigged referendum in 1955, Diem ousted Bao Dai and created the Republic of Vietnam (RVN) with himself as President. Diem had some credentials as a nationalist, but did not have a broad basis of popular support. The Ngo Dinh family were devout Catholics with a tradition of service to the imperial court and the church. In the early 1950s, Diem had lived in a seminary in the United States, where he established close relationships with leading Catholics, including the politically influential and vehemently anti-communist Archbishop of New York, Cardinal Francis Spellman. Apart from American Catholics, Diem's principal support came from the Vietnamese Catholics, about 800 000 in number, who 'regrouped' from the northern to the southern zone following the Geneva Accords. Before 1954, Catholicism, like communism, had been stronger in the north than the south: after the partition, Diem would rely heavily on the small but strongly anti-communist Catholic minority who, like him, had their roots north of the 17th parallel. He also had some support from landowners and the pro-Western middle class in the towns and cities, but much less from the peasant villages in rural areas, where most of the population lived.

Despite this narrow base of support, Diem initially had more success in his efforts to establish a credible state in South Vietnam than many in the West had dared hope. He crushed the Binh Xuyen, a Mafia-like organisation which ran gambling and vice in Saigon and to which Bao Dai had given control of the Saigon police, and moved effectively against some politico-religious sects and warlords. Diem also undertook a ruthless campaign to extirpate the cadres who had been left behind in the south when most of the communist forces had regrouped to the north. Diem's authoritarian measures created enduring dissent and resentment among non-communists, but in the short term they were brutally efficient, as many cadres were killed or imprisoned. Diem's supporters described the rebels as not Viet Minh but 'Viet Cong', or Vietnamese communists. Intended to be a disparaging dismissal of their claim to be a broad coalition of nationalists, the name stuck. The communists in the south appealed to Hanoi for desperately needed support, but the party's leaders could do little for their southern comrades, as they faced severe problems consolidating their own position in the north. A land reform program in 1956 ran out of control, with many peasants wrongly condemned as 'landlords' or 'rich peasants', leading to between 5000 and 15 000 deaths. Like both the Soviet Union and China, the DRV faced dissent from intellectuals seeking a less rigid form of communist rule.

Diem flatly refused to hold the elections scheduled for 1956, maintaining that the south was not bound by the Geneva Accords and that there was no possibility of a genuinely free election in the communist-controlled north. The United States supported this stand, while the Soviet Union gave only token support to the DRV, giving priority to 'peaceful co-existence' with the United States over support for the communists in Vietnam. For a time in 1957 the Soviet Union even contemplated the admission of both the RVN and the DRV to the United Nations. It seemed increasingly likely that the international community would tacitly accept that there were two Vietnams, just as there were two Germanys and two Koreas, each claiming to be the legitimate government of the entire country but in fact co-existing as ideological rivals.

In 1957–58, while the DRV worked to secure greater political and economic support from the communist bloc, Diem similarly sought to establish himself as a successful leader of a 'free world' country. In 1957 he visited the United States, where he was hailed by President Eisenhower as a 'miracle man', and later that year became the first foreign head of state to visit Australia. He was received with considerable pomp and ceremony by the government and hailed by the press as a highly successful leader who had done a great service to Australia as well as his own country by establishing the RVN as a viable entity and a stalwart fighter against communism in Southeast Asia. Evatt, as Leader of the Labor Opposition, joined the praise, saying that peace and democracy had been achieved in Vietnam, but the most ardent welcome came from the Catholic community, who acclaimed Diem as a bastion of Catholic Christianity. The Diem visit strengthened the already strong support given by Australian Catholics, especially those active in the DLP and the organisations associated with 'the Movement', to the Diem regime. The government had now come to accept that the RVN, or South Vietnam, was a viable state whose integrity and independence had to be defended, in Australia's own interests, against internal and external threats. The Australian diplomatic mission in Saigon was upgraded from a legation to an embassy, with the first ambassador arriving in 1959.

This public acclaim, and the confirmation of Australia's support for the Diem regime, came at the peak of his success and reputation. Much of Diem's apparent success was artificial and fragile, based on huge quantities of economic and military assistance from the United States. Much of the economic aid was not invested wisely but disbursed on the RVN's military and security services and consumer goods for the urban middle class. The military aid was used to create the Army of the Republic of Vietnam (ARVN), which was structured and trained as a large, conventional army, heavily reliant, like its American model, on technology, transport and firepower. It was designed to defend the RVN from a conventional invasion from the north, not to undertake counter-insurgency in the rural areas. The massive amount of American aid encouraged the growth of corruption in political and military circles, exacerbated by the Diem regime's promotion of political and military leaders on the basis of personal and political favouritism, especially towards Catholics, rather than on merit.

The desperate pleas of the southern communists for support from Hanoi eventually achieved their aim. In 1959, in response to reports by Le Duan, the communist leader with greatest experience of conditions in the south, the party formally decided to adopt a policy of armed struggle. Cadres who had 'regrouped' to the north after 1954 were now infiltrated back into the south to replenish the depleted numbers of the southern party. Groups responsible to the communist leaders in Hanoi were formed to organise the infiltration of people, arms and supplies, both through Laos and Cambodia and by sea, and to supply the communist forces from both North Vietnam and Laos fighting in Laos. In late 1960, following a standard communist tactic, the party established the National Liberation Front for the Liberation of South Vietnam (NLF), with the aim of uniting anti-Diem dissidents under communist leadership. The underground party in the south was reformed as the People's Revolutionary Party, to take the leading role in the NLF, and its forces were brought together as the People's Liberation Armed Forces (PLAF), under the command of a PAVN officer. The political and military organisations that would lead the revolution in the south were designed to be seen as independent, but were created and controlled by the communist party in Hanoi. The battle for the future of Vietnam was now joined, although few in the West were fully aware of the import of these developments.

AUSTRALIA, INDONESIA AND WEST NEW GUINEA[12]

In the late 1950s Australia's major focus of concern in Southeast Asia was neither Malaya nor Indochina but Indonesia's campaign to gain control of the western half of the island of New Guinea, which had been excluded from Indonesia's territory at the time of independence in 1949. President Sukarno and the Indonesian leadership were insistent that they should incorporate this last part of the former Netherlands East Indies into Indonesia. By the late 1950s Sukarno had become increasingly dictatorial, asserting that Indonesia required a 'guided democracy' rather than a European-style liberal democracy. The campaign to incorporate West New Guinea, by a combination of diplomatic, economic and military measures, gained him the support of both the rapidly growing PKI and the predominantly anti-communist Indonesian Army, which was also gaining increasing political and economic power. In his external policies also, Sukarno skilfully played the communist and anti-communist blocs off against each other, gaining financial and military support from both. Many Australians became increasingly troubled by his anti-Western rhetoric and growing links with the Soviet Union and China. Sukarno's ambition to acquire control of West New Guinea directly affected Australia, which had responsibility under a United Nations mandate for the eastern half of the island. Policy-makers feared that, if the Indonesian campaign were successful, Australia could find itself sharing an almost indefensible land border with a potentially hostile and pro-communist power in an area crucial to Australian defence. They hoped that the Dutch could retain control of West New Guinea until a satisfactory settlement could be achieved.

In 1957 the Australians and the Dutch issued a joint statement on cooperation between their respective territories, implying that the two halves of the island might achieve independence either separately or jointly. The international reaction, not only in Indonesia but throughout the newly independent countries in Asia and Africa, was hostile. While Sukarno's rhetoric was increasingly anti-Western and pro-Chinese, the Indonesians told Western governments that opposition to their claim was playing into the hands of China and the PKI. After a visit to Australia by the Indonesian Foreign Minister, Dr Subandrio, in 1959, Casey and Subandrio issued a communiqué stating that Australia would not oppose a transfer of sovereignty of West New Guinea from the Dutch to the Indonesians, if this were achieved by peaceful means. Across the political spectrum, from the left of the ALP to the DLP and the RSL, Casey's stance was denounced as a 'sellout', a capitulation to the Indonesians comparable with the appeasement of Nazi Germany at Munich in 1938.

The underlying problem for the Australian government was the sympathy shown by the United States to the argument put forward by Subandrio and other non-communist Indonesians – that West New Guinea might, in effect, be the price to pay for keeping Indonesia in friendly, non-communist hands. Despite the growing strength of the PKI, the Americans argued that Western interests would be best served by supporting Sukarno and facilitating his takeover of West New Guinea while developing close links with the Indonesian armed forces. After 1958, when Sukarno and the Indonesian Army had defeated rebellions in the 'outer islands' that had been supported by the CIA, the United

States had little option but to work as closely as possible with Sukarno and the head of the army, General Nasution.

The gulf between American and Australian policies on Indonesia and West New Guinea was particularly troublesome because Australia was moving closer to the United States in defence matters. In 1957, after a major review of defence policy, Menzies announced that Australia would organise its forces 'to fit ourselves for close cooperation with the United States in the South-East Asian area'.[13] Military equipment would, as far as possible, be standardised with the United States rather than with Britain. Menzies stressed the importance to Australia that 'the free countries of Southeast Asia' – meaning South Vietnam, Laos, Cambodia, Thailand and Malaya – should not fall to 'Communist aggression', and he emphasised the importance of SEATO and the military strength of the United States.

In 1959 the Defence Committee, the government's principal advisory body on defence policy, including both civilian officials and service chiefs, submitted a new assessment of Australian strategic policy. The Committee referred to the possibility that Australia might have to act independently of its allies in situations such as a conflict with Indonesia over West New Guinea while American and other allied forces were engaged elsewhere. The Committee (probably at the instigation of Sir Arthur Tange, the Secretary of the External Affairs Department) recommended that Australian forces develop the capacity to act independently, at least for a short time, without having to rely on allies for operational and logistic support. Cabinet firmly rejected this advice. Australian forces would be designed to act closely with allies, principally the United States, in collective defence arrangements such as SEATO, and only in Southeast Asia.[14] The divergent policies of the US and Australia towards West New Guinea established a major concern, seldom expressed publicly, for the Australian government. Australian defence policy was based on close cooperation with the United States in

Southeast Asia, but the Americans were taking a different stance on an area of extreme strategic sensitivity to the Australians. [In this context, the Australians were determined to do everything possible both to keep the United States committed to Southeast Asian security in general and to ensure that American policies supported Australian interests and aspirations with respect to both Indonesia and Indochina.] *

STAY in each other's fold

INDONESIA was the LINCHPIN of relying

By the end of the 1950s, Australian relations with Southeast Asia had entered a new phase. A new collective defence arrangement, SEATO, had been established, including both Australia's principal allies and some Asian nations. Australian forces were permanently stationed in the area as part of a Commonwealth Strategic Reserve, which the government liked to associate with SEATO. The Emergency was over and Malaya was an independent, pro-Western member of the Commonwealth, with excellent relations with Australia, although not a member of SEATO. Under Diem, the RVN seemed to be in a healthier state than anyone had thought possible in 1954 and Australia had committed itself to supporting its survival. Australian economic and defence policies were becoming ever more closely aligned with the United States, with beneficial results for the country's security and prosperity. The major flaw seemed to be the divergence between the United States and Australia over Indonesia and West New Guinea. With these successes and concerns in mind, Australia would face a new series of crises in the 1960s.

— FOUR —

THE CRISES OF THE EARLY 1960s

The Second Indochina War could be said to have begun in Laos even before the First Indochina War was over. The small landlocked kingdom provided little fertile ground for communism, but its position, bordering both parts of the partitioned Vietnam as well as China, Burma, Thailand and Cambodia, gave it enormous strategic significance. The Lao communist movement, known as the Pathet Lao, was heavily influenced by its Vietnamese counterpart, with whom it had strong ethnic and family links. Its leader, Prince Souvannouphong, a half-brother of the royalist leader Prince Souvanna Phouma, had spent several years in Vietnam, where he met Ho Chi Minh, formed close links with the Viet Minh, and married a Vietnamese. As noted earlier, the ability of the Viet Minh to use sanctuaries and supply lines in the eastern provinces of Laos, bordering northern Vietnam, had been a major asset in their war against the French, leading the French to make their ill-fated stand in 1954 at Dien Bien Phu, close to the Laotian border.

THE LAOS CRISES 1959–61[1]

The Geneva Accords of 1954 declared Laos to be neutral and free from foreign military forces, but it soon became clear that the DRV placed its strategic importance ahead of this provision. The United States, especially Dulles, decided that its responsibilities under the SEATO agreement required it to act similarly, placing a military mission under civilian cover. In the late 1950s Laos became the site of a proxy war between Hanoi and Washington. Observers commented on the bizarre contrast between, on the one hand, the almost comic opera nature of the conflict in a remote, landlocked country, where neither the Royal Lao forces nor their Pathet Lao opponents were militarily competent and both often avoided battle; and, on the other hand, the issues at stake in the global Cold War. When President Eisenhower discussed the state of the world when handing over to his successor, John F. Kennedy, in January 1961, Laos was an important topic, while Vietnam was barely mentioned.

While crises in Laos made world headlines from time to time, they were generally overshadowed by Cold War crises and other international developments in other parts of the world. A long-developing schism between the Soviet Union and China now became apparent, but did little to ease the problems faced by the West. In the late 1950s the Soviet Union had spoken of the need for 'peaceful co-existence' with the West, only to be scorned by Mao Zedong, who proclaimed Chinese support for 'wars of national liberation'. This opened the way for communist revolutionaries in Africa and Asia to play off the two most powerful communist governments for support, an exercise in which Ho and his colleagues proved highly skilful. In the early 1960s a renewal of Cold War confrontation between the United States and the Soviet Union, particularly in Europe and the Caribbean, dominated the concern of Western countries. In 1961 American support for an anti-communist willing to act alongside the United States even if neither of those conditions could be met. Because war was averted, this decision in principle never had to be implemented, and the public probably thought that the lines established by the Geneva Agreements would hold. At the highest levels of government, however, a major step had been taken in directing Australian policy towards a possible military involvement alongside the United States to counter the threat of communism in Indochina.

These discussions and decisions reinforced the lesson that Australia had become much closer to the United States than to Britain on policy towards Southeast Asia. Britain was not only extremely reluctant to become involved in any military commitment in Southeast Asia other than in direct defence of its own interests and responsibilities in Malaya and Borneo, but it was also engaged in a national debate about whether to abandon its global role and to concentrate its attention almost exclusively on Europe. The Australian government was concerned that the United States might similarly decide to pull out of Southeast Asia in order to give attention to other parts of the world, with grave implications for Australian security. Conscious of its own military weakness after years of severely constrained expenditure on defence, Australia had to demonstrate that it was willing to do everything it could to ensure that the United States would continue to commit its military and diplomatic power to ensuring the security of non-communist regimes in Southeast Asia.

In part, the Australian government was concerned, as a general matter of policy, to demonstrate that it was willing to pay the premium for its strategic insurance from the United States; in part, Australia was especially concerned about American policy towards Southeast Asia, the region of greatest direct importance to Australian security but of relatively low priority in American interests; and in part the government was moved by the even more particular concern over American policy towards Indonesia and West New Guinea. In 1962 the Menzies government was obliged to accept that, because of the clear direction of American policy, Australia had to accept the transfer of sovereignty over West New Guinea to Indonesia. The newly appointed Minister for External Affairs, Sir Garfield Barwick, and the diplomats of his department were working towards better relations with Sukarno and the Indonesians. They faced criticism from the Labor leader, Arthur Calwell, and the influential newspaper the *Sydney Morning Herald* that Australia was 'appeasing Indonesia'; but as Menzies told the Australian public, 'the hard facts of international life' meant that Australia had to accept decisions shaped by 'our great and powerful friends'.[4]

With these concerns in mind, Menzies and his colleagues became even more determined to do all they could to ensure American support for the security of Australia and its region. From the late 1950s Australia had been offering the United States the use of Australian facilities and territory for both defence and civilian projects, and several agreements were reached. The most important American proposal was for a naval communications station at North-West Cape in Western Australia to facilitate communications with US Navy submarines operating in the Indian Ocean and Southeast Asian waters. In 1962, shortly before an ANZUS Council meeting at which Australia would closely question the Secretary of State, Dean Rusk, over American determination to stand firmly in Indochina, the Australian government agreed to terms that gave the United States virtually total control of the North-West Cape station.[5]

While Australian policy was dominated by the desire to lock the United States into measures for the security of Southeast Asia, ministers continued to fear that the Americans might use excessively provocative tactics, including the use of nuclear weapons. This was still a major concern in the early 1960s, although hardly even hinted at in public discussion. As far as Australian political leaders, especially Menzies, were concerned, American power was so important to Australian security that any such fears had to be suppressed.

COMMITMENTS TO THAILAND AND VIETNAM 1962[6]

It was widely assumed in Washington that the Geneva Agreement on Laos merely postponed its takeover by the communists, making South Vietnam and Thailand the most vulnerable 'dominoes' of the Cold War conflict in Indochina. The position in South Vietnam was especially alarming, as the revolutionary forces grew extraordinarily rapidly after the 1959 decision to take up armed struggle. In 1959 there were estimated to be 2000 armed troops under communist command in the south. By the end of 1961 the regular units of the People's Liberation Armed Forces (or 'Viet Cong main force') had reached 17 000 and redoubled to 34 000 by the end of 1964. The combined total of the three elements of the PLAF – the main force, the regional forces and the village militia – was estimated to have grown from 7000 in early 1960 to 106 000 in late 1964. Most of the Viet Cong forces were recruited in the south, but they were augmented by the first troops to be infiltrated from the north. Initially, most of these were 'regroupees' who had moved north after the 1954 partition. Moving inconspicuously into PLAF units, they had a marked impact on the political motivation and military effectiveness of the southern forces that Diem had come close to wiping out in the late 1950s.

The appeal of the Viet Cong in the south was augmented by the policies of the Diem government in Saigon. The communists promised land reforms that would enable many rural peasants to have access to land currently controlled by a small number of wealthy landowners. The Diem government's favouritism to Catholics in promotions to sensitive military and political posts alienated many Buddhist groups, some of whom were infiltrated by communists and their sympathisers.

In 1961 President Kennedy sent Vice-President Lyndon B. Johnson on a mission to reassure American allies in Taiwan, the Philippines,

South Vietnam and Pakistan that the probable 'loss' of Laos did not imply any weakening of their security guarantees from the United States. Johnson, who publicly called Diem 'the Winston Churchill of Asia', reported to Kennedy that Thailand and South Vietnam were now the critical theatres in the global war against communism, and that Washington should make a major political, military and economic effort there, with the possibility of sending combat forces later. This was the first in a long series of missions to Vietnam by senior American officials, most of whom argued that the United States had to make a stand there in order to ensure the credibility of its alliances around the world. Following another mission by two senior advisers, General Maxwell Taylor and Walt Rostow, the Kennedy administration greatly increased its assistance to the Republic of Vietnam, especially in the numbers of military advisers. When Kennedy took office, there were fewer than 800 American advisers in Vietnam. By late 1962 there were 11 000 and by Kennedy's death in 1963 there were 16 000. The 'advisers' included pilots of helicopters and fixed-wing aircraft, who flew operational sorties that were officially described as 'training missions'. From late 1961 the Americans repeatedly indicated that they would welcome assistance in this build-up. Australian Army advisers who could assist in training the RVN forces in jungle and counter-insurgency warfare would be particularly welcome.

The story of the growth in the American commitment to South Vietnam under the Kennedy administration has often been told, but it is less often recalled that [in the early 1960s Thailand was seen as an equally important and vulnerable 'domino'.] Facing a communist insurgency in their northeastern provinces bordering Laos, and having placed their faith in SEATO as the means through which they would receive support from the United States, the Thais were alarmed to see the effectiveness of the alliance undermined by British and French policies. In 1962 a United States–Thai communiqué overturned the previously accepted rule that SEATO would act only by unanimous agreement. Instead,

SEATO obligations were stated to be 'individual as well as collective'. In other words, the United States could now take the Manila Treaty as the means by which it would act in Southeast Asia either unilaterally or with SEATO allies, but without requiring unanimous consent. Although not consulted, the Australian government was happy to agree with this formula. For the next several years, Menzies and his ministerial colleagues continued to contribute to SEATO programs and to assert that Australian actions in Southeast Asia were consistent with Australia's SEATO obligations.

In May 1962 these threads came together when Secretary of State Dean Rusk visited Canberra for the first ANZUS Council meeting since 1959, and the first to be held in Australia. The meeting coincided with a renewed outbreak of conflict in Laos, prompting the United States to strengthen its forces in Thailand in order to reassure the Thais and to seek the support of their SEATO allies. Leading the Australian delegation, Barwick pressed Rusk on American determination to defend South Vietnam. Rusk responded by seeking Australian assistance, particularly army advisers in jungle warfare and counter-insurgency.

Immediately afterwards the Australian government took important steps towards military involvement in Southeast Asia. It first resolved to give unequivocal support to American actions in Thailand and to send 'a small contingent' there. Reassured that the United States government was prepared to intervene in South Vietnam, either alone or with SEATO allies, Cabinet also decided to send Australian Army instructors to train the RVN forces. In each case, forces would be sent only at the request of the country they were to enter. The government saw these actions as consistent with its SEATO obligations, and preferred that any Australian intervention be as part of a SEATO force, but it would be prepared to act in support of the United States acting alone, if necessary. Although only instructors had been requested at this stage, Cabinet resolved to consider the implications of stationing service personnel anywhere in

Southeast Asia and of sending combat forces to support an operation conducted either by SEATO or by the United States alone. The Cabinet minute noted that its decision could be justified publicly by referring to Australia's role in the Malayan Emergency. There Australia had helped an independent government to defeat 'Communist bandits'; it should be prepared to help fight a similar insurgency in Vietnam, because the overthrow of the RVN government 'would pose the greatest possible threat to Australia'. Moreover, South Vietnam was, unlike Malaya, associated with SEATO, and Australia was prepared to meet its treaty obligations.

Although Rusk had pointed out that the United States already had 8000 advisers in Vietnam, Barwick initially emphasised that Australia would send no combat forces and only 'a handful' of instructors. Soon afterwards, the Minister for Defence, Athol Townley, announced the despatch of what would be known as the Australian Army Training Team Vietnam (AATTV), comprising 30 officers and senior non-commissioned officers. After a little delay, caused by the public insistence of the Malayan government that it would not be associated with any SEATO action, Townley announced that the 'contingent' to be sent to Thailand would be a squadron of RAAF Sabre jet fighters.

Australia's first military commitment to the Vietnam War received substantial press coverage, commenting on its significance in Australia's relations with the United States and with Asia. The prominent journalist Denis Warner wrote:

> Why is Australia getting involved in the Vietnam war?
>
> Partly because we think a Communist victory there would threaten the rest of Southeast Asia and jeopardise our security and partly because of the need to convince the Americans that we are more than paper allies.

Amplifying the second point, he added: 'It's a sort of life insurance cover we're taking out', possibly the first public use of this phrase with regard

76 AUSTRALIA AND THE VIETNAM WAR

to Austalia's involvement. Warner thus encapsulated both the 'domino theory' and 'insurance policy' elements of the government's motives.[7] The press coverage did not prompt public or parliamentary controversy at this time. While some on the left of the ALP occasionally raised questions about Laos, Vietnam and SEATO, the party as a whole was deeply divided on the American alliance and in no position to propose an alternative foreign policy to the government's.

THE RAAF SQUADRON IN THAILAND[8]

The squadron of eight Sabre fighters was taken from RAAF units stationed at Butterworth in Malaya. In response to Malayan sensitivities over association with SEATO, the aircraft were first flown to Singapore (still a British colony and not part of Malaya) before going on to Ubon, a Royal Thai Air Force base 80 kilometres from the border with Laos, where they were redesignated as No. 79 Squadron.

Britain and New Zealand also sent small air elements to Thailand in response to the 1962 crisis but these, along with American ground forces, were withdrawn after the Geneva Agreement was signed. The American air presence remained and, after 1965, conducted extensive operations against the enemy supply lines in Laos and the southern parts of the DRV. The RAAF Sabres also remained at Ubon until 1968, but were not involved in combat operations over Laos or either North or South Vietnam. Although placed on alert on several occasions, they were not involved in action over Thailand, but undertook reconnaissance and training missions.

THE TRAINING TEAM IN VIETNAM[9]

The Australian Army Training Team arrived in Vietnam in August 1962. The first Australian unit to be committed to Vietnam, 'the Team' would be the last to leave in 1972. More than half of the initial contingent had experience of combat in Malaya. The Team operated in small groups, mostly in the northern provinces of South Vietnam. Their initial deployment was in four groups, based at centres responsible for the training of, respectively, the regular soldiers of the ARVN; the regional troops of the Civil Guard and Self Defence Corps; the village defenders, border forces and trail watchers; and the Rangers, an ARVN special force. Another group served as the Team's headquarters.

The AATTV would remain in Vietnam for the next ten years, working closely with both American and RVN forces in a variety of locations throughout South Vietnam. Their numbers were increased from 30 to 83 in 1964, 100 in 1965 and more than 200 in the early 1970s. Initially, their role was designated solely as training, but it soon became apparent that they would be required to operate in combat. Their work won many accolades, including the only four Victoria Crosses awarded to Australians in Vietnam. For the most part, however, their story was little known in Australia until after the war, and their role was seldom mentioned in the public controversies over the Vietnam War.

The first commander of the AATTV, Colonel FP 'Ted' Serong, was a devout Catholic who shared the militant anti-communism of his schoolmate and lifelong friend, BA Santamaria. Serong devoted most of his life to fighting for the anti-communist cause in the jungles of Southeast Asia. He was appointed the first commandant of the Jungle Warfare Training Centre at Canungra in Queensland when it was reopened in 1955. For two years, from 1960 to 1962, he advised the Burmese Army on counter-insurgency tactics. From this position he was recalled by the Chief of the General Staff, Lieutenant General Sir Reginald Pollard, to head the AATTV. Serong's reputation as an expert on counter-insurgency in Southeast Asia led to his appointment as adviser to the Commander of the American forces in Vietnam, General Paul Harkins. At the end of his term as commander of the AATTV in 1965, and especially after his retirement from the army in 1968, Serong held a series of positions advising the Americans and the South Vietnamese. The nature and importance of his role in these positions would become one of the enduring minor controversies of Australia's involvement in the Vietnam War. Doubt has been cast on some of the claims made concerning his service in the later years of the war, but he made a commendable contribution in the 1950s and early 1960s, both in preparing the army for counter-insurgency operations in Southeast Asia and in leading the first contingent of the AATTV.[10]

The 1962 commitments of an RAAF squadron to Thailand and the Army Training Team to Vietnam, soon after the crises in Laos, led the government to reappraise its defence planning. The Defence Committee submitted a new appreciation of 'the Strategic Basis of Australian Defence Policy', the first since 1958. This paper saw dangers emerging from the growth in Chinese military strength, which was about to include a nuclear capability, and the threat posed by DRV forces to the RVN, Thailand, Laos and Cambodia. The paper also gave special attention to the precarious balance in Indonesia between the PKI, by now the largest communist party in the world outside the Soviet Union and China, and the anti-communist Indonesian Army. The Committee advised that there had been 'a significant and disturbing deterioration' in Australia's strategic position since 1958, underlining the importance of giving full support to SEATO and ANZUS. The Defence Committee warned the government:

> Unless Australia can support these treaty arrangements with force contributions commensurate with her vital interest in preventing a communist victory in Southeast Asia, and commensurate with her resources, it will become more difficult to encourage the United States to retain an effective military presence in Southeast Asia and to assist in our security in time of need.[11]

Under the ceiling placed on defence expenditure in 1955–56, the defence budget had declined from 3.6 per cent of gross national product to 2.8 per cent, while the comparable figures for the United States, the

United Kingdom and Canada were 10.25 per cent, 7 per cent and 4.3 per cent respectively. The government approved a marked increase in defence expenditure for the three years starting in 1962–63, all based on improving Australia's capacity to act with its allies in a limited war in Southeast Asia. All three services were to be strengthened in numbers and equipment, but the principal beneficiary was the army.

In January 1963, concerned especially by the trend of events in Indonesia and Indochina, the Cabinet formed the Foreign Affairs and Defence (FAD) Committee, enabling seven senior ministers to focus on the continuing demands of the crises to Australia's north.[12] It is likely that Menzies and some of his colleagues had in mind a desire to monitor the work of Barwick, who was appointed Minister for External Affairs after the 1961 election and whose diplomacy was thought in some circles to be unduly sympathetic towards Indonesia and abrasive towards both Britain and the United States. In effect, the FAD Committee was the peacetime equivalent of a War Cabinet, discussing strategic policies and taking decisions that excluded not only Parliament and the general public but also the outer ministry and even a large portion of the Cabinet. While the small FAD Committee could maintain the degree of confidentiality required for diplomatically sensitive decisions, its formation had the effect of limiting even more closely any significant discussion of the aims and means of Australian national security policy. Menzies and his senior ministers had already established the fundamental elements of Australian policy; there was little likelihood that those policies would be challenged in the years ahead.

CONFRONTATION 1963[13]

The FAD Committee faced both old and new challenges in its first year of operation. In 1963 Indonesia adopted a policy of 'Konfrontasi', or Confrontation, against the newly formed federation of Malaysia; the political and military position of the RVN deteriorated sharply, with a coup in November bringing the downfall and assassination of Diem; and the combination of these threats led to a further escalation of defence expenditure.

In 1961 the Malayan Prime Minister, Tunku Abdul Rahman, proposed the creation of a new federation of Malaysia, which would incorporate the current states of Malaya, Singapore, and the three British territories on the island of Borneo – the colonies of North Borneo (soon to be known as Sabah) and Sarawak and the Sultanate of Brunei. For the Tunku, Malaysia offered the strategic and economic benefits of a merger of Malaya and Singapore, and would allow Kuala Lumpur to oversee the internal security of Singapore, while the inclusion of the Borneo territories would ensure that the new federation would not be dominated by the ethnic Chinese population. In Singapore, the People's Action Party (PAP) led by Lee Kuan Yew had come to power in 1959 under constitutional arrangements that offered internal self-government and the promise of independence by 1963. The Malaysia proposal gave this entrepôt access to its natural hinterland on the peninsula, but it hastened the split between Lee's moderate wing of the PAP and the left wing, which departed to become the Barisan Sosialis (Socialist Front). Lee's future became tied to the proposal for Singapore to gain independence as part of Malaysia: its failure would have opened the way to an extreme left-wing government in Singapore closely aligned to communist China. For Sabah and Sarawak, Malaysia offered an economically, politically and ethnically attractive path to independence. For the status-conscious Sultan and the people of oil-rich Brunei, the advantages were less clear, and Brunei subsequently dropped out of the discussions before Malaysia was formed.

After initial hesitation, Britain strongly supported the Malaysia proposal. London saw the new federation as the means by which Britain could end its remaining colonial responsibilities and costly defence obligations in the region, with a good prospect of leaving behind a stable and friendly government. The Indonesians, who shared Borneo (in Indonesian, Kalimantan) with Sabah, Sarawak and Brunei, at first appeared unconcerned by the proposal, but by late 1962 grew increasingly hostile. Sukarno's 'guided democracy' required him to balance the China-aligned PKI and the anti-communist army. Both political opportunism and genuine ideological belief led him to present himself as a leader of the world's 'newly emerging forces' against the 'neo-colonialists and imperialists'. Denouncing Malaysia as a neo-colonialist plot by the British, and the Tunku as an imperialist stooge – with the implied threat of military action to promote Indonesia's interests – gained Sukarno the support of both the PKI and the army. To make matters more complicated, the Philippines also opposed the formation of Malaysia, claiming that, as the successor state to the Sultanate of Sulu, it was the rightful sovereign of Sabah.

Matters came to a head in December 1962 when a rebel group opposed to the formation of Malaysia attempted a revolt in Brunei, with an unclear degree of Indonesian support. The rebellion was quickly put down by British forces, aided by an RAAF transport aircraft that happened to be in Singapore at the time, but a war of words between the Malaysians and Indonesians ensued, culminating in the Indonesian declaration of a policy of Confrontation against Malaysia. Precisely what this meant was not defined, but comparisons were immediately drawn with the military, economic and political measures blended with bluff and deliberate ambiguity which had gained Indonesia success in its campaign to secure West New Guinea.

By this time Britain's support for the Malaysia proposal was leading to passionate denunciations of Sukarno. British officials compared him with Hitler and alleged that his expansionist ambitions included not only the Borneo territories and Portuguese Timor but also the Malayan peninsula, the Philippines, eastern New Guinea and much of Melanesia. Suggesting that Britain and Indonesia might soon be at war, the British government looked for support from the United States, Australia and New Zealand.

Menzies' immediate instinct was to support the British position. A principal aim of the forward defence strategy was to encourage Britain, as well as the United States, to remain committed to the security of Southeast Asia. Menzies' well-known Anglophilia was further encouraged at this time when he visited London to become a Knight of the Thistle, one of the higher orders of knighthood in the imperial system. By contrast, Barwick and his departmental officials in External Affairs were decidedly more cautious. They knew that Britain and the United States might withdraw from the region, but Australia and Indonesia would always be neighbours. Sceptical of British assertions about Sukarno's ambitions, they sought to avoid entrenching hostility between Australia and Indonesia, and to improve relations, even while expressing disapproval of the Indonesian campaign of subversion and infiltration. Barwick persuaded Cabinet to undertake a nuanced policy, supporting London and Kuala Lumpur in ensuring the creation of Malaysia but seeking to persuade, rather than to force, Indonesia and the Philippines to accept it. In the coming months, there were clear signs of tension between the External Affairs and Prime Minister's Departments, with Barwick's officials seeking a 'firm but friendly' attitude towards Indonesia while Menzies' department accused the diplomats of being 'over-sensitive' to Indonesia and 'flabby' in their support for Britain. Some Liberal Party parliamentarians were also critical of Barwick's policy, while Calwell and the *Sydney Morning Herald* continued to accuse the government of 'appeasing' Indonesia.

A further complication was the policy of the United States. The Americans, whose diplomacy had enabled the Indonesians to acquire West New Guinea without conflict, made it clear to Britain, Australia and New Zealand that Washington's first priority was to maintain its long-term relationship with Indonesia, and not to push it towards the communist bloc. The United States would support the creation of Malaysia, but saw this as a matter primarily for Britain and secondarily for Australia and New Zealand. Senior American officials were highly reluctant to indicate circumstances in which they might give military support to the Commonwealth countries.

From early 1963 until early 1964, before and after the official creation of Malaysia on 16 September 1963, Australia was engaged in a skilled and demanding exercise in diplomacy. Working closely with senior External Affairs officials in Canberra, including Tange, Keith Waller and Gordon Jockel, and two able heads of diplomatic missions, Keith Shann in Jakarta and Tom Critchley in Kuala Lumpur, Barwick sought energetically to persuade Sukarno that his confrontation of Malaysia would not be allowed to succeed, while simultaneously urging Malaysian and British officials to handle the creation of the new federation with minimal provocation. The policy was distinctly Australian, echoing neither the British nor the American position but being based on a perception of Australia's long-term national interests, 'refined but not defined' (as the diplomats liked to put it) by alliance considerations. While the Australians did not convince Sukarno to abandon Confrontation, he understood that Australia was not merely part of a British neo-colonialist plot. On the day Malaysia was created, rioters attacked the British Embassy in Jakarta, but the Australian Embassy was left untouched.

DEFENCE REVIEW 1963[14]

Indonesia's Confrontation policy brought about the 'quadripartite talks' between the United States, Britain, Australia and New Zealand for

THE COMMITMENT TO THE DEFENCE OF MALAYSIA[17]

While these decisions were being made, Australia came under pressure from Britain to commit itself to the defence of Malaysia. This, too, revealed a tension within the Australian government. Menzies and the service chiefs wanted a clear and strong commitment, while Barwick and his diplomats wanted to distance themselves from the British position. Eventually, a compromise was reached by which Australia associated itself with the Anglo–Malaysian Defence Agreement but without a formal treaty relationship. Before committing itself, Australia wanted to have Washington's assurance that if Australian forces became involved in serious conflict with Indonesia the ANZUS treaty would apply. After considerable pressure from the Australians on reluctant American officials, a level of assurance was given by the Americans. Soon after Malaysia was formed in September 1963, Menzies formally announced that Australia would support Britain and Malaysia against 'armed invasion or subversive activity – supported or directed or inspired from outside Malaysia'. Soon afterwards the Kennedy administration committed itself to a document which said that the United States would act under ANZUS if Indonesia attacked Australian forces in Malaysia, but only in the event of 'overt attack' and not in cases of 'subversion, guerrilla warfare or indirect aggression'. The use of American troops was excluded: any assistance would be limited to naval and air forces and logistic support. The Americans strongly urged diplomatic efforts to avoid the escalation of hostility. The document heavily emphasised the qualifications and limits on American support.[18]

The creation of Malaysia had not altered the sensitivities that the government had to consider over any use of the Australian forces committed to the British Commonwealth Far East Strategic Reserve. As had been the case in the 1950s, they were fulfilling their primary role by training in SEATO exercises, but were available for other tasks with specific government approval. Malaysia, like Malaya before it, was not a member of SEATO and did not wish to be associated with SEATO operations, but its government hoped to see the Australian elements of the Strategic Reserve, particularly the infantry battalion, engaged in anti-terrorist operations. The Australian government was prepared to see the battalion involved in anti-communist operations, but did not want its forces to become involved in domestic issues, such as conflicts arising from communal tensions on the Malayan peninsula (now known as West Malaysia) or the internal security of Singapore.

During the first year of Malaysia's existence, pressure from both London and Kuala Lumpur to give military support against the Indonesian Confrontation met an extremely cautious response. Menzies, the officials in his department and the service chiefs were generally more sympathetic to the British position than Barwick and the diplomats, but for the most part the External Affairs approach prevailed. Barwick and his department continued their energetic and independent diplomacy, in London and Washington as well as in Jakarta and Kuala Lumpur. They were aware of the American pressure to exercise restraint, but were principally motivated by their perception of Australia's long-term national interests.

In the latter months of 1963, British and Australian military planners held many discussions and developed plans for strong action in the event that Indonesia raised the level of Confrontation from small incursions into Sabah and Sarawak by 'volunteers' to overt aggression by regular forces, not only in Borneo but also possibly against the Malayan peninsula and Singapore. These plans included provision for attacks by front-line RAF aircraft on Indonesian territory, possibly using Australian airfields.

While much was discussed or planned, little was done on the ground. During the extensive discussions at political and military levels in late

1963 and early 1964, the British and Malaysian authorities indicated a wide range of forms of military support that they would welcome. The combative Chairman of the Chiefs of Staff Committee, Air Chief Marshal Sir Frederick Scherger, supported the British requests but was often overruled by the FAD Committee and Cabinet. As Barwick told the British, the Australians preferred a 'graduated response', providing only as much assistance as the level of threat required. The British consistently warned that Australian assistance might be 'too little, too late', but the Australians continued to believe that the British exaggerated the dangers posed by Indonesian activity. They were also conscious of the American pressure to act with the minimum of provocation.

The crucial question was always the desire by the British and Malaysian governments to see Australian combat troops, including an infantry battalion and a squadron of Special Air Service (SAS) troops, committed to Borneo. The first specific request along these lines was rejected in December 1963. After signs that the Indonesians were raising the level of guerrilla activity in Borneo, the government agreed in January 1964 to a Malaysian request that 3RAR, which had recently arrived as the infantry contribution to the Strategic Reserve, should serve on the Thai–Malayan border, where the remaining guerrillas of the Malayan Communist Party were still hiding. The patrols conducted by 3RAR served as good training for jungle operations, but led to no contacts with the enemy. Although this deployment allowed the Malaysian government to release a Malaysian battalion to serve in Borneo, it fell short of the direct commitment sought by London and Kuala Lumpur.

In April 1964 the British government specifically requested Australia to commit an infantry battalion and some SAS troops to Borneo. At the same time, the Malaysian government requested an extensive range of assistance, including army engineers, coastal minesweepers, helicopters and transport aircraft. The Australian government rejected the approach from London, but softened the blow by acceding to some of Kuala

Lumpur's requests, committing a squadron of army engineers and some RAN minesweepers. An ill-advised statement by Barwick, insisting that Australian servicemen in Malaysia were covered by the ANZUS guarantee, without referring to the qualifications imposed by Washington, made the commitment of the engineers unduly provocative to the Indonesians and therefore the Americans, causing some embarrassment to Menzies and his government.

In the following years, the army maintained a squadron of army engineers serving six-month tours of duty in Sabah, principally engaged in building an inland road and an airstrip in challenging climate and terrain. Similarly, six coastal minesweepers joined the extensive fleet of British, Malaysian and Singaporean vessels engaged in maritime patrols off the coasts of both West Malaysia and Borneo, principally to intercept Indonesian vessels on infiltration or sabotage missions. Later in the campaign, six larger RAN ships, destroyers and destroyer escorts, also served on similar patrols and other tasks. These were useful contributions to the Commonwealth efforts, but the refusal to send combat troops disappointed the British. The Australian insistence on the policy of 'graduated response' reflected the continuing divergence between British and Australian assessments of the Indonesian threat, an awareness of the American desire to see Confrontation handled with the minimum degree of provocation towards Sukarno, and a growing awareness that Australia might face further demands on its extremely limited defence resources.

Public discussion of foreign and defence policies in 1963 and 1964 was dominated by assessments of Confrontation. Was Sukarno a Hitler-like expansionist dictator who might pose a threat to the Australian-administered territories in New Guinea or even Australia itself? Was the PKI so influential, and were the links between Indonesia and China so close, that Sukarno was effectively an agent of communist expansionism, even if he himself was not a communist? Was conciliation of Indonesia an example of discreditable appeasement? How great was the risk that Confrontation might escalate, bringing Australia into open war with Indonesia? To what extent could Australia rely on American support under ANZUS in the event of such a conflict? These were the questions that dominated public debate and policy-makers' assessments in Australia in 1963 and 1964.

THE END OF DIEM, NOVEMBER 1963[19]

While Australians directed their attention to these questions, the great American debate on Vietnam was beginning. In January 1963 a large ARVN force with American advisers suffered heavy losses in a pitched battle with a smaller but substantial, well-armed and well-defended Viet Cong force at a hamlet called Bac. The 'battle of Ap Bac' (*ap* is the Vietnamese word for hamlet) was reported in the American press as demonstrating the incompetence and cowardice of the South Vietnamese forces, attributable largely to the inadequacies of officers who had been promoted on the basis of personal and political loyalty rather than military skill. This prompted considerable discussion in the United States, in the media and in political and military circles, about the ability of the Republic of Vietnam to succeed in its struggle against the mounting insurgency. Diem's attempt to create 'strategic hamlets' throughout South Vietnam, modelled on the 'new villages' that had played an important part in defeating the communist insurgency in Malaya, was also proving fruitless. Tensions between the RVN government and several Buddhist groups over Diem's favouritism towards Catholics were approaching a critical point. The pro-Catholic and anti-Buddhist policies were particularly associated with Diem's brother and closest associate, Ngo Dinh Nhu, and his wife, Madame

Nhu, who was effectively First Lady to the celibate President Diem. The effects of these and other policies of the Diem government were exacerbated by the infiltration of communists and their sympathisers into key political and military offices in South Vietnam.

The Australian government watched these developments with dismay, but with no desire to become more closely involved. Suggestions from American and RVN authorities that Australia might provide RAAF Dakota transport aircraft and pilots for use in Vietnam were quietly rejected. The RAAF wished to concentrate on its re-equipment program, while External Affairs was well aware of the Diem regime's faults, regarding support for it as, at best, a regrettable necessity of the global Cold War.[20]

In June 1963, in one of the most gruesome but most effective public relations events of the era, a Buddhist monk committed suicide by immolation. In front of an American photographer, he was doused with petrol, which was then ignited. The resulting photograph put South Vietnam on the front page of newspapers around the world. When other monks similarly suicided by self-immolation, Madame Nhu outraged world, and especially American, opinion by saying she welcomed these 'barbecues'. In August Nhu, breaking promises given to the Americans, instigated a military assault on Buddhist temples, leading to the incarceration of many monks.

The Australian government, like most Americans and the rest of the world, was unaware that these events precipitated an intense debate at the highest levels of the Kennedy administration. One group, in which the principal instigators were State Department officials, wanted Washington to encourage a coup in which Diem and Nhu would be replaced by a junta of generals, many of whom were seeking American support for such a move; another group strongly opposed this measure, insisting that the Americans should stand or fall with Diem (sometimes expressed as 'sink or swim with Ngo Dinh Diem'). The former group had their way. The coup took place, with the active involvement of the American ambassador in Saigon, Henry Cabot Lodge, and the Central Intelligence Agency, and Diem and Nhu were assassinated on 2 November.

American connivance in this coup was a critical step in the path towards war. By encouraging the generals, and by immediately recognising the government they established, the Americans could no longer claim to be supporting a government in South Vietnam which, for all its flaws, had some claims to legitimacy. They were now committed to supporting – if not creating – any anti-communist regime that could survive. Although heavily reliant on American political and financial support, Diem had persistently and stubbornly refused to take American advice: his successors could far more credibly be denounced by the communists as mere 'puppets' of the United States.

Australian support for American policy at the time of the coup also established a lasting pattern in a crucial period. While the Australian political and military leaders were closely questioning the assessments, policies and military strategies pursued by the British in Confrontation, they accepted uncritically what the United States said and did about events in Vietnam and its policies there. Australians were reasonably well informed about the policy-making process in London, and had substantial confidence in the abilities of, and popular support for, the Malaysian political and military leaders. By contrast, they had little information about developments behind the scenes in Washington and minimal confidence in Saigon's leadership. The forward defence policy was based on support for two different allies in two different theatres of actual or potential conflict, but a sharp contrast was emerging in the way that the Menzies government addressed the two developing crises.

Three weeks after the assassination of Ngo Dinh Diem, President Kennedy was himself assassinated, a year before he was due to face re-election. Almost immediately a counter-factual debate began that has never ended: would a re-elected President Kennedy, in his second term, have pulled the United States out of the conflict in Vietnam? Whatever the 'might-have-been', his successor, Lyndon Johnson, saw no such opportunity. Johnson's political ambitions were to establish the 'Great Society', a massive program of domestic reforms modelled on President Roosevelt's New Deal, and to advance the civil rights of African-Americans. In foreign policy, where he retained the advisers he had inherited from Kennedy, he saw no option but to continue Kennedy's policies, but without taking any major, controversial decisions before the election in November 1964. In the meantime he approved a number of covert measures, all designed to persuade Hanoi to reduce its support for the insurgency in the South.

A week after Kennedy's assassination, still in November 1963, the Menzies government was re-elected. Menzies had called the election a year before it was required, largely to take advantage of the divisions in the Labor Party over the alliance with the United States. These divisions had been dramatically displayed by a photograph of the leader and deputy leader of the Labor Party, Arthur Calwell and Gough Whitlam, waiting outside a Canberra hotel while the party's federal conference – later described by the government as '36 faceless men' – decided its policy on the North-West Cape communications station. Having survived for two years with a majority of two (and only one on the floor of the House of Representatives after providing a Speaker), Menzies gained a comfortable majority of 22. The result indicated firm public support, not only for the government's attitude to the American alliance but also for its strengthening of Australian defence capacities, especially with an eye to possible conflict with Indonesia in Malaysia and Papua New Guinea. After a period of uncertainty, in which Barwick and other senior ministers had been jockeying to place themselves as Menzies' successor, it also placed Menzies back in firm control of the Liberal Party, the Cabinet, and the Parliament. His authority, especially over policies towards Australia's 'great and powerful friends' and towards Southeast Asia, was at its peak.

TWO CONFLICTS, TWO ALLIES[21]

The year from late 1963 to late 1964 aroused increasing anxiety among Australian policy-makers as they watched disturbing events in both Indochina and Confrontation, hoping to influence the policies of their two great allies. In the presidential election campaign Johnson portrayed himself as the candidate best equipped to keep American forces out of a foreign war and his conservative Republican opponent, Senator Barry Goldwater, as more likely to escalate tensions. The Australians knew little of the covert measures by which Johnson hoped to stave off defeat in Vietnam, but they were aware that many American policy-makers had concluded that their current strategy of counter-insurgency using large numbers of American advisers was failing because the enemy had easy access to supplies of men and weapons while there was no government in Saigon with a strong basis of popular support. The Americans would therefore be forced to consider direct intervention with large-scale American forces, not a decision that Johnson would contemplate before the presidential election. President de Gaulle continued his pressure for 'neutralisation' of Southeast Asia, and many American allies in Europe and elsewhere urged the Americans to seek a negotiated end to the conflict, but Washington felt that it was in too weak a position to enter negotiations.

Ironically, Hanoi also felt that it was in a weaker position than it had hoped to be. Despite the political turmoil in Saigon, neither the Viet Cong's political wing, the NLF, nor its military wing, the PLAF, had achieved as much in 1963 as Hanoi had hoped. In late 1963 and early 1964 the central committee of the communist party decided to escalate the role of northern forces in promoting revolution in the south. This decision was taken despite advice from the Soviets, who after the Cuban missile crisis of 1962 were returning to a policy of 'peaceful co-existence' with the West. To augment the 'regroupees', the DRV began to infiltrate regular soldiers of the PAVN, at first as individuals who joined the PLAF (or 'Viet Cong') and then as formed units of the PAVN. The Ho Chi Minh trail through Laos was upgraded. Hanoi was preparing to strike a decisive blow in 1965 against the struggling RVN.

The Johnson administration was in no mood to consult allies, although it sought their support for whatever decisions it took. The Australian government could do little but hope that the United States would stand firm. Furthermore, in the early months of 1964 tension grew between Canberra and Washington over Confrontation. Diplomatic initiatives suggested that the Americans wanted to resolve the tensions between Indonesia, Malaysia and the Philippines in ways that, to Australian eyes, conceded too much to Sukarno. Sharp exchanges passed between Barwick and Rusk. The Americans were also angered by Barwick's public statements about the application of ANZUS to Confrontation, believing that Australia was trying to embroil the United States in an area that affected Australia's interests more directly than America's. The Americans reiterated their view that they would support Australia only if it raised its level of military effort across Southeast Asia.

In this context Australia was required to respond to a campaign by Johnson and Rusk for ['more flags'] in Vietnam. The administration pressed all its allies around the world, especially the members of SEATO, to support the American effort in Vietnam. Numerous forms of military and civilian aid were requested, in order to show that the Americans were not exercising 'American imperialism' but leading an international campaign against communist aggression. Most American allies failed to respond as Washington had hoped but Australia, acutely conscious of the need for American support over Confrontation, felt obliged to be more positive. The size of the Army Training Team was more than doubled, from 30 to 83. The government also recognised that members of the Team would accompany ARVN soldiers into combat, which would inevitably lead to Australian casualties. The government also committed a flight of Caribou transport aircraft, which were still in the process of being supplied from the Canadian manufacturer under the RAAF's acquisition program. In the ensuing months, RAAF Transport Flight Vietnam (RTFV) was built up to six Caribous with pilots and groundcrew. It was based at a US Army aviation base at Vung Tau but was placed under the operational control of the US Air Force. Nicknamed 'Wallaby Airlines', the RTFV gained a reputation for determined and effective, if unglamorous, service.

In April 1964 Barwick was appointed Chief Justice of the High Court, the country's highest judicial position. His successor as Minister for External Affairs was Paul Hasluck, who had been privately critical of Barwick's diplomacy, especially his handling of the American alliance. Although Hasluck had himself served in the Department of External Affairs in the 1940s, he was also critical of many of the attitudes and policies that were popular among his former colleagues. Garry Woodard, a diplomat who served under both Hasluck and Barwick, has proposed a counterfactual similar to that relating to Kennedy – that if Barwick had remained at External Affairs for another year, Australia might not have entered the Vietnam War.[22] This is perhaps an unduly bold claim, because decisions on peace and war are in the last resort taken by the Prime Minister and Menzies was clearly the dominant influence on Vietnam policy, but Barwick might certainly have had some influence on the way in which the commitment was shaped. Hasluck, it seems, was used by Menzies to counter the efforts by External Affairs to limit Australia's military commitments in Southeast Asia and to take a robust attitude to the management of the American alliance. At an important moment, Hasluck rebuked the Australian ambassador in Saigon for taking what he called an unduly 'academic' approach to the developing crisis. Australian diplomats were left in no doubt that they were expected to take the threat to the RVN as a threat to Australia's own security.

Unlike most of the Australian public and many policy-makers in Canberra, Hasluck also began to favour the American view that the critical position in South Vietnam was a more important threat to security than Confrontation, as he reported after touring Southeast Asia early in his tenure. In confidential documents he discussed, in a fairly open-minded way, many issues that would soon be seen as critical, such as the relationship between the DRV and China, Hanoi's role in instigating the rebellion of the Viet Cong in the south, and the ability of the United States to sustain a long conflict on Asian soil. In his public statements, by contrast, he asserted dogmatic and unequivocal support for the official American position on these issues.

The Australian support was still based on minimal information about events in Vietnam or the development of American policy. In August 1964 reports of two apparently unprovoked attacks by North Vietnamese forces on United States naval vessels in the Gulf of Tonkin led to the adoption of a congressional declaration, permitting the administration to take 'all necessary measures' to defend American interests. This cleared the way for the administration to act as it saw fit, circumventing the constitutional provision requiring congressional approval to go to war. The Australian government again gave immediate support for the American policy, while unaware that the supposed second attack almost certainly did not occur and that the first was probably provoked by the covert measures that Johnson had approved earlier in the year.

In the same month as the Gulf of Tonkin incident, the Indonesians landed paratroops on the Malayan peninsula. The forces were pitifully small and quickly rounded up, an exercise in which Australian soldiers of 3RAR were involved, but the step indicated that the Indonesians were preparing to escalate Confrontation. Sukarno declared that Indonesia was beginning a 'year of living dangerously' and his public statements became increasingly hostile to the West and sympathetic to China, leading to his announcement on 1 January that Indonesia was withdrawing from the United Nations in protest at the election of Malaysia to a non-permanent seat on the Security Council. Political tensions within Malaysia were also rising, as the UMNO leaders in Kuala Lumpur became increasingly suspicious that Lee Kuan Yew aspired to become Prime Minister of Malaysia. Naval action by a British vessel, perhaps modelled on the Gulf of Tonkin incident, seemed designed to provoke the Indonesians.

Although little noticed at the time, changes were also taking place among those groups in Australia who dissented from Australian foreign policy. The Communist Party was not only weaker than in earlier years but was also splintering into three groups, one aligned with Moscow, one with Beijing and the third assertively Australian. The foundations were being laid for a protest movement that would draw on a wider social base than the communist-front Peace Council of the 1950s.

The defence review initiated in 1963 culminated in the last months of 1964. A strategic assessment by the Defence Committee in late October described Indonesia as the 'only direct threat to Australia and its territories' and cited the commitments that Australia was most likely to face as, first, an escalation of Indonesia's Confrontation of Malaysia; second, a possible extension of Confrontation into New Guinea; and, as a less prominent third, a commitment to the mainland of Southeast Asia. The Defence Committee appeared to think that South Vietnam might be beyond recovery, so that any Australian involvement on the mainland, either under SEATO or in collaboration with the United States, would probably be in Thailand, after South Vietnam and Laos had already succumbed to the communists. Menzies and his Cabinet colleagues were even more concerned than their official advisers by the possibility that Australian forces might have to act against hostile Indonesian activities in New Guinea without any military assistance from the United States.

On that basis, the government overruled any remaining objections to the introduction of conscription to strengthen the army's numbers more rapidly than had been envisaged the previous year. Having reluctantly accepted that this expansion could be achieved only by conscription, the army secured the form that suited its needs. The national service scheme would be highly selective, taking about one in eight of the 20-year-old males of each cohort. Those selected by ballot would be liable for two years' full-time service, followed by three years on the reserve, and would be liable for 'overseas service as required'. When Menzies referred to Australia's potential military commitments in announcing the results of the defence review to Parliament on 10 November, he discussed Indonesia, Malaysia and Papua New Guinea at much greater length than Laos and South Vietnam, referring pointedly to the strengthening of the Pacific Islands Regiment and improvements to airfields in New Guinea. On the following day, Remembrance Day 1964, the government introduced the legislation that became the National Service Act.

All of this was seen at the time as, in the words of one newspaper editorial, 'preparing against war with Indonesia'. That impression was confirmed by other decisions which indicated that the government was making a long-term commitment to the defence of Malaysia and Papua New Guinea against Indonesia, but was prepared to make only short-term commitments in Vietnam. The government was waiting to see whether President Johnson would stand firm in South Vietnam, but it was preparing to take whatever military actions might be necessary against Indonesia, with or without support from the United States.

JB 'Ben' Chifley, Prime Minister 1945–49.

Percy Spender, Minister for External Affairs 1949–51.

RG Casey, Minister for External Affairs 1951–60.

RG Menzies, Prime Minister 1949–66.

The UK High Commissioner in Australia, Lord Carrington, the US Secretary of State, John Foster Dulles, and the UK Commonwealth Secretary, Lord Home, at the Australian War Memorial during the SEATO Council meeting in 1957.

Senior representatives of eight countries attend the SEATO Council of Ministers in Canberra in 1957.

Prime Minister Robert Menzies with the Malayan Prime Minister, Tunku Abdul Rahman, in 1959.

Prime Minister Robert Menzies and his wife, Dame Pattie Menzies, with Indonesia's President Sukarno in Jakarta in 1959.

In 1957 President Ngo Dinh Diem became the first foreign head of state to visit Australia.

The Indonesian Foreign Minister, Dr Subandrio, and his wife were greeted by Casey when they visited Australia in 1959.

US Secretary of State Dean Rusk and Prime Minister RG Menzies in 1962.

The ANZUS Council in Canberra in 1962. The Australian representatives (centre, from left) were Sir Arthur Tange, Secretary of the External Affairs Department; Sir Garfield Barwick, Minister for External Affairs; and Air Chief Marshal Sir Frederick Scherger, Chairman of the Chiefs of Staff Committee. At right is US Secretary of State Dean Rusk.

Sir Garfield Barwick, Minister for External Affairs 1961–64.

Arthur Calwell, Leader of the Labor Party Opposition 1960–67.

Dr Jim Cairns, prominent Labor politician and protest movement leader in the 1960s and 1970s.

Paul (later Sir Paul) Hasluck, Minister for External Affairs 1964–69.

The self-immolation of a Buddhist monk in 1963 placed the crisis in South Vietnam on the world's front pages.

This photograph of the execution of a Viet Cong cadre by the Saigon police chief during the 1968 Tet offensive had a profound impact on public opinion throughout the world.

The Australian ambassador to the United States, Keith (later Sir Keith) Waller, with President Lyndon B Johnson, 1965.

Malcolm Fraser, visiting Vietnam as Minister for the Army in 1967, took a close interest in the Army's civic action program.

Establishing the 1st Australian Logistic Support Group in the sand dunes at Vung Tau in 1966.

By 1969 the logistic base at Vung Tau had evolved into a sprawling complex, including supply facilities, troops' recreational amenities including a swimming pool, and a hospital with helipad.

Prime Minister Harold Holt visits 1 RAR at Bien Hoa, 1966.

< The commanding officer of 5 RAR, Lieutenant Colonel John Warr (left), and the 5 RAR intelligence officer, Captain Robert O'Neill, plan a cordon-and-search operation in 1967.

> The Chief of the General Staff, Lieutenant General Tom Daly, visits troops at a fire support base in 1969.

Prime Minister John Gorton visits the troops of 3RAR at Nui Dat, 1968.

> Warrant Officer Jock Richardson of 4RAR/NZ emerges from a Viet Cong bunker with a bag of enemy grenades, 1968.

Private Gordon Condon of 7RAR carries an infantryman's heavy load, including an M16 rifle and an M79 grenade launcher.

Soldiers of 7RAR await helicopters at Nui Dat base at the start of an operation, 1970.

Minister for Defence Malcolm Fraser (centre) and General John Wilton (left) welcomed by Australian and Vietnamese officials at Tan Son Nhut airport in 1970.

Dr Jim Cairns urges the 70 000 protesters at the Melbourne Moratorium demonstration on 8 May 1970 not to take provocative or violent action.

The five howitzers of an Australian artillery battery fire simultaneously from Fire Support Base Pamela in support of 3 RAR, 1971.

An Australian Centurion tank in the border areas of Phuoc Tuy and Long Khanh provinces, 1971.

An airstrike on the Long Hai hills, the location of the enemy base known as the Minh Dam Secret Zone, 1971.

From *To Long Tan: The Australian Army and the Vietnam War 1950–1965*, AWM, 1993.

— FIVE —

COMMITMENTS TO CONFRONTATION AND VIETNAM 1965

In late 1964 and early 1965, the deepening crisis in South Vietnam commanded the world's attention. President Johnson, who won a resounding victory in the November election, was confronted by overwhelming evidence that the policy he had inherited of trying to preserve a non-communist South Vietnam without a major intervention by American forces was failing. The PLAF, strengthened by the infiltration of about 10 000 PAVN regulars from the north during 1964, dominated most of the rural areas and were close to strangling the towns and cities. A series of well-timed strikes by the PLAF demonstrated the military weakness of the ARVN forces and the vulnerability of their American advisers. The assassination of Diem had not brought stability but had initiated a seemingly endless series of coups, with each new government less convincing than its predecessor. Factional strife in Saigon politics was reaching nearly terminal levels, including Buddhists against Catholics, civilians against military, and young officers against older officers. Principal participants included the current strong man, Nguyen Khanh; the leaders of some Buddhist groups; a military faction led by a Catholic general, Nguyen Van Thieu, and the head of the RVN Air Force, Nguyen Cao Ky; and the American ambassador, General Maxwell Taylor, who replaced Henry Cabot Lodge. Some factions were known to have made contact with the NLF with a view to forming a 'neutralist' government.

THE TWO CRISES DEEPEN[1]

With South Vietnam clearly on the verge of collapse, the Johnson administration came under enormous pressure within the United States and around the world. 'Hawks' advised the president to bomb North Vietnam, to introduce American combat troops to South Vietnam, or both; 'doves' urged him to salvage the best settlement he could by negotiation, possibly through the United Nations or a reconvened Geneva Conference. The disastrous consequences of either course were extensively canvassed. Drastic military action might lead to the direct involvement of China's forces, as in the Korean War, precipitating a wider war in which both sides would have nuclear weapons. Although the Johnson administration underestimated the domestic political costs, it was already clear that intervention with large-scale forces would be controversial, divisive and expensive, reducing the president's political capital and his ability to create 'the Great Society'. On the other hand, negotiations would almost certainly lead to a thinly disguised surrender of South Vietnam and at least some of the other 'dominoes'. The credibility of American alliances and security guarantees around the world would be severely weakened, undermining the strength of the West across the globe. Johnson could expect to be accused of 'losing Vietnam' or even 'losing Southeast Asia', just as the Truman administration had been accused of 'losing China'. It was possible that he might even be impeached.

Australian commentators followed the American and global debate on Vietnam with an eye to the implications for Australian security. Some argued that South Vietnam was the critical theatre in the West's confrontation of communist expansionism, that its defence was vital to Australia's security, that 'neutralisation' would only lead to a communist victory, and that Australia must be prepared to give military support to the United States. Others agonised over the possible options without being able to suggest a satisfactory solution. Books and articles by Denis Warner, a correspondent with considerable knowledge of Southeast Asia and anti-communist views, were scathingly critical not only of the Diem regime but also of the French and American governments, which had created a Vietnamese army designed for conventional warfare rather than counter-insurgency, relying too heavily on American-style technology such as artillery and air support. Warner said that South Vietnam had become an 'un-country', held together only by the American presence. In December 1964 he wrote that the war had been lost, that the communists had gained their greatest success since taking China in 1949, and that all the United States could now do was to help those who wanted to escape from a communist Vietnam.[2]

Even at this time Australians were more concerned about the Indonesian Confrontation, which escalated sharply at the same time. In late 1964 the Indonesians raised the level of their military challenge to Malaysia, moving brigades of regular troops to Borneo, facing the borders of Sabah and Sarawak. Sukarno's ideological pronouncements were more extreme. Relations between the Indonesian and Chinese governments became increasingly close, as Sukarno's confrontation of 'neo-colonialism and imperialism' meshed with Mao's support for 'wars of national liberation'. There was much talk of a 'Beijing–Jakarta axis', uncomfortably reminiscent of the Rome–Berlin axis that had done much to precipitate the 1939–45 war. Sukarno spoke grandiosely of a Beijing–Jakarta–Hanoi–Phnom Penh–Pyongyang axis, directly linking

Confrontation with Vietnam and implying that there was a concerted union of anti-Western forces. The decision to withdraw from the United Nations, where the Nationalist government on Taiwan and not the communist government in Beijing held the China seat, and the growth in the PKI suggested that the risk of a pro-Chinese communist takeover in Indonesia loomed ever larger.

The Australian government therefore faced its most acute crisis in foreign and defence policy since 1945. It was under pressure from its two most powerful allies to assist them in two separate theatres of conflict in Southeast Asia, to which the two powers had markedly different approaches. The British continued to assert the importance of Confrontation, while resisting pressure to become involved in Vietnam. The Labour government led by Harold Wilson, which had replaced the Conservatives in 1964, was even more determined to seek a diplomatic rather than a military solution to the Vietnam crisis, although some of its leading ministers attracted left-wing criticism by defending American policies. The Americans now acknowledged that Sukarno's increasingly close links with the Chinese were a major concern. Instead of arguing that a firm policy would drive Sukarno into China's arms, they argued that the collapse of South Vietnam would only encourage the PKI and discourage the non-communist elements in Jakarta. The deterioration in Confrontation was therefore, in the American view, a further reason to stand firm in South Vietnam.

Australian ministers were now inclined to accept this view and to press it on the British. The longstanding Australian hope that Britain, the United States, Australia and New Zealand could coordinate their military and political efforts in the region continued to be frustrated. To the Australians, the Americans repeated that it would look as if a 'white men's club' was trying to determine the future of Asia. Privately, they maintained their longstanding reluctance to share their military and political plans even with close allies, especially when those plans were uncertain. Australia therefore had to continue to plan 'separately with two different allies for two different campaigns'.³ In each case Australian ministers and diplomats pressed their ally to maintain a 'robust' stand, while emphasising that Australia would find it difficult to make military commitments simultaneously to both conflicts, as well as a potential commitment to counter any possible Indonesian actions in Papua New Guinea.

Discussions with Washington were frustrating, as the Australians received vague, confused and often contradictory responses to their questions about American policy. It gradually became evident that Johnson's principal advisers were divided. Most, including those closest to Johnson, were hawkish, but divided in their recommendations over the use of air power or combat troops. There was less support for a diplomatic solution. What gradually emerged was a series of decisions that were essentially designed not to gain victory — assuming there was a satisfactory definition of 'victory' — but simply to stave off defeat in South Vietnam.

Johnson was initially inclined to make any major assistance to the Saigon government conditional on its achieving greater political stability and military effectiveness. On this point, he was gradually worn down by his advisers. The Australians threw their weight behind those who argued that a strong American military stance should not wait for political stability, but would help to achieve it. There is little evidence to show that the Australian view was of any significant influence: the argument was fought by American agencies and individuals, based on their assessments of American national interests, amid an intense global debate about the likely policy and strategy of the United States. The American hawks were pleased that at least one ally was indicating support for strong military commitment in Vietnam, but this was of marginal importance in the administration's political calculations. Assurances that the Americans would inform and consult the Australians had little meaning, when the administration was itself ['at its wit's end',] as one official candidly admitted, in its efforts to arrive at a credible strategy.⁴

Australia's approach to Vietnam at this time was dominated by the effort to ensure that the United States did not withdraw or agree to negotiations, which were regarded as a virtual admission of defeat. To many policy-makers, the experience of two world wars showed that the crucial question was to get the United States involved in a war: once committed, its military, industrial and economic strength would, they thought, inevitably ensure victory. Menzies had been prime minister from 1939 to 1941, when Britain and its empire had been at war without the United States. To Menzies and others in positions of influence it was inconceivable that the United States, once committed to a war, could lose. The combination of this confidence and the American reluctance to discuss their plans ensured that in this crucial period American and Australian policy-makers did not hold any constructive discussion about the aims and means that should shape an effective American strategy or the most effective contribution that Australia and other allies could make to that strategy.

When the United States government approached Australia for support, there was little coherence or consistency in the requests. In December a senior State Department official, William Bundy, told the Australian and New Zealand ambassadors in Washington, [Keith Waller] and George Laking, that the United States was considering a bombing campaign against the DRV supply routes in Laos and possibly in the southern part of North Vietnam, just above the demilitarised zone. Consideration was also being given to the introduction of combat troops, possibly US Marines, in which case Australian and New Zealand ground forces would be welcome. More specifically, Bundy suggested that the Americans would welcome a further 200 Australian military advisers, in addition to the 83 currently posted to the AATTV.⁵

A few days later President Johnson wrote to Menzies, requesting the 200 advisers and various forms of other assistance, including hospital ships and other naval vessels that Australia simply did not possess, but indicating that combat forces were not yet required. By this time the Australian service chiefs had already advised the government that it would be difficult to meet the request for more advisers, as these would have to come from precisely the ranks, experienced junior officers and senior non-commissioned officers, who would be needed to train the first intakes of national servicemen. The service chiefs advised that Australia would be better placed to offer an infantry battalion of about 750 troops, together with an SAS squadron of about 100 and other logistic and headquarters elements. Australia was therefore moving towards the commitment of an infantry battalion before the Americans had either called for Australian combat troops or decided the nature of their own commitment. The Americans foreshadowed military staff talks in Honolulu to resolve the nature of Australian and New Zealand contributions to the American military effort, but the date of these talks was postponed while the Americans tried to frame their strategy.

From late 1964 onwards, Menzies kept Vietnam policy increasingly within his own hands. In marked contrast with policy on Confrontation – on which the diplomats of External Affairs had had considerable influence, especially under Barwick as Minister – Menzies largely bypassed the Defence Committee, which included civilian officials of the Prime Minister's, Defence and External Affairs departments, and placed increasing reliance on the chiefs of staff. The Chairman of the Chiefs of Staff Committee, Air Chief Marshal Sir Frederick Scherger, had a long history of supporting vigorous military intervention in both Indochina and Indonesia. The Chief of the General Staff was Lieutenant General Sir John Wilton, the former head of SEATO's military planning office in Bangkok. Both as the professional head of the army from 1963 to 1966 and then as Scherger's successor as Chairman of the

Chiefs of Staff Committee, Wilton was and would remain a consistent supporter of the Vietnam commitment. The diplomats in External Affairs and senior civilians in Defence, by contrast, were concerned over the lack of a clear American strategy, but were unable to communicate their concerns to the highest level.

In December 1964 Menzies discussed President Johnson's letter with the Cabinet. The records are unclear, but it seems likely that the ministers took a provisional decision: Australia would offer a battalion, if that would help to ensure that the United States took a strong military stand in South Vietnam. Little hint of this was made public, as any Australian action depended on the highly uncertain direction of American policy. In the following months, few ministers, let alone other parliamentarians or the general public, were privy to the government's deliberations on Vietnam policy; at the final stages, even some hesitancy in the FAD Committee was overruled.[6]

As noted in Chapter 2, Menzies had handled a request from the British in 1950 for military assistance in the Malayan Emergency with great caution. He was sensitive to political opinion not only in Australia but also in Asian countries emerging from European colonialism; he wanted an assurance that Australia's great power ally had political and military strategies with a strong chance of success; he questioned whether orthodox military tactics, especially bombing, would be effective against insurgents in Southeast Asian jungles. In 1965, after dominating Australian politics for 15 years, Menzies took a very different approach to an Australian commitment to Vietnam. The caution and the questioning were set aside. Menzies had evidently decided that the preservation of an independent, non-communist South Vietnam was essential to Australia's security, as well as in the interests of maintaining a healthy alliance relationship with the United States. Australia should therefore do all that it could, militarily as well as diplomatically, to ensure that the United States took a firm stand in South Vietnam. He was encouraged by indications that the commitment of even a small number of Australian combat troops would have a profound effect in Washington, reinforcing the hawks in the private and public debates over the policy of the United States. He did not question, and he ensured that others did not question, whether the United States had a viable political and military strategy: the effectiveness of American military power was simply assumed.

Menzies evidently thought a commitment to Vietnam, in close alliance with the United States, would have broad popular support, with opposition limited largely to communists and their allies, some clergy and other pacifists, and some radical fringe groups. Some commentators who were critical of any involvement in Vietnam, on the grounds that the West was opposing nationalism rather than communism, had expressed similar views about Malaya and had been proved wrong. Menzies also expected that he could, once again, divide the Labor Party, driving a wedge between the right and left wings. Subsequent events would indicate that he had failed to understand not only the nature of the conflict in Vietnam and the limits on America's capacity to affect the outcome there, but also the changing nature of Australian society.

THE COMMITMENT OF A BATTALION TO CONFRONTATION[7]

In December 1964 and January 1965 both the British and Malaysian governments renewed their pressure on Australia to contribute combat troops to Borneo in order to meet the heightened threat from the Indonesians. After Cabinet and FAD Committee meetings that discussed both Vietnam and Confrontation, Australia committed 3RAR, the battalion serving with the Strategic Reserve on the Malayan peninsula, as well as about 100 SAS troops. The decision was taken in January and announced in February. The government had already agreed that, if British plans for more aggressive action against Indonesia, including bombing, had to be activated, RAAF aircraft would be available and Darwin could be used as a base. The government also agreed that the RAN ships operating off the Indonesian coast would adopt the new British policy of patrolling closer to the shore, recognising only a 3-mile limit for territorial waters rather than the 12 miles claimed by the Indonesians. RAN destroyers and destroyer escorts had already been added to the coastal minesweepers committed in 1964. By the time Confrontation ended, six minesweepers and six destroyers or destroyer escorts had served in Borneo and West Malaysian waters.

Britain had phrased its request for troops and other support in general terms, respecting the Australian policy of 'graduated response', which had led to the rejections of several similar requests since late 1963. The Malaysian government was more forthright. Kuala Lumpur asked for two Australian battalions, both 3RAR and another to come from Australia. The government could not agree to the additional battalion, knowing that it was highly likely that at least one of the other two RAR battalions would be committed to Vietnam. The other was held for possible service either in the SEATO area or in Papua New Guinea.

The Australian government agreed to commit infantry and SAS troops to Borneo only after strict assurances that it would be closely consulted over any actions that would involve Australian forces in combat. To this longstanding concern was added a new element. Since mid-1964, the British and Malaysian troops in Borneo had been authorised to cross the border and operate on Indonesian territory in what was known as Operation Claret. To avoid charges of aggression, and to reduce Indonesian embarrassment, Claret operations were a closely kept secret. Any casualties were described as having taken place on Malaysian soil. At this time, as part of the strengthening of British policy, the troops were allowed to operate up to 10 000 yards (9.1 kilometres) inside the Indonesian border, instead of the previous limit of 3000 yards (2.7 kilometres). The government was concerned about the involvement of Australian troops in Claret operations, fearing that the Indonesians might retaliate on the Papua New Guinea border. It finally accepted that Australians would act under the same rules of engagement as the British and Malaysian forces, but urged special care in their deployment.

The Australians emphasised to both the British and the Americans their difficulty in making simultaneous commitments to Vietnam and Confrontation. They told the British that the two campaigns were now becoming 'a common threat',[8] with the implication that the British position in Malaysia was dependent on the American stance in Vietnam.

In short, the Australian government's first public reaction to the renewed pressure from two allies for support in two campaigns was the commitment of an infantry battalion, an SAS squadron and other elements to Confrontation. This commitment came 16 months after the formation of Malaysia and Menzies' announcement of a decision in principle to give military support there, if required. Throughout that time the Menzies government had been highly cautious, maintaining a policy of 'graduated response' and resisting pressure from both Conservative and Labour governments in London, as well as from Kuala Lumpur, for a greater commitment. Even when committing combat troops, the government decided to maintain its aid program in Indonesia and the intake of Indonesian students to Australia. The government's handling of Confrontation, including the commitment of the infantry battalion, was broadly supported by the public and the Labor Opposition: the only critics were those who pressed the government to do more, rather than less, to oppose Indonesian ambitions. But Menzies and his government did not share with the public its knowledge that it was highly likely that another battalion would soon be sent to Vietnam, nor its fear that yet another might be required in Papua New Guinea.

THE COMMITMENT OF A BATTALION TO VIETNAM[9]

In February and March 1965 the Johnson administration began to implement the bombing campaign against North Vietnam that had been canvassed for some months. By the time Operation Rolling Thunder was ended in 1968, American planes would drop more bombs on North Vietnam than had been expended in the entire Korean War or the Pacific theatre of the Second World War. Hasluck immediately issued a statement, welcoming the action as a fitting response to the infiltration from North Vietnam into South Vietnam. More remarkably, the Labor Party also adopted a resolution that effectively backed the bombing program, seeing it as a step towards a negotiated settlement that would achieve a genuinely democratic South Vietnam. The Labor Party also supported the government's commitment of the infantry battalion and the SAS squadron to Borneo.

The staff talks in Honolulu between military representatives of the United States, Australia and New Zealand, which had been foreshadowed since early December, finally took place from 30 March to 1 April. The host was Admiral USG Sharp, Commander-in-Chief of Pacific Command, and the Australian and New Zealand delegations were led by, respectively, Scherger and Rear Admiral Sir Peter Phipps, New Zealand's Chief of the Defence Staff. Scherger's brief for the talks, prepared by the officials on the Defence Committee and endorsed by the ministers of the FAD Committee, emphasised that Australia's participation in the talks was 'exploratory and on a "no-commitment" basis'.[10] Scherger was directed to seek detailed information on the Americans' military objectives and operational concepts, and to ask how they would cope with the difficulties of fighting in a civil war in which it was hard to distinguish friend from foe, with the anti-American and anti-foreign propaganda generated by intervention by foreign forces, and with the danger that the RVN forces would leave the fighting to their allies. He was also instructed to gain much more information on the likely responses by the DRV, the NLF and China, and on American assessments of the strategic importance of South Vietnam. The brief scarcely mentioned the proposal to send a battalion, but it discussed at some length the serious political and military position in Vietnam.

Scherger did not follow his brief. Admiral Sharp indicated that the Americans were considering a number of radically different strategic approaches. One envisaged basing United States forces in a series of coastal enclaves at Da Nang, Qhi Nhon, Nha Trang and Saigon–Vung Tau, each with a major airfield. Another plan envisaged placing two or three divisions in Laos around the 17th parallel, to cut off infiltration from North to South Vietnam; a third would have placed between 70 000 and 90 000 troops in the northern provinces of South Vietnam and Thailand, to deny strategically important areas to the enemy. No decision had been taken on which, if any, of these radically different strategies would be adopted. Scherger's report consequently gave vague answers, or none at all, to the questions raised in his brief. Nevertheless he gave the impression that the Americans were likely to adopt an enclave strategy, with the role of the forces extending beyond base security to counter-insurgency. According to Scherger, the Americans wanted to have an Australian battalion, preferably with a New Zealand element, to serve with the US Marines in the Da Nang enclave. He recommended that Australia offer a battalion.

The New Zealand representatives were startled by Scherger's conduct at the Honolulu talks. Rear Admiral Phipps reported that Scherger had seemed more anxious than Sharp to have Australia involved, that he made no secret of his intention to recommend that Australia send a battalion, and that he expected Cabinet to agree. In conversation Scherger indicated that he thought the Eisenhower administration should have accepted Radford's advice on using air power to save the French at Dien

Bien Phu in 1954, instead of the 'chicken-hearted' British approach. The New Zealanders speculated that Scherger's assertiveness, and his willingness to go far beyond his official brief, could only be based on his close association with Menzies and knowledge of his private views.

For their part, the New Zealand government had foreseen disaster in any escalation of American involvement. They hoped to avoid or minimise military involvement by persuading the Americans that maintaining their role in Confrontation was New Zealand's most effective contribution to the security of Southeast Asia. In the following weeks, the Australian enthusiasm to be involved in Vietnam made this approach untenable. [To maintain credibility as an ANZUS partner, New Zealand became a highly reluctant contributor to the Vietnam commitment.[11]]

While Scherger was in Honolulu, Hasluck was seeking further information on American policy through the Australian embassy in Washington. Senior officials there indicated that the United States still had no clear ideas on its political aims or military strategy in Vietnam. It was possible that the Australians might be asked to provide a battalion to serve with the Marines, but the only specific request was for 150 additional army instructors to train the Regional Forces, the provincial militia who supported the ARVN. Hasluck and External Affairs officials were also concerned that American escalation could lead to further increases in support from the Soviet Union and China for the DRV and damage the standing of the United States in the numerous diplomatic initiatives being taken to start peace negotiations.

At a meeting of the FAD Committee on 7 April, Scherger reported that the Americans hoped that an Australian battalion would join the Marines in Da Nang. Hasluck, in contrast to his actions over the previous 12 months, now suggested that Australian forces were being dispersed too widely across Southeast Asia. He pressed for delay, to await the outcome of several attempts to start peace negotiations. Hasluck was supported by the Minister for Labour and National Service, William

McMahon, who had joined the FAD Committee after the introduction of the conscription system, for which he had ministerial responsibility. Their views were overruled by the other four members of the Committee – Menzies, Deputy Prime Minister John McEwen, Treasurer Harold Holt, and Minister for Defence Senator Shane Paltridge. Menzies reiterated his view that it was in Australia's own security interests, as well as in the interests of the American alliance, to help the United States keep South Vietnam out of communist hands. The psychological impact on the United States would be 'phenomenally valuable', he said, and Australia was 'looking for a way in and not a way out'. The Committee therefore decided not to send the additional 150 instructors, who were needed to implement the new national service scheme, but to offer a battalion.[12] After a short delay while the Australians assessed the implications of a major speech by Johnson at Johns Hopkins University, the Australian ambassador in Washington conveyed the Australian offer on 13 April to Rusk, who expressed deep appreciation.

A fundamental principle of forward defence had been that any intervention in a Southeast Asian country, alongside either Britain or the United States, must be at the invitation of the country concerned. It was therefore essential that Australia be able to say that the commitment of a battalion, and potentially other forces, to Vietnam was at the invitation of the RVN government. This was no easy matter, for the current RVN Prime Minister, Dr Phan Huy Quat, had serious reservations about the entry of foreign combat troops, as did the American ambassador, Maxwell Taylor. The Australian ambassador in Saigon, David Anderson, insisted that the RVN government should be genuinely consulted, not only about the commitment of the battalion but also about its role and its relationship with American and RVN forces. For more than two weeks, the government had to keep its decision secret until complex, triangular discussions between Saigon, Washington and Canberra could secure the necessary request. Finally, Quat and Anderson agreed at a meeting on 28 April that the Australian battalion, like the other external forces, would be used for base security and to be a mobile reserve for major combat operations; they would not be used for counter-subversion and pacification, which would be conducted by Vietnamese forces. On that basis, the battalion would be welcome. It was an acceptance by the RVN of an Australian offer, but the Saigon government agreed that the Australian government could say that it was 'in receipt of a request' from the RVN.[13]

Throughout April American strategy was still in a state of flux. By late April the Americans had decided that they wanted the Australian battalion to serve not with the US Marines at Da Nang but with a US Army airborne brigade at an enclave to be centred on the air base at Bien Hoa, just east of Saigon. The Americans also wanted the Australians to be engaged in base security and conventional operations, not pacification. General William Westmoreland, who had succeeded General Harkins as commander of US forces in Vietnam in 1964, envisaged an international mobile reserve force combining American, RVN, Korean, Filipino and Australian units.

THE ANNOUNCEMENT AND PARLIAMENTARY REACTION[14]

In March and April 1965 the leaders of many countries and institutions, including the Pope, the Secretary-General of the United Nations, and the governments of Britain, France, Canada and India, were urging Washington and Hanoi to engage in negotiations towards a peaceful resolution of the Vietnam crisis. Menzies' obvious reluctance to support these calls was the principal focus of criticism from the Opposition. In March a group of Anglican bishops issued a public letter to Menzies, urging him to join the many international efforts to encourage negotiations towards 'an honourable and peaceful settlement'. Menzies' blistering reply contended that the United States was courageously and generously accepting the responsibility for protecting 'human freedom' against 'atheistic and materialistic Communism'. He asked rhetorically how the United States could negotiate with the Viet Cong, who were 'determined upon revolution by violence', with the DRV, which had shown that it would be bound by no agreement, or with China, 'the home of aggression'. In early April, after the FAD Committee had confirmed its decision to offer the battalion but before it could be announced, the bishops returned to the fray, contending that both North and South Vietnam, the United States and China had all breached the Geneva Accords, that Hanoi's political views were not necessarily identical with Beijing's, and that it was idealistic to see the war as a crusade for freedom against 'atheistic and materialistic Communism'. The heads of the Prime Minister's and External Affairs Departments, Sir John Bunting and Sir James Plimsoll, urged Menzies to send a short and 'unbelligerent' reply, because 'some aspects of the Vietnam situation … are so hazy that anything written, no matter how carefully, can be open to rebuttal'. Menzies rejected this advice and sent another vigorously argued retort, repeating a recent statement in Parliament that he was opposed to suggestions that

> the United States, instead of fighting, should negotiate … with an enemy which has violated its obligations … with a country that has ignored its international obligations … and … with people who will keep on shooting when the Americans have stopped shooting. That seems to me a fantasy, and if I am the only Prime Minister left to denounce it, I denounce it.[15]

The exchange marked the first major round in the debate that was to dominate Australian politics for years to come. As some commentators noted, the bishops had drawn from Menzies a more fully argued statement of the government's case than he had ever given to Parliament. They had also shown that the government's policies on Vietnam would not be as readily accepted as most of Menzies' foreign policies had been for the previous 15 years. Menzies had another audience in mind. He ensured that the text of the letters was promptly conveyed to President Johnson, who replied gratefully that 'your words give me strength'. Johnson knew that the United States had one ally who was prepared to stand against the worldwide clamour to enter negotiations rather than to intervene with combat forces.

When Menzies told the House of Representatives on the evening of 29 April that Australia had committed a battalion to Vietnam, Calwell and Whitlam had left Canberra for a political commitment in Sydney, having been assured that no announcement was expected. These circumstances gave an air of deceit and deviousness to the decision, especially as something remarkably similar had occurred when Menzies had announced the defection of Vladimir Petrov in 1954. The problem had in fact arisen from a combination of the long delay in securing the RVN's official request for the battalion, poor cable communications between Saigon and Canberra, and McMahon's notorious propensity to leak government secrets to a favoured journalist. At the time, and for years afterwards, many Labor leaders and supporters aimed much of their criticism at the 'deceit' involved in the commitment, contending that there had been no 'request' from the RVN government and that Australia was only responding to pressure from the United States. Given that the RVN had approved the intervention, albeit by accepting an offer rather than by initiating a request, that there had been a history of requests by the RVN for assistance from foreign countries, including Australia, and that Menzies and his government made no secret of the fact that they were more concerned about Washington's opinions than Saigon's, the Opposition's attention to the issue of the 'request' was an unfortunate distraction from the more serious weaknesses in the government's case. They would have been better advised to ask whether the RVN had a government with political credibility and military capacity on which a Western intervention could be based; or whether the United States had a coherent political and military strategy, within which Australia could make an appropriate and cost-effective contribution.

During the drafting of Menzies' statement, Plimsoll noted that, while there was wide agreement that Australia should accept military commitments in Malaysia, this was not true of Vietnam. He suggested that Menzies might include the following sentences:

> The take-over of South Vietnam would be a direct military threat to Australia and all the countries of South and South-East Asia. It must be seen as part of a thrust by Communist China between the Indian and Pacific Oceans, exploiting weaknesses in the multi-racial and economically underdeveloped countries of the region.

Menzies included this passage, but omitted the clause beginning 'exploiting weaknesses'. With this omission, the two sentences gave the inaccurate and unfortunate impression that Australia was intervening in Vietnam in order to meet a direct military threat from China. Menzies and his ministers did place the survival or fall of the RVN in the context of the expansion of Chinese influence, but they saw it as a political rather than a military threat, while official assessments had seen Indonesia as the only country that might pose a direct military threat to Australia. The suggestion from Plimsoll, who had not been involved in policy-making on Vietnam and who had just returned from India – a country that did regard China as a military threat – together with Menzies' decision to abbreviate the passage for rhetorical effect, gave rise to the two most quoted sentences in the statement. They gave a false impression of Australia's strategic thinking, which distorted the debate on the Vietnam commitment for years to come.[16]

The parliamentary debate on Menzies' statement began with a speech by Calwell. Carefully crafted to unite the left and right wings of the party, it was probably the finest of his long political career. On the nature of the war itself, Calwell said that while there had been aggression from North Vietnam, '[t]he war in South Vietnam is a civil war, aided and abetted by the North Vietnamese Government, but neither created nor principally maintained by it'. Most of the Viet Cong were from the south; the RVN government had no base of popular support; and if northern support were cut off, the Viet Cong would not collapse. Secondly, Calwell agreed that 'China must be stopped', but he said the threat from China was political rather than military, and could only be met by nationalism and the great non-Christian religions. Thirdly, he agreed that the United States must not be humiliated in Asia, but that humiliation could come from being bogged down in Vietnam, as France had been, leading to withdrawal or an escalated war. Consequently Australia should support those, like the British and Canadian Prime Ministers, who had urged the United States to enter negotiations. The speech was elegant, effective and often prescient.[17]

Menzies' response was focused on Australia's relationship with the United States. After noting that the Labor Party had previously supported American motives, he argued that Labor now wanted Australia to tell the Americans that 'American soldiers … can go and fight and die in South Vietnam, but that is not for us'.[18]

Calwell's speech had ensured that Labor was united in opposition to the war, but different emphases were evident in those of other Labor leaders. Unlike Calwell, Dr Jim Cairns regarded North and South Vietnam as two parts of one country, and questioned the degree of control the north exercised over the revolution in the south. Whitlam, by contrast, strongly supported the American alliance, said that America's motives were 'above dispute', but said Australian forces would be better employed in the Malaysia–Indonesia–Papua New Guinea area. 'The Government's sin', he concluded, 'is to have acted militarily without having prepared the ground diplomatically'.

REACTIONS AT HOME AND ABROAD[19]

The first reactions to Australia's commitment to Vietnam, both internationally and within Australia, were surprisingly mixed and muted, with less support from supposed friends and less criticism from potential enemies than might have been predicted. The government continued to argue that the commitment 'flowed from' its SEATO obligations, although the disunity of the SEATO members was increasingly obvious. Only Thailand and the Philippines gave strong support to the Australian commitment: both countries would themselves send troops. Pakistan and France distanced themselves from SEATO. The New Zealand government's reluctance to be involved was overridden by the Australian decision: in late May it committed an artillery battery to support the Australian battalion. In Britain a Labour government was trying to maintain its 'special relationship' with the United States and to initiate peace negotiations, preferably by reconvening the Geneva Conference. Labour's left wing was highly critical of American policy but the robustly anti-communist Defence Secretary, Denis Healey, said he was happy to see the Australian commitment. In the RVN itself, civilian and military leaders were disappointingly cool in response, although the increasingly powerful Minister for Defence, General Thieu, expressed warm appreciation. The Prime Minister of Laos, heading a precarious coalition that was officially neutralist, welcomed the Australian decision, while Prince Norodom Sihanouk, the effective ruler of Cambodia, was remarkably restrained in his public criticism. Tunku Abdul Rahman publicly expressed support, but Lee Kuan Yew in Singapore was deliberately ambiguous. In Indonesia Sukarno's denunciation of the United States was becoming more extreme, but he did not comment on Australia's decision. Japan, like most European allies of the United States, was caught between a deep unease over Vietnam and a reluctance to criticise the United States. The Soviet Union criticised the Australian decision, but said it would not be allowed to affect the Australian–Soviet relationship. China, predictably, condemned the 'reckless decision'.

Both the DRV in Hanoi and the NLF in South Vietnam vehemently denounced the commitment, calling on the Australian people to stop the 'reactionary clique' from providing 'Australian youth as cannon-fodder for the U.S. aggressors'. The Vietnamese communists' undisguised interest in encouraging domestic opposition to the commitment reflected the importance they placed on Western public opinion as a crucial battlefield in the war.

In the Australian community the general mood was acceptance, with an uneasy sense of foreboding. Opinion polls suggested that a majority accepted the government's case that the fall of South Vietnam would expose Thailand and Malaysia to external threat. Most newspapers were sombre but supportive, describing the commitment as 'grave' but necessary. The principal exception was *The Australian*, founded the previous year by Rupert Murdoch, which strongly criticised it as 'reckless' and 'wrong'. The militant left of the trade union movement was counter-balanced by an equally vehement anti-communist right. The leaders of the ACTU acted to ensure that the militant left unions, such as the Seamen's Union, did not do anything that might rebound against the Labor Party, such as action affecting supplies to the troops or trade with the United States. The principal spokesmen for the Anglican and Catholic hierarchies supported the commitment. Even after the assassination of Diem, many Catholic activists within the DLP and the NCC continued to give emphatic support to the commitment. Within the universities there were expressions of support for government policy.

Nevertheless, there were early indications of the protests to come. Academics with a detailed knowledge of China and Southeast Asia challenged the accuracy of the government's analyses. Many commentators, even those broadly sympathetic to the government's policies, strongly criticised the way in which it had been handled, alleging that ministers, especially Menzies and Hasluck, were arrogant, insensitive to public opinion, and unwilling or unable to argue a coherent case. A number were concerned that the government did not have a convincing defence strategy, and that the nation's meagre defence resources were being divided between at least two, potentially more, conflicts in the region. Some clergy and prominent laymen, mostly in Protestant denominations but even a few Catholics, expressed doubts about the morality as well as the strategic wisdom of the commitment.

Where there was dissent, it was usually expressed in moderate forms. Australian protesters soon established the practice of borrowing forms of protest from the United States and adapting them to Australian conditions. Some clergy, for example, sought to emulate an advertisement in the *New York Times* by 2500 ministers, priests and rabbis, denouncing President Johnson's policies. In the American spring of 1965 the distinctive form of anti-war protest was the 'teach-in'. The teach-ins were long, often all-night, forums on university campuses, where thousands of academic staff and students heard speakers, also predominantly staff and students, debate the war. The American teach-ins were protests rather than debates, but the teach-ins at Australian universities in the southern winter of 1965 were markedly different in tone. The organising committees ensured that presentations were balanced between supporters and critics of the government's policy, principally academics and journalists. Hundreds of students attended many hours of debate, applauding those who gave well-informed and well-delivered speeches, whether for or against the Vietnam commitment. The most effective critics were historians and political scientists with expertise on Asian affairs, such as CP Fitzgerald, JD Legge and Macmahon Ball, churchmen such as Alan Walker and Bishop Moyes, and Dr Cairns, who was rapidly becoming a leader of the anti-war movement outside Parliament. The most convincing supporters of the government's policy were journalists such as Denis Warner and Peter Samuels, academics like Geoffrey Fairbairn and Owen Harries, and a backbench Liberal parliamentarian, TEF Hughes. Government ministers, most notably Hasluck, proved remarkably inept in defending the government's policies in the teach-ins and other forums.[20]

In contrast to the even-handed nature of the teach-ins, there were a few early examples of radical protest by groups prepared to display civil disobedience and to express support for the DRV and the NLF. After one protest in Sydney turned into a near-riot, leaders of anti-war groups, aware of the counter-productive effect of such militancy, worked to build broad coalitions in support of non-violent opposition to the commitment.

The first intakes into the selective national service system took place in 1965, so the first conscripts would not be available for overseas service – in Malaysia, Vietnam, Papua New Guinea or anywhere else – until 1966. The battalion committed to Vietnam in April 1965 was therefore composed entirely of regulars. Opposition to the war and opposition to conscription were still two separate streams of dissent.

The initial opposition to conscription was also predominantly moderate in tone. In reaction to the National Service Act of November 1964, young men in Australia's major cities formed the Youth Campaign Against Conscription (YCAC). The YCAC groups were closely aligned with the Labor Party; their rallies and demonstrations were usually orderly, even good-humoured at times. Knowing that Calwell's antipathy to conscription was stronger and more visceral than his opposition to the Vietnam War, YCAC's initial aim was to help Labor to victory at the election due in late 1966. Another prominent group founded in 1965 was Save Our Sons (SOS). Predominantly middle-aged and middle-class women with sons liable for conscription, members of SOS dressed respectably and behaved impeccably at their demonstrations, for example at army barracks when new intakes of national servicemen were inducted. Both YCAC and SOS mobilised new constituencies of support for the Labor Party.[21]

These first signs of significant dissent evidently caught the government by surprise. After years in which its foreign and defence policies had been accepted almost without question, it was remarkably inept at explaining them when challenged. Menzies and his colleagues seemed confident that the Vietnam commitment would be popular electorally and expose the divisions within the Labor Party over the American alliance. They evidently thought that criticism would only come from communists and the small numbers of clergy and others who had long been willing to join communist fronts. In fact, the communist movement in Australia was splintering and losing its effectiveness, while dissent was emerging from new sources. In Parliament and outside, the government's efforts to defend the Vietnam commitment were clumsy and often counter-productive. Its own supporters criticised the excessive secrecy with which it made decisions and its ineptitude in explaining them. By the end of 1965 it was evident that, while a majority of the electorate supported the government's policy, opinion-forming circles were beginning to turn against it.

OPERATIONS IN CONFRONTATION[22]

The battalion committed in January 1965 to operate in Borneo was 3RAR. The operational capacity of the regiment had been affected by the army's short-lived experiment in the early 1960s with a reorganised structure known as Pentropic, under which battalions would be larger, with five rifle companies instead of four.[23] As the British never adopted this system – the Americans having abandoned their version before the Australians adopted it – deployment to Malaysia required the army for some time to maintain two different forms of organisation simultaneously. The battalion recovered quickly from the disruption caused by the adoption and abandonment of the new structure. With its traditional organisation, it fitted well into the environment of Commonwealth units. By May 1965 there were 12 battalions in Borneo: one Australian, four British (one of which was soon to be replaced by a New Zealand battalion), four Gurkha and three Malaysian.

The operations in Borneo comprised a continual series of reconnaissance, ambush and fighting patrols on both sides of the Malaysian–Indonesian border. A distinctive feature was the use of company bases, typically housing a rifle company with supporting artillery or mortars. From these bases, patrols were usually conducted by platoons, or sometimes sections. (Numbers varied, but a company normally comprised about 120 men, a platoon about 30, and a section about 10; the entire battalion, including headquarters and support units, comprised about 800 men.) During its four-month tour in Borneo, 3RAR conducted 30 Claret operations across the Indonesian border, of which 12 were reconnaissance and 18 ambush or fighting patrols, and had four successful contacts. The battalion lost three killed in action, all to mines laid by the enemy. As Jeffrey Grey has recorded, 'The fighting in Borneo in 1965 was a war of companies and platoons, a conflict at sub-unit level in a trying climate and difficult terrain', to which the 'officers and men of 3RAR had proven … well suited'.[24]

The SAS squadron operated separately from the infantry battalion, but in a similar manner. Most of its operations were four-man patrols. On the Malaysian side of the border these were primarily to monitor the border crossing-points used by the enemy, as well as 'hearts and minds' operations with the local people, who responded with useful intelligence. Patrols across the border were airlifted in and out, but otherwise moved entirely on foot. The principal purpose was to obtain intelligence on the enemy without being detected, although one patrol joined with a Gurkha unit in a successful attack on an Indonesian position, and another successfully ambushed a boat carrying Indonesian troops. The only fatality suffered by the squadron was a member of a patrol who was gored by an elephant. The British commanders in Borneo valued the work of the SAS as the 'eyes and ears' of the Commonwealth force.

1RAR AT BIEN HOA[25]

This was the type of war in Southeast Asia for which the army was trained and equipped and in which it had developed skills from experience in the Malayan Emergency and Confrontation: working with British and other Commonwealth forces, operating cautiously and silently in small sub-units, countering small-scale enemy forces with their own techniques, ambushing insurgents while avoiding being ambushed. The first battalion committed to Vietnam encountered a very different war, in scale and nature. The PLAF forces, by this time reinforced with formed units of the PAVN, were poised to strike a decisive blow, driving a wedge through the central provinces of South Vietnam. The uncertainties over whether the United States would intervene, and if so with what strategy and operational methods, meant that little detailed planning had been done to prepare the Australian battalion for its new environment. Scherger had failed to take the opportunity of the staff talks at Honolulu to seek information about, or influence on, American strategy. In the following days the military planners were constrained by tight security provisions and extremely limited time in which to assess the size and nature of the force to be sent. Not until the troops were en route to Vietnam on board HMAS *Sydney*, a former aircraft carrier modified to become a troop transport, did they learn their destination.

The battalion, 1RAR, with the support of a battery of New Zealand artillery, was sent to operate at Bien Hoa with the US Army's 173rd Airborne Brigade (Separate), a formation of about 3000 men, designed to operate as an independent task force. In addition to two battalions of infantry, trained to deploy by air and to parachute into operations, the brigade included artillery, armoured, engineer, logistic and other support units. It was trained to operate in conventional rather than counter-insurgency warfare, to deploy quickly, to use its considerable assets of mobility, technology and firepower, and to get out quickly having accomplished its mission. It would accept casualties in the process of bringing the enemy to battle, when it would expect to inflict greater casualties. The brigade's patrols were noisy and blatant, designed to provoke the enemy into reaction. The sharp contrast in operational styles of the Australians and the Americans was exacerbated by different staff methods and military terminology.

Tensions between the Australian and American military commanders also arose over the limits placed by the Australian authorities on 1RAR's role. Initially it was confined to operations to protect the security of the Bien Hoa base. Following pressure from Westmoreland, the role was extended to include participation in 'search-and-destroy' operations designed to assault the enemy's base areas and to keep him off balance, at first to stem the communist offensive and then to take the offensive. The army's chief, Wilton, was deeply concerned at the possible implications of the employment of the Australian battalion in the brigade's operations. From his own experience in the Korean War and from what he saw in Vietnam, Wilton thought American brigade commanders used their troops recklessly: he did not want Australians to be caught up in their 'meat-grinder' tactics. After extensive, high-level negotiations between military authorities in Saigon, Canberra and Washington, compromises were reached. The Australian battalion participated in some major operations at some distance from Bien Hoa, including the

Iron Triangle north of Saigon, but not as far afield as Westmoreland would have wished. The Australians acquitted themselves well in these operations, but at some cost.

Over time, some American commanders came to respect the Australians' patient application of small-unit counter-insurgency tactics. For their part, the Australians came to recognise that Vietnam was a very different campaign from those in Malaya or Borneo, and that they had a lot to learn about large operations requiring coordination of infantry with artillery, armour, combat engineers, and support from helicopters and fixed-wing aircraft.

From an early stage in 1RAR's service in Vietnam, the army began to press for two major changes to the commitment. First, it sought to make the battalion more effective in its current role by adding an artillery battery (in addition to the New Zealand battery), an engineer troop, an army aviation reconnaissance flight and logistic support elements. The change – in military parlance, from a battalion to a battalion group – would raise the total Australian strength from about 1100 to about 1400 men.

More importantly, the army, led by Wilton, sought the commitment of at least one more battalion, so that the Australian commitment would take the form of a task force of two or more battalions. Such a task force would be able to operate with a greater degree of independence from the American military, relying to a greater degree on its own operational methods and doctrines. The Defence Committee advised the government that a second battalion could be made available in early 1966, but it would require the inclusion of conscripts from the new national service scheme, the intake for which would have to be maintained at its 1965 level, instead of reducing it as had previously been foreshadowed. Wilton recommended that planning for a two-battalion task force, to be despatched in early 1966, commence immediately.[26]

THE MALAYSIA–SINGAPORE SPLIT AND THE COMMITMENT OF A BATTALION GROUP[27]

This recommendation from the army coincided with renewed pressure from Washington. In July, in what was widely seen as a crucial step in the escalation of the American commitment in Vietnam, Johnson responded to a request from Westmoreland to commit substantial numbers of additional American troops to Vietnam. The process was begun, by which the American commitment would eventually reach more than 500 000 personnel 'in-country' in mid-1969. Johnson's attempt to conceal the full extent and impact of this decision was a major element in the growing mistrust of official American statements on the war, which came to be known as 'the credibility gap'. In an effort to make the American escalation more acceptable to domestic and international public opinion, Johnson asked Australia to increase its assistance, without specifying what form that increase should take.

The government's consideration of these pressures was complicated by a new element of uncertainty in Southeast Asia. As noted earlier, a principal motive for the creation of Malaysia was the desire to include Singapore in a federation with the Malayan states. In 1965 there were signs of increasing tension between the Malay-dominated Alliance government in Kuala Lumpur and Lee Kuan Yew in Singapore. Tunku Abdul Rahman and his UMNO particularly disliked the intention of Lee's People's Action Party to contest elections on the peninsula. The tension aroused concern both in Britain, because the separation of Singapore from Malaysia would cast doubts on the future of the British defence establishments in Singapore, and in Australia, where it would raise new doubts about the British commitment to keep its forces in Southeast Asia, a fundamental aim of the forward defence policy. In August the feared separation took place. Despite vigorous efforts by

British and Australian diplomats, Singapore was effectively evicted from Malaysia.

Amid these pressures, the FAD Committee decided to raise the Vietnam commitment to a battalion group, committing an artillery battery, a troop of combat engineers and an army aviation reconnaissance flight to support 1RAR. It also maintained the higher level of national service intake that would be required by a second battalion, but explicitly instructed the army not to make any plans for a two-battalion task force. Amid the intense controversy over the American commitment to Vietnam, and with the added concerns over the implications of the split between Malaysia and Singapore, the government was determined to suppress any suggestion of an increased Australian commitment to Vietnam. As had been the case with the initial commitment of the battalion, military planning was again subordinated to the requirements of domestic and international politics, a practice that greatly increased the pressures on those who were required to serve.

THE INDONESIAN COUP AND ITS IMPACT ON AUSTRALIAN POLICY[28]

The commitment of large numbers of combat troops by the United States and its allies to South Vietnam and the separation of Singapore from Malaysia did not end the crises of 1965. In late August India and Pakistan fought another in their series of small wars over Kashmir. Although a member of SEATO, Pakistan was supported by China in the South Asian conflict, so the Kashmir dispute was interpreted by some in Australia as another example of the extension of Chinese influence.

More important to Australia were events in Indonesia. Rivalry between the PKI and the anti-communist army had been building for months, but few expected the events of the night of 30 September–

1 October. A group of officers, apparently attempting a coup d'état in the interests of the PKI, killed six leading generals and narrowly missed their principal target, General Nasution. Army units, led by a general little known to the outside world named Suharto, retaliated. The army soon controlled Jakarta, but took some time to extend their control to central and eastern Java and the rest of the country. In the following months Indonesia experienced an horrific bloodbath as anti-communist forces, including militant Muslims as well as the army, slaughtered and jailed hundreds of thousands of real or alleged communists.

The coup and counter-coup came as a shock to the world. Although much remains the subject of controversy and speculation, it appears that Australian and American authorities were not involved, other than perhaps to provide information to the army about PKI members. It is now clear that the events on and after 30 September constituted a major turning-point in the politics of Indonesia and all of Southeast Asia, but their immediate effect was to underline the widespread fears and uncertainty. Although the PKI was effectively destroyed, Sukarno retained much of his personal charisma and his title of President, while Suharto moved slowly and carefully to remove him from effective power and to consolidate the army's control. In March 1966 Suharto took many of the presidential powers from Sukarno, but let him retain the title; in March 1967 Suharto became Acting President; and only in March 1968 did he formally become President, the office he would hold for the next 30 years.

Australia and its allies knew that the Indonesian Army had never been as enthusiastic as the PKI over Confrontation, in which the Commonwealth forces had in any case gained the upper hand by 1965. Nevertheless, many months passed before the impact of the coup on Indonesian policy became clear. Not until August 1966 did the Indonesians and Malaysians formally end Confrontation. Until that time, and even afterwards, there were occasional clashes between their armed forces. Australian authorities watched events in Indonesia carefully, hoping that the dominant forces would adopt policies friendlier to the West, but without any great confidence until well into 1966. They long retained the fear that Indonesia might revert to the aggressive policies of 'the year of living dangerously'.

A major element in the Australian motivation for the commitment to Vietnam was the contention that Australia needed to support the United States there, in order to ensure American support if Confrontation were to become a major conflict, perhaps including clashes between Indonesian and Australian forces in New Guinea. By 1965 support in Vietnam was seen as necessary to ensure that the anti-communist forces in Indonesia did not lose heart in their struggle against the PKI. The events on and after 30 September therefore made a considerable impact on much of the rationale for the Australian commitment. The timing of these events was crucial. Had the Indonesian coup and counter-coup taken place a year or two earlier, it is possible that Australian policy in Vietnam might have taken a different course. But in late 1965 and early 1966, the events of September–October in Indonesia, following the separation of Singapore from Malaysia and the hostilities between India and Pakistan, only underlined the unpredictability and danger of politics in South and Southeast Asia. In that atmosphere, Australia continued to seek the closest possible relations with its ultimate protector, the United States. By the time that Australians could be confident that Indonesia was a bulwark against communist threats instead of a potentially dangerous neighbour, Australia had become too deeply committed to the conflict in Vietnam to extricate itself.

THE TASK FORCE AND THE ELECTION 1966

A NEW PRIME MINISTER[1]

On Australia Day, 26 January 1966, Harold Holt succeeded Robert Menzies as Prime Minister. Having won seven successive elections and established a record-breaking term of 16 successive years as Prime Minister, in addition to his two years in 1939–1941, Menzies had retired at a time of his own choosing. Paul Hasluck remained as Minister for External Affairs, while [Allen Fairhall] had succeeded Athol Townley, who had died a few days earlier, as Minister for Defence. A new appointee to the ministry, Malcolm Fraser, became Minister for the Army. These men would be the most important shapers of Australia's policies in Vietnam for the next two years, a period in which the commitment took on a markedly different tone.

As a member of Parliament since 1935, deputy leader of the Liberal Party since 1958, and a longstanding and trusted colleague of Menzies,

Holt had long seemed his mentor's most likely successor. He had earned a reputation as a moderate and reformist minister in economic portfolios, establishing good relations with the union movement as Minister for Labour and National Service (1940–41 and 1949–58), moderating the implementation of the White Australia policy as Minister for Immigration (1949–56), and preparing the introduction of decimal currency as Treasurer (1958–66). Although a member of the FAD Committee of Cabinet since its creation in 1963, his role in this area had generally been to give unequivocal support to Menzies. At the important meeting of the Committee on 7 April 1965, Holt had said that, 'whatever the final outcome of United States intervention in Vietnam', Australia had to give its maximum possible contribution.[2]

After his accession to the prime ministership, Holt quickly identified himself with Australia's war in Vietnam to an even greater extent than had Menzies. He portrayed the commitment as the price that Australia and the United States had to pay in order to protect the growing prosperity and future development of the non-communist countries of Asia, of vital importance to Australia's future. Menzies had long been noted for his enthusiasm for visiting London and Washington, and his obvious discomfort on his relatively few visits to Asian capitals. Holt, by contrast, made a point of visiting Asia, especially Southeast Asia, not only for his first overseas trip as Prime Minister but also on three occasions in his first 15 months. He was always accompanied by a large party from the Australian media: his purpose was to bring the attention of the Australian people to the progress made by non-communist countries such as South Korea, Taiwan, Malaysia and Thailand. When he did visit London, he urged the British government to remain committed to Asia. In his first weeks as Prime Minister, Holt also received a series of high-ranking foreign visitors, including the Vice-President of the United States and the Prime Minister of Thailand, underlining his commitment to the anti-communist cause in Southeast Asia.

Hasluck later said that he, Fairhall and senior public servants had to 'nurse' Holt, whom they considered naive and inexperienced in foreign affairs.[3] In Hasluck's opinion Holt did not understand that Australia's policies and commitments were based not on the warmth of official meetings and welcoming crowds but on considerations of hard political power, especially that of the United States, and on American willingness to shape its policies towards Asia, particularly Indonesia, in Australia's interests. Hasluck probably thought that Holt did not realise the differences between the government's vigorously pro-American and anti-communist rhetoric and the practical limits it would place on its military and diplomatic commitments. Soon after becoming Prime Minister, Holt agreed to establish an Australian embassy to the anti-communist Republic of China on Taiwan, a measure that the Menzies government had consistently resisted while recognising that government as the legitimate ruler of China and refusing recognition of the communist government in Beijing. Holt, it seemed, took at face value the government's longstanding rhetoric about the American alliance and its importance in shaping a bright future for a non-communist Asia.

In one of its first decisions under Holt's leadership, the government in March decided to increase the Australian commitment to Vietnam to a two-battalion task force.[4] Although six months earlier the government had prohibited the army from making even provisional plans for such a commitment, the fears that had shaped this caution had now subsided. The split between Malaysia and Singapore had not made as serious an impact on regional affairs as had been feared, while the dramatic events in Indonesia seemed to offer a prospect, albeit still uncertain, of an end to Confrontation and an Indonesian government more sympathetic to the West. Moreover, a defence review in the United Kingdom suggested that the British government would not withdraw its forces from 'east of Suez'.

In this environment the government acceded to the continuing American pressure to send another battalion, accepting the army's recommendation to create an Australian task force, to be designated the 1st Australian Task Force (1ATF), with two infantry battalions and additional combat and logistic units.⁵ The task force would not only operate with a greater degree of independence from American military tactics and operational methods; it would also be a more distinctive national contribution to the allied effort. The government noted that this measure would give Australian officers a greater level of command experience. Even now, the government still had in mind the possibility of a military commitment closer to Australia, for the Cabinet minute noted that the task force could readily be transferred from Vietnam to operate elsewhere – for example, in Papua New Guinea. Together with the flight of RAAF Caribou transport aircraft and the 100 members of the Training Team already in Vietnam, the decision to create the task force tripled the Australian commitment to about 4500 men.

To raise the battalions, substantial numbers of national servicemen from the first intakes of the new selective service scheme would be required. At first it appeared that some battalions would have a majority of national servicemen, but the government insisted that no battalion should have more than 50 per cent of conscripts. For the remainder of the Vietnam commitment, the RAR battalions and other combat units in Vietnam would normally comprise roughly equal numbers of regulars and national servicemen.

In Australian politics, two separate sources of dissent – the war itself and conscription for overseas service – were now joined. The selective national service scheme, which had been introduced because of concerns over actual or potential commitments in Indonesia, Malaysia and Papua New Guinea as much as those in Indochina, would henceforth be associated in the public mind exclusively with Vietnam.

Having postponed the decision on the task force from August 1965 to early 1966, the government delayed the announcement until 8 March, so that Holt could make it on the first day he faced Parliament as Prime Minister. This increased Holt's personal association with the Vietnam commitment, but the further delay exacerbated the army's difficulties in planning the task force. Despite the embargo of August 1965 on any planning, and the further delays in early 1966, the government still required the task force to arrive in June, a previously established target date. Firm limits were also placed on the size of the task force and its major components, using figures that had been provisionally suggested in 1965, without consultation with allies or with the officers and men currently serving with 1RAR. These constraints required the army to plan the commitment of the task force in great haste and with inadequate information. When operational experience indicated additional requirements, the ceiling on numbers created considerable difficulties. As a result, the task force would be deficient in many of the capabilities it required, placing additional pressure on those who were sent.

OPERATIONS IN BORNEO[6]

Early in 1966 4RAR arrived in Borneo to serve a six-month tour, as 3RAR had the previous year. 4RAR had been raised in 1964, with a view towards service in Southeast Asia, following the 1963 defence review. For much of the year uncertainty remained over the future of Confrontation, while Suharto moved slowly and cautiously to assert the army's, and his own, political pre-eminence. After negotiations between the Malaysians and Indonesians started, and even after they signed a peace accord officially ending Confrontation in August 1966, clashes continued. Throughout this time there were signs of divisions within the political and military leadership in Jakarta, and also between leaders in Jakarta and commanders on the ground in Borneo. While some in the Indonesian Army were far from enthusiastic about Confrontation, others could see continuing benefit for the army in taking a leading role in a national campaign.

As Confrontation slowly wound down, Sarawak faced security threats from within its borders as much as from Indonesian aggression. With irregular as well as regular forces operating across the border, the distinction between internal and external threats to Malaysian security was not always clear, but the Australian government continued to insist that its forces were to be used only against external aggression, and were not to be drawn into matters of internal security. The operations of 4RAR were therefore subjected to even closer oversight than those of 3RAR in 1965, with occasional instructions to act with 'extreme care'.

Like its predecessor, 4RAR generally operated from company bases in patrols of platoon size, gaining further experience in small-unit tactics and working effectively with its British and Malaysian partners. The battalion conducted a number of Claret operations, which achieved some notable successes but remained secret. The SAS squadron also confirmed its skills in reconnaissance missions. These operations confirmed the Australians' ability and confidence in their style of jungle warfare.

In 1966 Indonesia's Confrontation of Malaysia, the conflict that had dominated Australian official concerns, media coverage and public discussion in 1963 and 1964, and to which the Australian government had committed an infantry battalion and an SAS squadron in early 1965, virtually disappeared from sight and even from public memory. Among policy-makers in Canberra the fear of renewed Indonesian militancy, especially on the border with the Australian-administered territories in New Guinea, persisted into 1967 and long afterwards; but as far as the Australian public, and most people involved in politics, were concerned, the preoccupation with Indonesia was over. The Vietnam commitment had taken on a life of its own to become the dominant issue in Australian political life, where it would remain for the next several years. The 'Vietnam era' in Australian political and social life had begun.

THE LONG ELECTION CAMPAIGN[7]

The battlelines for the election due at the end of the year were soon drawn: unusually in Australian politics, it would be fought on foreign and defence policies. While Holt portrayed the Vietnam commitment as defending the prosperity and development of non-communist Asian countries, the Labor Party was united in opposition to the war, albeit with different emphases from its left and right wings, and Calwell expressed his visceral antipathy towards conscription for overseas military service. The period from early March to late November 1966 was effectively one long election campaign, fought on the issues of Vietnam and conscription.

The government's public defence of its policies remained ineffective. Even its supporters criticised the parliamentary statements by Holt and Hasluck, and the official pamphlets issued by the government, as cliché-ridden, and lacking strong evidence and clear argument to support its case. While parliamentary debate in 1966 was dominated by arguments over the war and conscription, much of the real debate took place outside. After the government and its critics had issued pamphlets arguing their respective cases in 1965, the first books on the issue appeared in 1966. Dr Cairns published a widely read book, *Living with Asia*, which argued that Australia should learn to live with 'the revolution' in Asia. The book gained considerable popularity among critics of the war, and established Dr Cairns' status as the leader of the anti-war movement outside Parliament, but its impact was reduced by its elastic use of the word 'revolution' and its inattention to the dramatic changes in Indonesian politics.

To counter the views expressed at the 1965 teach-ins by academic and other critics, conservative scholars, politicians and journalists from a number of Asian and Western countries supported the American and Australian stance in a collection of essays entitled *Vietnam: Seen from East and West*. They argued that the power of China and North Vietnam presented a threat to many countries in the region, and that opponents of the Vietnam commitment were making the same mistake as the advocates of the appeasement of Hitler in the 1930s.

From the better-informed and more thoughtful commentators, two competing arguments emerged. On the one hand, as one journalist put it, 'Vietnam was already too far gone'. In other words, the strength of the communist forces in South Vietnam and the weakness of the RVN's position were such that even the commitment of massive numbers of American and allied troops could not succeed: the costs would outweigh any possible benefits in the global struggle against communism. On the other hand, the Western intervention, even if ultimately unsuccessful, could nevertheless serve an important purpose if it gained time for countries like Malaysia, Singapore, Thailand and the Philippines to consolidate their growing political, economic and military strength. The writer and commentator Donald Horne had recently published a widely read book, *The Lucky Country*, which among other things criticised Australia's understanding of Asia. In his contribution to *Vietnam: Seen from East and West*, Horne was among those who argued that if the Americans had pulled out of Vietnam in 1965 the Indonesian Army might not have had the courage to fight back against the attempted coup in Jakarta on 30 September. On these grounds, even though the intervention might fail, it was still 'worth giving it a go'.[8] Decades later, Australians would still debate the respective merits of those two arguments.

During 1966 the tone of protests, on the streets and on university campuses, became markedly more radical and sometimes violent. A number of controversies, hotly debated in Parliament and the media, kept the war and conscription in the headlines and contributed to a growing feeling that Vietnam was something new to Australian experience – a particularly cruel and dirty war. Many of these individual controversies lingered for years in public memory, especially among political activists.

One consequence of the haste with which forces were committed to Vietnam was that no provision had been made to detain wrongdoers among the Australian troops: Australian military law was, as a contemporary observer noted, 'confused, anomalous and anachronistic'.⁹ These failures contributed to the uproar created when an artillery officer sentenced a persistently disobedient soldier to be handcuffed to a stake in a weapon pit for 21 days. The constraints on planning also led to the government needing civilian cargo vessels to transport stores and material for the task force. The militant, communist-led Seamen's Union initially refused to provide crews for two ships, but they were overruled by the leadership of the Australian Council of Trade Unions. The ACTU realised that, no matter what unionists thought of the merits of the conflict, failure to support Australian servicemen overseas would only discredit the union movement and its political allies in the ALP.

The death of the first national serviceman in Vietnam, Private Errol Noack, occurred within days of the arrival of the first elements of the task force. The reaction was sharp, but short, and probably would have been greater if the public had known that Noack was a casualty of 'friendly fire', killed when two companies of the same battalion had fired on each other during an early operational patrol, each thinking the other was Viet Cong.

When 1RAR paraded through Sydney on their return from service in Vietnam, they were welcomed by an enthusiastic crowd variously estimated at between 300 000 and 500 000. What remained in the memory, especially of many veterans, was the act of a lone woman protester who drenched herself in red paint, ran into the parade and smeared paint on to the commander of 1RAR and several of his men.

When a schoolboy was asked to leave Sydney Grammar School over his objections to compulsory participation in the school's cadet unit after refusing to take part in a simulated 'search-and-destroy' mission against a Viet Cong-style enemy, the Minister for the Army, Malcolm Fraser, quoted in Parliament information from ASIO concerning the boy's mother's association with communist-influenced peace organisations. The government's handling of the matter was widely criticised even by supporters of the Vietnam commitment.

In October the press reported comments by the Secretary of the Department of the Army, Bruce White. Thinking he was addressing a private meeting, White said that bombing North Vietnam would not end the war in the south and that the Australians had been glad to leave Bien Hoa because the Americans took risks the Australians could not afford while the South Vietnamese Army lacked good leaders. Such views were known to be widely held, but they were highly sensitive in the pre-election atmosphere.

In November William White, who had been called up in the first national service ballot and whose claim to be a conscientious objector had been refused, was taken into military custody. A photograph of this intelligent and articulate schoolteacher being dragged through a crowd of demonstrators by four burly policemen turned White into a folk hero and symbolic figure for many in the growing protest movement.

The publicity given to these and other episodes encouraged those who opposed the war and conscription to believe that the Labor Party would win the election and reverse the commitment. Their hopes were ill-founded, for the intensity of the opposition from articulate sections of society was not matched by the breadth of support for their views. Moreover, the Labor Party was weakened by clear divisions between Calwell and his ambitious deputy, Gough Whitlam. Calwell's statements were intensely emotional, while Whitlam was more cautious in his approach. His statements were carefully calibrated, expressing sympathy for the dilemma faced by the United States, describing the war as unwinnable rather than immoral, and distancing himself from the extra-parliamentary protest movement. He was sensitive to the conservatism of the Australian electorate on foreign policy, especially the American alliance, but his caution led his left-wing colleagues to question the depth of his commitment to opposing the war.

THE ESTABLISHMENT OF THE TASK FORCE IN PHUOC TUY[10]

In August 1965, just before the government imposed its embargo on planning for the commitment of a task force, Australian and American military leaders in South Vietnam had identified its destination. Phuoc Tuy province, a coastal province to the southeast of Saigon, fulfilled the criteria that General Wilton had established. It was an area of significant enemy activity, so that Australia could be seen to be pulling its weight; it was a geographically distinct area, with which Australia could identify its national effort; it was not contiguous with the borders of Cambodia, Laos or the demilitarised zone; and it offered reasonably secure access by sea and air. At its southernmost point the port of Vung Tau lay on a sandy peninsula (known to the French as Cap St Jacques). The shallow-water port of Vung Tau gave the RVN's allies an alternative access point to the often congested Saigon River, making Route 15, which linked Vung Tau with Saigon through the provincial capital Ba Ria and Bien Hoa, a strategically important highway. Much of Phuoc Tuy was flat, with rice paddies and rubber plantations as well as uncultivated jungle, most of which was less dense than the rainforest experienced by the Australians in Malaya and Borneo.

Phuoc Tuy had been a centre of communist activity against the French during the First Indochina War. By 1965 the communists had political

Phuoc Tuy province, showing districts and main Australian areas of operations, 1966–71.

cadres and guerrilla units in most towns and villages, including Long Tan and Long Phuoc in the centre of the province, while their regional and main force units had established base areas in the Long Hai hills in the south (known by the Viet Cong as the Minh Dam Secret Zone, after the local guerrilla leaders in the First Indochina War), the May Tao mountains in the northeast, the Nui Dinh and Nui Thi Vai hills in the west, near Route 15, and the Hat Dich region in the northwest. The main enemies of the task force for the next five years would be the D445 Provincial Mobile Battalion and 274 and 275 Main Force Regiments, which formed the Viet Cong 5 Division. By the time the Australian task force arrived in 1966, the Saigon government could count on support only in Ba Ria and the village of Binh Gia, established by about 8000 Catholic 'regroupees' after the 1954 partition. Among the remainder of the population of around 100 000 people, opinion was divided between supporters of the Viet Cong and those who were sullenly neutral, hoping that someone would bring greater security and better living conditions.

Although Australian political and military leaders often spoke as if the task force's role was the security of Phuoc Tuy province, the reality was more complex. South Vietnam had been divided for military purposes into four tactical zones, from I Corps Tactical Zone in the north, closest to the demilitarised zone, to IV Corps Tactical Zone, covering the Mekong Delta region in the far south. Phuoc Tuy, like Saigon and the adjacent provinces including Bien Hoa, lay within the III Corps Tactical Zone. The American and Australian military commanders agreed on several roles for the task force: to secure its tactical area of responsibility (TAOR), which initially covered most but not all of Phuoc Tuy province; to provide security to Route 15; to conduct other operations as required in Phuoc Tuy; and to conduct other operations as required in III Corps Tactical Zone.

These arrangements left many issues to be resolved. The task force was not responsible for all security operations in the province, for American advisers continued to work with ARVN units. Nor was it responsible for security of the whole province, for its TAOR did not extend to the province's borders until later. The other operations within the province included those in support of pacification operations, which were consistent with Australian counter-insurgency doctrine (although not with the agreement with the RVN government in April 1965, about which no one seemed concerned). Nevertheless, the way was left open for Australian troops to be involved in out-of-province operations in close collaboration with United States forces against large PLAF or PAVN main force units, despite Wilton's determination that Australians not be bound to the Americans' 'meat-grinder' tactics.

Australian operations in Malaya and Borneo were conducted under clear hierarchical command structures, bringing a high degree of coordination to the military, civilian and police agencies of all the national forces involved. No such coordination was possible in Vietnam, where there were pronounced tensions and mistrust between agencies of the various nations involved, as well as between different national forces. The Australian task force operated within a complex network of command and control arrangements involving American, Vietnamese, Australian and New Zealand agencies. Although a principal reason for establishing the task force was to ensure that Australians operated with more autonomy than 1RAR had experienced with 173rd Airborne Brigade, it was placed under the operational control of II Field Force Vietnam (II FFV), the US command responsible for III Corps Tactical Zone. Overall command of all national forces in Vietnam was given to the Commander Australian Force Vietnam (COMAFV), with headquarters in Saigon. His was a quasi-diplomatic role, ensuring that Australia's military actions were consistent with national directives. Because the Australian force had air force and later naval elements, AFV was technically a joint command, but Australia did not have a joint command structure. As the Australian contribution was overwhelmingly from the army, the position of COMAFV was always held by a major general, despite an attempt by the RAAF to rotate the position between the services. As a compromise, the head of the RAAF component at AFV was also designated Deputy Commander of AFV. On joint service matters, COMAFV reported to the Chairman of the Chiefs of Staff Committee, General Sir John Wilton. Although the most senior position in the armed forces was only the chairman of a committee who did not have command over the individual services, Wilton became the effective overall commander after he became Chairman of the Chiefs of Staff Committee in 1966. In Canberra, each of the three armed services had its own department and minister, supposedly subordinate to the Minister for Defence, as well as its own uniformed chief, and inter-service tensions were common. Task force commanders, in short, were obliged to develop their operational concepts in an environment that presented not only the challenges of an entrenched enemy, able to fight both guerrilla and main force operations, but also many military and political constraints, some embodied in written directives and others dictated by forceful personalities.

One of the first decisions made by the task force created an enduring controversy. The task force base was established at Nui Dat, a small elevated area in the middle of the province, while the logistic force, the 1st Australian Logistic Support Group (1ALSG), was located on the sand dunes of Vung Tau. Locating the combat elements at Nui Dat, rather than close to an urban centre such as Ba Ria or Vung Tau, was intended to make a statement about the Australians' intention to

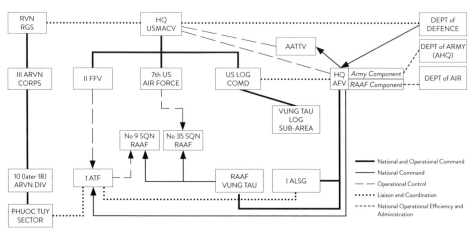

From *To Long Tan: The Australian Army and the Vietnam War 1950–1965*, AWM, 1993.

Command and control of the Australian force in Vietnam

have a lasting impact on the province by separating the guerrillas from the population. Vietnamese of all political opinions expressed gratitude that the Australians had not been associated with the inevitable social effects of locating a force of foreign soldiers close to a town. But it did give rise to several problems. To ensure the security of the base, an area around it had to be cleared of settlements. This required the removal and relocation of two villages, Long Tan and Long Phuoc. The forced relocation only increased the villagers' entrenched allegiance to the Viet Cong. Exposed in the middle of the province, the base needed to retain a substantial proportion of its combat elements for its own security. At any time only one battalion was available for operations, while the other remained at the base. The helicopters of the RAAF's No. 9 Squadron were designated to support the task force, but they were based at Vung Tau, where they could be fuelled and serviced, reducing the speed with which they could be deployed. The separation of the task force from its logistic support required frequent transport of supplies between Nui Dat and Vung Tau, adding to the burden of security requirements as well as involving double handling of matériel.

The two battalions initially committed to the task force, 5RAR and 6RAR, were soon heavily engaged in a demanding program of patrols to extend control beyond the tactical area of responsibility. A pattern was established of 'one battalion out and one battalion in': that is, one battalion operating beyond the boundaries of the TAOR and the other remaining on stand-by in the base or patrolling its immediate environs. Civic action also began with a series of medical visits to a local village. The deserted village of Long Phuoc, which the Viet Cong continued to use as a base after its population had been forcibly removed, was destroyed.

By August severe signs of strain were showing. Sub-units, such as companies and platoons, were under-strength, having lost men to illness, battle casualties, or rest and recuperation. There had been indications, difficult to interpret, that the enemy might be preparing to challenge the task force before it became securely lodged.

THE BATTLE OF LONG TAN

The challenge came in mid-August.[11] In the early hours of 17 August the base received mortar fire, which wounded 24 soldiers, two seriously, and caused some damage. The commanding officer of 6RAR, Lieutenant Colonel Colin Townsend, sent B Company to locate the mortar positions. They found the positions, but the Viet Cong had gone. On Townsend's orders, B Company followed the Viet Cong tracks, staying out until the following morning when they were relieved by D Company. In the afternoon of 18 August, the three platoons of D Company were following tracks when they encountered a small group of enemy. Thinking they were attacking a small Viet Cong unit, they moved forward in an extended formation. They soon discovered that they were outnumbered by a highly professional force. They had encountered the well-armed and highly skilled Viet Cong 275 Regiment, reinforced with North Vietnamese regulars and supported by the D445 Provincial Battalion. D Company called in artillery support, which was highly effective despite the extremely difficult weather conditions, the extended Australian positions, and the Viet Cong tactic of engaging at close range, known as 'holding the enemy's belt while punching with the other fist'. D Company's ammunition was close to running out, until resupplied by two helicopters of RAAF's No. 9 Squadron, flying in appalling weather conditions. Finally, as the enemy appeared to be preparing for a final assault, the armoured personnel carriers of 3 APC Troop with their .50 calibre machine-guns arrived, carrying A Company of 6RAR. The enemy withdrew.

D Company comprised about 100 men, many of whom, including two platoon commanders, were national servicemen. The entire company was narrowly saved from disaster by the courage and training of the infantry, both experienced regulars and young national servicemen; the skill and dedication of the New Zealand artillery battery, with support from two Australian batteries and US Army medium batteries; the willingness of two RAAF helicopter pilots to fly in ammunition in dangerous flying conditions; and the timely arrival of reinforcements in the armoured personnel carriers. The task force lost 17 killed and another who later died of wounds, including 11 national servicemen. After the battle 245 enemy bodies were counted, with possibly a similar number of bodies removed. The enemy had clearly hoped for a decisive victory, which would have had a considerable impact on Australian public opinion. Instead, the task force had established itself at Nui Dat, where it was never again directly challenged.

For years afterwards veterans and others debated the enemy's intentions at Long Tan, particularly in attacking the base with mortars in the early hours of 17 August. Was it an attempt to 'lure the tiger from the mountains', a frequent Viet Cong tactic of taking provocative action with a view to ambushing the force that was sent out of the base? Or was it the prelude to a full-scale assault on the base, with the aim of causing so many casualties that Australian public opinion would turn against the war? Or was it an encounter battle, where both sides stumbled into contact, neither knowing what it was facing? The debate continues to this day.

The battle of Long Tan soon acquired symbolic significance, eventually coming to stand for the whole Australian commitment. In Australia, 18 August was celebrated as Long Tan Day, and later Vietnam Veterans' Day. The nation is entitled to celebrate a victory, but it was, as the Duke of Wellington famously said of the Battle of Waterloo, 'the nearest-run thing you ever saw'. The battle had not been sought by the Australians nor was it fought on their terms. Disaster was avoided and a tactical victory gained, but narrowly. While they had achieved a great deal, the Australians were learning some hard lessons about a war that was very different from anything they had previously experienced or for which they had been trained and equipped.

LONG TAN - a PYRRIC victory?

RELATIONS WITH ALLIES AND ENEMIES[12]

By the end of 1966, after the task force had been in Phuoc Tuy only six months, some of the major characteristics of Australia's military experience of the Vietnam War were already evident. The Australians had to learn, rapidly and under pressure from enemies and allies, how to operate in a very different environment from Malaya or Borneo. They had to learn how to deploy their limited resources between pacification operations, operations against main force units, and security operations around the base and along the major roads. Infantrymen had to learn how to operate effectively with artillery, with armoured units, and with air support. Their previous experience of working with artillery and with helicopters and fixed-wing aircraft was on a different scale and level of complexity. Senior officers began to debate whether to ask for a squadron of Centurion tanks, which some thought would be a great asset.

The most obvious need was simply for more men. By the end of the year the commander of the Australian Force Vietnam, Major General K Mackay, had prepared a request for an additional 940 soldiers for the task force. About half of these were required to make up deficiencies in the staffing of the units that had been committed to the task force. They included an 82-man civil affairs unit, as well as additional numbers for logistics units at Vung Tau and the headquarters of both AFV in Saigon and the task force at Nui Dat. The other half were needed to make up for the deficiencies of infantry and other combat units, who were going into the field under-strength because of battle casualties, sickness, and authorised rest and recuperation. To compensate for deficiencies arising from the constraints on planning, the task force needed nearly a thousand more soldiers just to enable its existing units to carry out their current tasks, even before considering additional units or capabilities.

In 1966 and 1967, the relationship between the army and the RAAF was described by one officer at the task force headquarters as one of 'conflict, friction, antagonism, ill-will, lack of co-operation'.[13] The problems started at the top. The leadership of the RAAF gave priority to fighters and bombers over rotary-winged aircraft, whereas the army's leaders were impressed by the value to the US Army of the support from helicopters in a wide range of roles, including direct battlefield support. In 1965, when 1RAR was serving at Bien Hoa, Wilton suggested that the RAAF send two helicopters and aircrew to Vietnam to study the tactics and techniques of airmobile operations. Wilton was angered when the Chief of Air Staff, Air Marshal Alister Murdoch, refused, saying that the experience to be gained from US-style operations was doubtful, there would be complications in control, and the RAAF was already gaining useful experience in operations in Malaysia. Relations were not improved when it was announced, without consultation with the RAAF, that eight RAAF Iroquois helicopters, one-third of the RAAF's total helicopter fleet, would be committed in support of the task force. Having been 'dragooned' into an unexpected commitment of its limited resources, the Department of Air issued directives that prescribed the helicopters to be used only in airlift operations to areas that were relatively secure and free from expected enemy resistance. To army officers who had witnessed the American system, where the army had control of large numbers of helicopters, where battlefield risks were accepted and where casualties were expected, these directives seemed quite inappropriate. The Australian helicopters initially sent were not equipped with door-mountings for guns or armour-plated protection.

The army–RAAF relationship was improved by the courage and skill of the two pilots of No. 9 Squadron who flew valuable ammunition to the soldiers of D Company, 6RAR, at a critical stage of the Battle of Long Tan. Battalions who served in the subsequent years of the task force's operations, and most especially the SAS squadrons who depended heavily on the helicopters for the insertion and extraction of their patrols, often in hazardous conditions, formed a healthy rapport with the No. 9 Squadron pilots. Both the pilots and the groundcrew adjusted to local conditions. Nevertheless, the early tensions cast a long shadow.

Even more important than relations between the Australian services were relations between the Australian and American commanders.[14] In January 1967 Brigadier Stuart Graham succeeded Brigadier OD Jackson as commander of the task force and Major General D 'Tim' Vincent took over from Mackay as commander of the Australian forces in Vietnam. In a series of meetings at this time, General Westmoreland expressed his considerable dissatisfaction with the Australians' operational methods. He was directing United States forces to conduct large operations designed to kill as many enemy as possible, often with many American casualties. The Australians, by contrast, were operating in their traditional mode, searching methodically, moving silently, sometimes taking days to clear a relatively small area. In Australian minds, this was the most effective way to achieve an enduring result, but to the American general it was insufficiently aggressive. Westmoreland also criticised the small number of troops who could be engaged in operations at any one time because a significant number had to remain to protect the base. His own preference would have been to include the Australian battalions in a mobile reserve force, able to take part with American, South Vietnamese and other units in large formations seeking to kill large numbers of the enemy in a war of attrition. Although Wilton admired Westmoreland, he had pressed for the creation of the task force precisely in order to ensure that Australians were not included in such operations.

Westmoreland also criticised the Australian policy of unit rotation for infantry and artillery units. The Australians believed that cohesion, teamwork and confidence between all ranks were greatly enhanced when the infantry battalions and artillery batteries trained together, arrived together, fought together, and left together at the end of their 12-month tour. In all other units, the majority of the force, personnel changed over on an individual basis. Westmoreland said that rotation by units caused the major combat units to be ineffective for a month each year, as a departing battalion wound down its activity in its last two weeks and its replacement took another two weeks to acclimatise before undertaking major operations. The Australian commanders listened politely to all these complaints and maintained their own practice. On one point, the Australian and American commanders were agreed: the task force needed more soldiers, most importantly a third battalion, in order to be more effective.

Relations with the people of Phuoc Tuy province remained problematic.[15] Many villagers were clearly hostile, and clearing the villages of Long Tan and Long Phuoc in order to secure the base at Nui Dat only increased that hostility. The Australians, like the RVN government, could count on support only in Ba Ria and the Catholic village, Binh Gia. Probably most Vietnamese in the rural areas wanted to be left to till their fields in peace, without a heavy burden of taxes from the government, the Viet Cong or both. The first efforts by the task force in civic action were well intentioned, but did not owe a great deal to the initiative or wishes of the local people.

By the end of 1966 it was already clear that there was relatively little connection between the war being fought by the task force in Phuoc Tuy province, let alone other Australian forces in Vietnam, and the war that was being debated on television, in Parliament, in universities and on the streets, in Australia and around the world. That war was overwhelmingly the war being fought by the American forces. The dominance of the American media, reporting primarily to an American audience, ensured that emphasis, even though the South Vietnamese forces were actually taking greater losses than American forces.

'ALL THE WAY WITH LBJ'[16]

In June 1966 Holt visited Washington and London. Just before he was due to arrive in Washington for an informal, personal meeting with Johnson, news broke that the United States had started a bombing campaign against oil installations around Hanoi and the north's principal seaport, Haiphong. Johnson came under stronger criticism, in the United States and around the world, than he had expected. Holt immediately announced his support, but Britain's Prime Minister Harold Wilson, under increasing pressure from the Labour Party's left wing, attacked the bombing campaign even while trying to give some general support to the United States. Johnson, who was remarkably sensitive to criticism, transformed the proposed, relatively informal meeting with Holt into a full-scale state visit. At a formal welcoming ceremony on the south lawn of the White House, Holt, clearly delighted at the warmth of Johnson's welcome, unequivocally reaffirmed Australia's support for the United States in Vietnam and, in an impromptu peroration, adopted Johnson's 1964 campaign slogan for his own purposes:

> And so, sir, in the lonelier and perhaps even more disheartening moments which come to any national leader, I hope there will be a corner of your heart and mind which takes cheer from the fact that you have an admiring friend, a staunch friend that will be all the way with LBJ.[17]

THE forerunners to Tony Blair's POODLE

Holt's personal and political rapport with Johnson was underlined by the contrasting tone of his visit to London, where he publicly took issue with the Wilson government for criticising the bombing raids and for turning away from its military engagement with Southeast Asia.

*[Holt's 'all the way with LBJ' remark was denounced by the media and the Opposition at the time and has ever since been quoted against any Australian Prime Minister regarded as subservient to the United States.] At the time Holt himself was happy to identify himself unreservedly with American policy in Vietnam, but as a former Treasurer and as a member of the FAD Committee since its creation Holt should have been well aware that Australia's military capacity was severely limited and that the recent growth in defence expenditure was creating severe fiscal strains. Australia's support for its allies was always stronger in public rhetoric and diplomatic encouragement than in military commitment, as the 'graduated response' to British pleas for support in Confrontation had demonstrated. The next 18 months would reveal that Australia was by no means 'all the way' with American policy.

In the short term, however, Holt drew substantial political rewards. In October Johnson became the first incumbent President of the United States to visit Australia. Although organised at short notice, the visit was a triumph for Johnson, who performed brilliantly before the hundreds of thousands of Australians who gave him an extraordinarily warm welcome in Canberra, Melbourne, Sydney, Brisbane and Townsville. He told delighted crowds that 'every American – and LBJ – is with Australia all the way'. The small number of protesters, some of whom threw paint or tried to lie in front of the presidential motorcade, served only to underline the breadth and depth of the Australian public's warmth towards its greatest ally. (In 1968, the Premier of New South Wales, Bob [later Sir Robert] Askin, asserted that he had told Johnson that he wished he had told the driver of the car carrying Johnson and himself to run over the protesters lying on the road. This was reported as Askin having said: 'Run the bastards over'. Whatever Askin did or did not say in 1966, he was probably expressing a widely held opinion about protesters.) Holt himself made few notable contributions to public or private discussions, but he was content to bask in Johnson's reflected glory.

Immediately afterwards, Johnson and Holt attended a conference in Manila of the seven 'free world' nations contributing forces to the war – Australia, New Zealand, Thailand, the Philippines, South Korea, the United States and the Republic of Vietnam. The conference was designed to show that the war was being fought by a coalition of nations who were determined to defend freedom against North Vietnamese aggression and who were as committed to social and economic reform as to military measures, but the impact of this conference on Australian public opinion was completely overshadowed by that of Holt's 'all the way with LBJ' statement and Johnson's triumphal visit to Australia. In Australian minds, Vietnam was now associated almost exclusively with the American alliance, as if Australia had entered in response to pressure from the United States rather than as an expression of Australia's own concerns over the future of Southeast Asia.

THE COMMITMENT CONFIRMED AND INCREASED[18]

As the long election campaign over the Vietnam War and conscription came to its conclusion, further divisions appeared between Calwell and Whitlam over the speed with which a Labor government would withdraw conscripts and regular troops from Vietnam. This had a greater effect than the formation of a Liberal Reform Group by businessmen and professionals who opposed the government's policies on the Vietnam War and conscription while supporting its domestic policies. The election on 26 November 1966 gave an unequivocal endorsement to the government's policies. The Liberal Party gained nine seats, its coalition partner the Country Party gained one, and a Labor member who left the party over his support for the government's defence policies won his seat as an Independent. The coalition won 56.9 per cent of the two-party preferred vote, while the ALP was reduced to 41 of the 124 seats in the House of Representatives. At his first attempt, Holt had won a bigger electoral victory than Menzies had ever achieved and had gained the largest House of Representatives majority in Australia's electoral history to that time.

In the immediate aftermath of his electoral triumph, Holt remained overwhelmingly positive about the commitment. In early December the government received the request from the commander of the Australian Force Vietnam, Major General Mackay, for an additional 940 soldiers to make up for deficiencies in the staffing of the units committed to the task force. Before Mackay's request was received in Canberra, Holt by-passed the Minister for Defence, Fairhall, and personally directed the Defence Department to prepare a report on additional forces for Vietnam. Holt was so eager to increase the commitment that ministers and officials speculated that he might have given a secret undertaking to President Johnson. There is no hard evidence for such a view, but the Americans had long made it clear that an increase to the Australian commitment would be most welcome. Whatever the reason, Holt clearly wanted to add a third battalion to the task force. This would double the operational effectiveness of the task force, as two battalions rather than one could be on operations while one defended the base, but the army did not want to commit a third battalion yet. To sustain a three-battalion commitment in Vietnam, as well as one serving in Malaysia, would require the army to raise a ninth infantry battalion. This was beyond the army's current organisational capacity, but ministers and officials had to work hard to persuade Holt to put the idea aside.

In its first decision after the election, Cabinet decided to send the 940 men requested by Mackay, but not the third battalion. Consideration was also given to sending a squadron of Centurion tanks or, alternatively, a cavalry squadron of light armoured vehicles, but both options were rejected. The government also decided to increase the RAAF commitment by sending No. 2 Squadron of eight Canberra bombers. From the RAN, the government committed HMAS *Hobart*, one of the navy's new DDG-class guided-missile destroyers of American design, and a clearance diving team of six personnel. In all, 1700 personnel were added to the Australian commitment.

In the early weeks of 1967 fortune continued to favour Holt's optimism.[19] In January the RVN Prime Minister, Air Vice Marshal Nguyen Cao Ky, visited Australia. Ky had gained a reputation for provocatively brash comments, most notoriously praising Hitler as a nationalist leader. In his last days before resigning the Labor leadership, Calwell denounced Ky as 'a moral and social leper' and 'a little Quisling gangster'. With the benefit of advice from Richard Woolcott, an External Affairs official with considerable expertise in media relations, Ky handled the Australian press with skill and aplomb, turning a potential public relations disaster into a modest success. In February Holt visited New Zealand, where Prime Minister Keith Holyoake informed him that he was considering detaching an infantry company from the Commonwealth Strategic Reserve to serve in Vietnam. Holt demurred at first, not wanting to weaken the Commonwealth's commitment to Malaysia, but soon afterwards the Australians agreed to an arrangement under which first one, then two New Zealand infantry companies were incorporated into RAR battalions, which were designated ANZAC battalions. In March and April Holt made his third visit to East and Southeast Asia in the first 15 months of his tenure, becoming the first Australian Prime Minister to visit Cambodia, Laos, South Korea and Taiwan, the location of the nationalist Republic of China, which

Australia recognised as the government of all China. Once again, his purpose was simply to encourage Australians to look beyond the conflict in Vietnam to a prosperous and secure future in Asia.

— : —

By the summer of 1966–67, a new Prime Minister had gained a massive electoral endorsement for the Vietnam commitment and conscription policies with which he had wholeheartedly identified himself; he had established a warm political and personal rapport with the President of the United States; his views on Australia's relations with its region were gaining respect; and the task force had established itself in its allocated province of South Vietnam, having beaten off a vigorous challenge from the enemy. The autumn and winter of 1967 would bring a very different atmosphere.

— SEVEN —

ESCALATION OF THE COMMITMENT, ESCALATION OF CONTROVERSY 1967

The increase in the Australian commitment to Vietnam in December 1966 owed much to Holt's personal enthusiasm. In late 1967 the Holt government made another increase, but in a very different atmosphere. The change in mood was based on developments in the different arenas in which Australia's Vietnam War was being fought, arenas that often seemed to have little relationship to each other: Australian politics, both inside and outside Parliament; the global battle for Western public opinion; the course of the war between Hanoi and Washington; and the small war being fought by the Australian task force in Phuoc Tuy province.

THE ESCALATION OF DISSENT[1]

After the triumphs of 1966, everything seemed to go wrong for Holt in 1967. A friendly man who liked to be liked, Holt could not impose discipline on the swollen ranks of the parliamentary Liberal Party; he failed to replace tired and incompetent ministers with new blood; he could not end a damaging feud between the second- and third-ranking ministers, John McEwen and William McMahon; he allowed minor issues, such as a dispute over the use of the RAAF's VIP aircraft, to escalate to damaging proportions; and his own appearances in the House of Representatives lacked authority. On the other side of the House, Calwell's resignation and the election of Whitlam as Labor's leader, with Lance Barnard as a loyal and quietly effective deputy, gave the Opposition new confidence. On the floor of the House of Representatives, Whitlam soon demonstrated superiority over Holt in debate. As part of a long-term plan to restore the Labor Party's electoral standing, Whitlam established a 'shadow cabinet', with Whitlam and Barnard taking responsibility for foreign affairs and defence. Victory in by-elections in July and September enhanced Whitlam's standing with his parliamentary colleagues, but he faced strong opposition from the party's extra-parliamentary left wing, especially those who controlled the Victorian branch. Policy over Vietnam acquired symbolic importance in this intra-party struggle. After visiting Vietnam, Barnard suggested that Labor might need to reassess its policy in the light of 'current realities': he had formed the view that Australians did not understand the extent of involvement by the North Vietnamese Army, that the South Vietnamese Army was carrying much of the fighting and taking heavy casualties, and that an American withdrawal would lead to chaos. He was denounced by FE Chamberlain, a powerful member of Labor's extra-parliamentary old guard, who condemned the 'unjust, filthy and unwinnable war' in Vietnam.[2]

More importantly, changes were taking place in Australian society, undermining much of the support that the Menzies and Holt governments had traditionally enjoyed, especially in foreign and defence policies. By the mid-1960s, a generation of Australians had come to adulthood with no personal experience of the world wars and the 1930s depression that had shaped the views of their elders. A new middle class, largely shaped by a significant growth in university education, sought the expansion of education and welfare programs. Some young Australians drew inspiration from the counter-culture being shaped by radical students and intellectuals in American and European universities. Across the country, middle-class Australians challenged the traditional values of established institutions. Their views were given voice in new current affairs programs on radio and television, notably *This Day Tonight*, which first appeared on ABC television in 1967.

The protest movement in Australia drew encouragement from the growth in mass protest in major American cities. Tens of thousands attended anti-war rallies in New York and San Francisco, and 50 000 demonstrators marched on the Pentagon in Washington. During 1967 two distinct streams of dissent appeared over the Vietnam War. The moderate wing continued to argue about the strategic and legal justification for the war, but focused especially on two arguments. One concerned the means used by the American forces. The bombing of North Vietnam, they contended, caused civilian casualties, especially among children. Protesters particularly condemned the use of napalm, a flammable petroleum jelly that burned the flesh of its victims, causing hideous and often fatal injuries. American protesters chanted: 'Hey, hey, LBJ, how many kids did you kill today?' The moderate protesters also contended that the National Liberation Front should be recognised as an independent party in peace negotiations, not as a mere creature of Hanoi. In July the Labor Party's federal conference adopted a compromise between the right and left wings, stating that a Labor government would ask its allies to stop bombing North Vietnam, recognise the NLF as a party to negotiations, and transform the war in the south into 'holding operations'.

The moderate wing of the protest movement generally used legal tactics with a view to changing the government's policies within the framework of Australia's political and social institutions. This was not enough for the militant protesters, who sought revolution rather than reform. Many identified with the 'new left', a worldwide neo-Marxist intellectual movement, based in universities rather than trade unions. In Sydney and Melbourne, students formed groups called Students for a Democratic Society (SDS), adopting the name of radical student groups in the United States. Intense rivalries not only affected relations between the new and old left but also divided the new left, as Maoists, Trostskyites, Leninists, anarchists, socialists and social democrats argued over ideology and tactics. In Melbourne Maoists hailed the cultural revolution, then causing turmoil in China; in Sydney Trotskyites dominated; in Brisbane, anarchists and libertarians were most influential. The respective merits of gurus such as Mao Zedong, Jean-Paul Sartre, Che Guevara, Frantz Fanon and Herbert Marcuse were vigorously debated. The world's media made household names of revolutionary student leaders such as Mario Savio in California, Tariq Ali in London, Daniel Cohn-Bendit in Paris and Rudi Dutschke in Berlin. In Australia, the media focused on radicals such as Brian Laver in Brisbane, Bob Gould and Mike Jones in Sydney, and Albert Langer and Michael Hyde in Melbourne.

The moderate and militant wings of the protest movement came into conflict over both aims and tactics. The militants aimed to provoke confrontation with the police and other authorities, as a step towards the eventual overthrow of institutions such as Parliament; the moderates regarded these tactics as counter-productive. The militants did not want simply to withdraw from the war: they supported the other side, which they characterised as a noble, peasant rebellion against American imperialism. A favourite chant was: 'One side right, One side wrong, Victory to the Viet Cong'. Most controversially, the Monash University Labor Club sponsored a committee to raise money to support the NLF. It is not clear how much money was actually sent to the NLF, but the proposal attracted considerable publicity, mostly hostile. Members of the Labor Clubs at Monash and other Australian universities were far to the left of the Labor Party, to whose leaders they were an embarrassment, while other students opposed giving aid to the NLF. The concept of openly supporting the enemy infuriated many Australians, including the troops.

In previous years, the government had had little difficulty in coping with opposition to its foreign policies from traditional critics, such as communists, left-wing unions, and a small number of clerics, academics and pacifists. The growth of radical dissent and its manifestation in violent demonstrations on university campuses and city streets was another matter, especially when it was combined with protest from more respectable groups in society, expressing more limited aims and using legitimate tactics. [The world was changing, and the Vietnam War was becoming a symbol of the changes, which established institutions found hard to comprehend, let alone to counter.]

THE WAR OF ATTRITION[3]

By early 1967, doubts were appearing at the highest levels concerning American policy in Vietnam. The intervention of United States and allied forces in 1965 had blunted the thrust of the PAVN–PLAF offensive, which had threatened to cut South Vietnam in two, but had not deterred the communist leadership in Hanoi from its goal of uniting Vietnam under communist rule. Communist leaders spoke often of their willingness to continue their struggle until victory, even if it should take 20 years or more. Although few signs were allowed to appear publicly, there were intense struggles within the central committee in Hanoi, but from the early 1960s until the mid-1970s those contests were usually won by those who were utterly determined to continue the struggle without compromise. Ho Chi Minh himself was becoming more of a figurehead, while the driving force in the communist party leadership was [Le Duan,] who never wavered in his determination to incorporate the south into a country under a hard-line communist regime.

Although many in the West, including Australia, could not imagine that a small, third-world country could prevail against the might of the United States, the communists enjoyed a number of strategic advantages:

> the advanced stage reached by communist revolutionary warfare in Vietnam before the allied intervention; the ability of the North Vietnamese to match American strength increases; the increasing supplies of modern armaments from communist bloc countries; the active communist sanctuaries in Cambodia, Laos and China; and the self-imposed constraints on the selection of [bombing] targets by the Americans.[4]

In sheer numbers, the communists were able to more than replace their heavy losses by infiltration from the north and recruitment in the south. Moreover, while large numbers of American troops were despatched to Vietnam, many were logistic and other support units. In combat forces, the communists probably held a numerical advantage. The South Vietnamese Army (ARVN) was ostensibly large, but the numbers were often inflated, and its military capacity was badly affected by corruption, poor leadership and low morale. The Regional Forces and Popular Forces, responsible for security in the rural villages and hamlets, were under-resourced and poorly motivated.

The Vietnamese communists received substantial support from both the Soviet Union and China throughout the war, playing off the two rivals for leadership of world communism against each other and overriding counsels of caution or moderation that either might offer. At the time and ever since, much attention was given to the supplies sent

[alt. supply Route *]

from North Vietnam through Laos along the Ho Chi Minh trail into the northern provinces of South Vietnam. Less reported, but of comparable importance, was the ['Sihanouk trail'] through Cambodia. Matériel from the Soviet Union, China and other communist countries came into the Cambodian port of Sihanoukville (Kompong Som) and was then transported through the 'rear areas' of the PAVN and PLAF in eastern Cambodia and across the border into the southern provinces of South Vietnam, including Phuoc Tuy. The communist forces also received substantial supplies through the port of Haiphong, from where they were infiltrated into South Vietnam either along the Ho Chi Minh trail or by sea on the South Vietnamese coast. In 1959, when the communists in Hanoi decided to adopt armed struggle in the south, they had established units to facilitate maritime infiltration as well as to handle relations with Laos and Cambodia, even before establishing the National Liberation Front.

The bombing campaign against North Vietnam, Operation Rolling Thunder, cost the Americans heavily, largely due to the anti-aircraft weapons and operators provided by the Soviet Union and China, but inflicted disproportionately small damage on the enemy. Most of the communists' war matériel was manufactured in the Soviet Union or China, so the Rolling Thunder campaign had few military targets of any strategic importance. It cost civilian lives, which only reinforced the determination of the North Vietnamese people. The Americans ruled out any land attack on North Vietnam, fearing that any such attack would bring Chinese forces into the war, as Beijing had threatened. Until late in the war, attacks on the communist sanctuaries in Cambodia and Laos were also excluded, as was the mining of Haiphong harbour.

The United States thus faced many constraints in confronting a different type of warfare from that for which it was trained and equipped. The American strategy was based on attrition, with the aim

U.S. approach

of gaining [a 'kill ratio'] that would achieve the ['crossover point',] when more of the enemy were killed than could be replaced by infiltration or recruitment. This strategy led to the importance of the 'body count', by which success or failure was measured by the comparative numbers of killed on each side. The primary instrument of the strategy was the conduct of search-and-destroy operations, in which large forces took the war to the enemy's main force units in their base areas, to disrupt and destroy them before they could attack government positions. Behind this shield, ARVN troops were given the principal role in pacification operations, in a program known as Revolutionary Development. A lower priority was allocated to small-unit operations designed to counter local guerrilla forces and eliminate the Viet Cong infrastructure (VCI), the underground political operatives of the NLF.

In accordance with this strategic approach, Australia was under pressure from the Americans, through both political and military channels, to increase the size of its commitment and to adopt American tactics. Johnson and his senior officials repeatedly told the Australians that every extra serviceman committed by Australia helped the administration to gain congressional support for the far greater numbers of United States troops that were being requested by Westmoreland. The growing protest movement in the United States was fuelled by the high cost in American lives of Westmoreland's tactics, especially in some major operations in late 1966 and early 1967, but this only increased the American pressure to secure the largest possible commitment from its allies. Westmoreland continued to indicate that he wanted to use the Australian troops as part of a large mobile reserve, to take part in 'big unit' battles wherever they were to take place rather than to focus on pacification and anti-guerrilla operations in Phuoc Tuy province. Australian commanders, for the most part, wanted to maintain their preferred operational methods.

BRITISH WITHDRAWAL, AMERICAN PRESSURE[5]

In the autumn and winter of 1967, another element of Australian strategic policy was under threat. The British government advised that, contrary to the assurances they had given only a year earlier, they would accelerate the withdrawal of British forces from east of Suez, with all forces to be removed by the mid-1970s. Working with the governments of Malaysia, Singapore, New Zealand and the United States, the Australian government argued vigorously against the British policy. In one of the many personal messages between heads of government at this time, Holt personally told Wilson that 'the next century will be the century of Asia' and that 'a new Asia [was] emerging, in which we can all find hope for a brighter future'.[6] The strong diplomatic pressure was to no avail: the British government announced its new policy in July. This was a major blow to Australia's forward defence posture, and cast doubt upon all of Australia's regional policies. The government foresaw demands for an increased Australian contribution to the defence of the Malaysia–Singapore region. It also feared that the British decision might turn the Americans towards withdrawal from Vietnam.

As the government was assessing its current and potential defence demands, the Treasurer, William McMahon, pointed out that defence expenditure had increased by an annual average of 22 per cent over the past four years, much of it in purchases from the United States, placing heavy burdens on the balance of payments and overseas debt. In preparing the 1967–68 budget, McMahon wanted to reduce the burden of defence expenditure on the rest of the economy, just as Australia was coming under renewed pressure from Washington. With the war effectively in a stalemate, the United States Congress was becoming increasingly reluctant to accede to Westmoreland's requests for further troop commitments. While Holt and his colleagues were absorbing the effects of the British announcement, President Johnson despatched two close advisers, Clark Clifford and General Maxwell Taylor, on a mission to seek further assistance from the countries that were already contributing troops to Vietnam. Clifford and Taylor told the Australian Cabinet that Johnson had to ask Congress to raise taxes in order to pay for the war. Additional help from allies like Australia and New Zealand would have a disproportionate effect in Washington. As Clifford said in Wellington, 'one additional New Zealand soldier might produce fifty Americans'. Holt demurred, suggesting that a strong Australian economy would contribute more to the stability of the region than an economy weakened by excessive expenditure on defence. Later in the year McMahon was summoned from New York to the White House, where Johnson applied extraordinarily strong pressure on him for more Australian support. The Defense Secretary, Robert McNamara, told him that none of America's allies was bearing its fair share of the defence burden.

THE NEW TASK FORCE COMMANDER

In January 1967 Brigadier Stuart Graham succeeded Brigadier Jackson as commander of the task force in Phuoc Tuy province. Like his successors, Graham faced the challenge of two demanding roles: 'almost continuous conventional operations in depth to destroy or neutralise the enemy's main and regional forces in their remote base and logistical areas; [and] uninterrupted pacification and reconstruction programmes to "remove the claws" of the Viet Cong local forces and infrastructure and to eliminate the NLF's influence in the towns and villages'.[7] In addition, the task force had to ensure the security of the base at Nui Dat, which was growing in size and complexity until it resembled a small Australian town set in a predominantly hostile region.[8] Operations to secure the roads between Nui Dat and Vung Tau as well as other roads in the province were a further burden. Two battalions were insufficient to meet all these demands.

Many of the task force operations were either 'cordon-and-search' or 'search-and-destroy' missions. In the former, an Australian battalion surrounded a village and, with South Vietnamese forces, searched the buildings and grounds while interrogating the inhabitants. Viet Cong cadres were handed to the South Vietnamese authorities; enemy arms, food supplies and documents were removed and destroyed. In search-and-destroy operations, also known as 'reconnaissance-in-force', small or large units were deployed, often with artillery and air support, to locate and eliminate enemy units. An analysis of the first six months of operations by the intelligence officer of 5RAR, Captain Robert O'Neill, at the direction of the battalion commander, Lieutenant Colonel John Warr, concluded that cordon-and-search operations yielded the best results with the fewest Australian casualties.[9] Nevertheless, both battalions were required to undertake search-and-destroy operations. Usually the enemy avoided contact, eluding the Australian patrols and the firepower they could bring to bear. When they did resist the costs could be heavy, as 6RAR discovered on Operation Bribie in February 1967 when it encountered the Viet Cong's D445 Battalion, reinforced by North Vietnamese regulars. 6RAR lost six soldiers killed and 27 wounded. At one point Australian soldiers charged with fixed bayonets against enemy machine-guns. Although Graham claimed that Operation Bribie had achieved a good deal, most of the soldiers thought that they 'had been soundly thrashed'.[10]

Immediately afterwards, 5RAR conducted Operation Renmark, a search-and-destroy mission against the PLAF base in the Long Hai hills. The operation was recalled soon after an armoured personnel carrier hit a mine, causing horrific casualties. In all, Operation Renmark cost seven killed and 26 wounded, including two who later died of wounds. Operations conducted by later task force commanders against the Long Hai hills proved similarly costly and unsuccessful. The PLAF could later claim that the Minh Dam Secret Zone remained a secure base throughout the Second Indochina War, as it had been in the First.

These and other similar experiences reinforced the feeling that, despite the bravery and skill of the troops, the task force had neither the numbers nor the military capabilities it needed. Senior officers in Saigon and Canberra debated whether the greater need was a third battalion group or a squadron of tanks. By the middle of the year, the army was pressing the government to supply one or the other, or preferably both.

THE MINEFIELD[11]

The shortfall of 'troops to task', in the jargon of military planners, led to another fateful decision. In keeping with the Australian doctrine of separating the guerrillas from the people, and particularly to disrupt the food supply routes between the base in the Long Hai hills, enemy sanctuary areas to the east and the rice-growing areas around Dat Do, Brigadier Graham ordered the building of a minefield, stretching about 11 kilometres from a hill north of Dat Do known as the Horseshoe to the coast near the village of Lang Phuoc Hai. The minefield comprised two lines of barbed wire about 100 metres apart, between which were laid about 22 600 mines, of which 12 700 were fitted with anti-lifting devices. In accordance with the 'fundamental military principle that the minefield had to be kept under continual observation, using patrols by day and night', the intention was that South Vietnamese forces should be responsible for patrolling one side of the fence and the Australian task force the other side.[12]

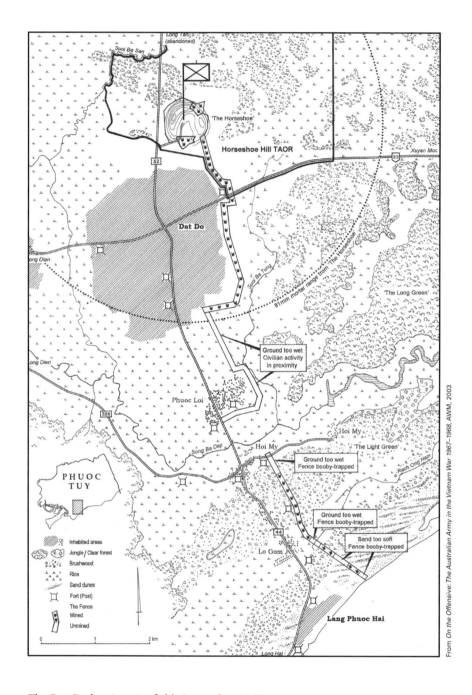

The Dat Do barrier minefield, September 1967

For several months, the minefield successfully disrupted the Viet Cong communications and food supply routes. According to the communist histories, the Minh Dam base was isolated and the guerrillas in the Long Dat district 'had to dig for roots and pick leaves in the jungle to eat'.[13] After a little time, however, it became evident that neither the South Vietnamese nor the Australian forces were patrolling their respective sides, rendering the minefield an ineffective barrier. With extraordinary courage and ingenuity, the Viet Cong discovered how to neutralise the anti-lifting devices and lift the mines. Guerrillas, both men and women, removed the mines and used them against the Australians. By the end of 1967 thousands of mines had been lifted: many were re-laid in areas where the Australians operated, especially around the Minh Dam base in the Long Hai hills.

For the next four years, especially in 1969 and 1970, mines were a major source of casualties for the task force, causing a large number of horrific wounds, some fatal, others requiring amputations. The widespread belief that 'half our casualties were due to our mines' was probably an exaggeration. The Viet Cong had other sources of mines, which had been inflicting casualties on the task force even before the Dat Do minefield was laid. The most plausible estimate is that mines from the minefield caused about 11 per cent of all Australian deaths and 8 per cent of all injuries. Nevertheless, the knowledge that a considerable number of casualties came from mines lifted from the Australian-laid minefield had a profound impact on morale within the task force, affecting all ranks from the task force commander to private soldiers. It also affected political opinion in Australia: the Opposition cited it as 'a tragic example of the waste and futility of Australian participation in the Vietnam war', while it undermined the confidence of the commitment's supporters in the army and the government.[14]

The barrier minefield is generally considered to have been the greatest blunder committed by the task force. Much of the criticism was directed at Brigadier Graham, the task force commander, who insisted on the measure against advice from many subordinates. Some Australians blamed the South Vietnamese for failing to patrol the western side of the fence; they often overlooked the fact that the task force failed to patrol the eastern side. While there was merit in the idea of cutting Viet Cong supply routes, the planning, preparation and implementation had been seriously flawed. As historian Ashley Ekins has stated, the minefield was 'a failure on many levels; command, communications, liaison with allies, staff work and field operations'.[15] Another historian, Greg Lockhart, has contended that the minefield demonstrated that Australia's senior political and military leaders were all 'immured in an imperial mind-set'.[16] Without accepting that terminology, it is fair to conclude that the minefield 'reflected a serious underestimation of the Viet Cong, their ability and ingenuity, their tenacity and dedication and, not least, the cost they were prepared to pay for victory'.[17]

The decision-making on the minefield, like that on the siting of the base at Nui Dat, also reflected the lack of clarity in the command arrangements for the Australian force in Vietnam. Not only were the relationships with American and RVN authorities complex and often tense but the Australians' own command hierarchy also suffered from 'the ill-defined roles and relationships between the chiefs of staff, the Defence Committee, individual ministers and senior officials'. As the biographer of Lieutenant General Sir Thomas Daly, CGS from 1966 to 1971, has noted, 'soldiers paid the price'.[18]

Another attempt to apply the counter-insurgency doctrines that the Australians had learned in the Malayan Emergency was Operation Ainslie, the forced resettlement of a group of hamlets known locally as [Slope 30]. The creation of 'new villages' had been one of the key elements in the successful strategy in Malaya, moving squatters into villages where they were offered greater physical and economic security. The creation of 'strategic hamlets' in Vietnam in the early 1960s, in an attempt to emulate this tactic, had proved counter-productive. The Vietnamese farmers had resented being separated from their ancestral lands, rendering them more sympathetic to the Viet Cong than to the government, and corrupt officials appropriated a large proportion of the resources designated for the program. The official who was appointed by President Diem's brother, Ngo Dinh Nhu, to administer the program was later revealed to be a communist agent. A subsequent attempt to create 'New Life' hamlets proved similarly unsuccessful for many of the same reasons.

Slope 30 was not merely sympathetic to the Viet Cong: it was an important staging point in the logistic network supplying Viet Cong units in Phuoc Tuy province. Graham decided 'to clear Slope 30 lock, stock and barrel', to resettle the occupants in a newly constructed village named Ap Suoi Nghe, and to raze everything in the deserted hamlets. The operation proved to be 'poorly conceived and misguided',[19] creating more resentment among the villagers. The land in the new site proved less fertile than at Slope 30, and the corruption and indifference of the local RVN officials ensured that the resettlement process was deeply flawed.

Despite the Australian preference for pacification operations, Westmoreland continued to seek Australian involvement in large operations conducted by massed formations. The task force continued to find that search-and-destroy operations were usually ineffective, as the Viet Cong eluded the Australian infantry. In July 1967 the task force was given the task of planning and executing Operation Paddington, a massive operation by Australian standards, using the equivalent of nine battalions of American, South Vietnamese and Australian troops, with considerable support from artillery, armour, close air support and B-52 bombing. The aim was to trap and destroy the Viet Cong's 274 Regiment, but the results were minimal. Once again, the enemy proved too elusive, avoiding confrontation with the huge, noisy and cumbersome allied formations.

The Viet Cong did not always avoid battle if they held a numerical advantage. In August, 7RAR conducted a search-and-destroy operation in the Hat Dich area, a Viet Cong base area. A company had a brief contact, killing two of the enemy. After similar contacts, Viet Cong units usually withdrew and avoided further losses, but on this occasion the enemy, a company of 274 Regiment, counter-attacked. They were probably fighting a rearguard action, holding up the Australians while the rest of their battalion escaped. The unexpected encounter became an intense, two-hour firefight between two evenly matched opponents. Both sides used grenades, machine-guns and small arms, but the Viet Cong had the advantage of rocket-propelled grenades. Despite the Viet Cong tactic of 'hugging the enemy', artillery support from the Australian–New Zealand battery and an American artillery battalion proved crucial in what became known as 'the battle of Suoi Chau Pha'. These and other operations underlined the need for tanks, as well as a third battalion.

THE THIRD BATTALION

In August 1967 the pressure on the Holt government came to a head. The burden of defence expenditure was proving painful, but the demands were only increasing. From Saigon, the commander of the Australian force was pressing the case for a third battalion, a squadron of tanks, and additional helicopter support. The Americans were exerting heavy pressure for more troops: Washington politics dictated that numbers of infantry were more important than smaller, specialised elements such as tanks. Senior military and civilian officials debated whether the higher priority should be given to the tanks or the battalion. At a critical stage the task force commander, Graham, sent a disconcerting and unexpected message recommending against tanks. It transpired that he had been unaware of recent modifications to the Centurions, and that he was trying to place priority on the third battalion, if it came to a choice. Overhanging these discussions were the uncertain implications of the British withdrawal for Australia's commitments to Malaysia and Singapore, coupled with apprehension about possible Indonesian designs on the Australian-administered territories in Papua New Guinea, a longstanding concern that had not been removed by the end of Confrontation. A strategic appreciation warned that the most serious scenario Australia might have to face was 'a Borneo type confrontation in Papua/New Guinea, leading to a possible limited war'.[20]

After intense debate, Cabinet decided in early September that it had no choice but to put support for the American alliance ahead of its other concerns. It agreed to commit the third battalion, the tank squadron, a joint RAAF–RAN contribution of four helicopters and eight pilots, and some other units and personnel. The government did not immediately convey this decision to the Americans because the ministers hoped that it could be used to gain two important concessions from Washington – more favourable terms for the controversial purchase of F-111 aircraft for the RAAF and a stronger statement of American support for the Australian commitment in Malaysia and Singapore. The pressure from Washington was such that in early October Holt sent a personal message to Johnson advising him of the decision, which would bring the total Australian commitment in Vietnam to more than 8000 personnel. He emphasised that this was no easy decision, especially in light of Australia's continuing commitment to Malaysia and Singapore. Holt told Johnson that Australia was 'at the full stretch of our present and planned military capacity'.[21] This, in short, would be the last increase in the Australian commitment.

The Holt government's attitude to this last escalation of the Australian commitment had an ironic outcome. In early 1968 Clark Clifford was appointed Secretary of Defense, replacing Robert McNamara, who had left the Pentagon in a virtual admission of failure in Vietnam. Clifford soon came to the conclusion that the war could not be won, given the limitations within which the United States was fighting, and he turned the Johnson administration in its last year in office towards withdrawal. In 1969, soon after leaving office, he wrote that his visit to Australia and other regional allies in 1967 had initiated his doubts. If the Australians had sent 300 000 troops overseas in the Second World War but were extremely reluctant to send more than 7000 to Vietnam, he thought, perhaps the United States was exaggerating the danger of a communist victory in Vietnam. The politically astute lawyer had realised that, by 1967, Australia was far from 'all the way' in its commitment to Vietnam. The Holt government, renowned then and ever since as a champion of the Vietnam commitment, had helped to turn the United States government away from escalation and towards withdrawal.[22]

ANZAC IN VIETNAM

When the first two battalions of the task force, 5RAR and 6RAR, ended their tours in mid-1967, they were replaced by 7RAR and 2RAR. During its tour, 2RAR's strength was enhanced by the arrival of the two New Zealand infantry companies, the first of which, as mentioned in Chapter 6, had been promised by Prime Minister Holyoake earlier in the year. The two companies, known as V (Victor) Company and W (Whiskey) Company, were integrated into 2RAR, which was officially designated 2RAR/NZ (ANZAC). The battalion now had a total of six rifle companies instead of the Australian standard of four (or the five of the abandoned Pentropic formation). Successors to the original V and W companies were similarly integrated into the later tours of 2RAR's successors, 4RAR and 6RAR, which were also designated ANZAC battalions, until 4RAR/NZ (ANZAC) became the last battalion of the task force to leave Vietnam in December 1971.[23]

This was the first time that Australian and New Zealand infantry had fought in the same battalion, and the first time that New Zealand infantry had served under an Australian battalion commander. A New Zealand officer was appointed deputy battalion commander. For the most part, this unprecedented degree of ANZAC collaboration was regarded as a success, although tensions sometimes rose beyond the traditional trans-Tasman rivalry. New Zealand had not introduced conscription, so all the New Zealand soldiers were regulars. Many were Maori who, living up to their reputation as excellent jungle fighters, moved silently and shot with great accuracy, but were inclined to indiscipline in camp. One of the ANZAC battalion commanders found that the battalion worked more smoothly when a Maori was appointed deputy commander.

The soldiers of the New Zealand artillery battery that had preceded the two infantry companies had earned a high reputation for their performance at the battle of Long Tan and on other occasions. This esteem was damaged by 'friendly fire' incidents, especially one in February 1967, when artillery rounds from the New Zealand battery fell on D Company, 6RAR – by a bitter irony, the company that had fought heroically at Long Tan. Four Australians were killed, including Warrant Officer 2 Jack Kirby, who had been decorated for his courage at Long Tan and who 'had become a mixture of hero, idol, mascot and good luck charm' for D Company. The error was caused by mechanical failure on an artillery plotting instrument, a fault that had been detected earlier but not corrected.[24]

THE TASK FORCE AND ITS THIRD COMMANDER

In October 1967 Brigadier Graham ended his tour as task force commander, returning to Australia where he was soon afterwards promoted major general and Deputy Chief of the General Staff. His successor, Brigadier RL Hughes, initially followed Graham's preference for pacification operations. He phased out the cordon-and-search operations using a battalion or even the whole task force and replaced them with 'acorn' operations, in which a platoon or company of Australians would accompany South Vietnamese police and intelligence units into a village to apprehend individuals and small groups who were suspected of being part of the Viet Cong infrastructure. Acorn operations initially proved an effective way of identifying members of the VCI, who were handed over to the South Vietnamese interrogation and judicial authorities. To the frustration of the Australians, however, many of those detained were subsequently released. The RVN judges, police and other officials were justifiably frightened of assassination by the ruthless security service of the Viet Cong, which reportedly carried out more than 6500 assassinations and 10 600 abductions in 1968 alone.[25]

During Hughes' tour as task force commander, the third battalion, 3RAR, and the tank squadron arrived at the expanding base at Nui Dat. With the added strength of these units, Hughes adopted a more aggressive approach than his predecessors, undertaking more major operations than any other task force commander, including search-and-destroy and reconnaissance-in-force operations in the base areas used by the PLAF main force elements near the borders of Phuoc Tuy. In circumstances discussed in the next chapter, he was also willing to deploy the task force beyond Phuoc Tuy.

THE COMMITMENT OF THREE SERVICES

As the Holt government's decisions in 1966 and 1967 were implemented, the Australian commitment grew in numbers and the range of skills. By the end of 1967 Australia had become the only ally of South Vietnam other than the United States to contribute combat forces and support elements of all three armed services. At peak strength in mid-1969, of the total of about 8000 personnel, nearly 7000 were from the army, of whom more than 5000 were in the task force. The infantry component of the task force included three battalions, one of which was augmented by two New Zealand companies. They were supported by armour, artillery, engineers, army aviation, signals and other units, as well as the logistics support group at Vung Tau and the helicopters of the RAAF's No. 9 Squadron. Combat units comprised about half regulars and half national servicemen, a combination that most battalion commanders and other senior officers found highly satisfactory. The army hierarchy knew that there would be no further increases to the commitment, but for the most part they were satisfied that initial deficiencies and weaknesses had been resolved and that a well balanced force was in place.

The RAAF and RAN contributions were also approaching their peak, both in combat forces and in the vital but unspectacular and often neglected role of logistic support. From the first deployment of 1RAR in 1965, the principal transport of troops and equipment between Australia and Vietnam was by HMAS *Sydney*. The role of the 'Vung Tau ferry' was supplemented by two vessels chartered in 1966 from the Australian National Line, the *Jeparit* and the *Boonaroo*. When members of the Seamen's Union refused in February 1967 to crew ships supporting the forces in Vietnam, the *Boonaroo* was commissioned into the RAN as HMAS *Boonaroo* for its only mission. *Jeparit* made a total of 47 trips to and from Vietnam, first as a chartered vessel, then with a mixed RAN–civilian crew, and finally as HMAS *Jeparit*. Four ships of the army's 32 Small Ships Squadron also contributed to the logistic support of the task force.[26]

The RAN's other commitments were not directly linked to the task force but were integrated into United States forces and placed under their operational control. In March 1967 HMAS *Hobart* became the first of the DDG-class guided-missile destroyers to join the US Navy ships 'on the gun-line' in the Gulf of Tonkin. Fully integrated into the task units formed by the US Navy's Seventh Fleet, *Hobart* provided naval gunfire support to ground forces and contributed to maritime surveillance and interception. This initiated a commitment maintained by *Hobart*, its sister ships HMAS *Brisbane* and HMAS *Perth*, and the older *Daring*-class destroyer HMAS *Vendetta*, until late 1971.[27]

The first contingent of the six-man clearance diving team also arrived in early 1967. Under the operational control of the US Naval Forces within the US Military Assistance Command Vietnam, this small but highly specialised team worked with its American counterparts to protect allied shipping from the mines laid by the enemy, as well as assisting in salvage and disposal of unsafe ordnance.[28] The RAN helicopter aircrew and groundcrew, committed in mid-1967, were designated the RAN Helicopter Flight Vietnam (RANHFV) and integrated into the 135th Assault Helicopter Company, a US Army unit that operated in the troop-carrying, ground support and medical evacuation roles, supporting allied units in the III Corps and sometimes IV Corps areas of South Vietnam. Based from December 1967 at Black Horse, an American base near Xuan Loc, the RAN pilots and their American colleagues sometimes flew in direct support of the Australian task force, but more commonly its sorties were associated with US Army and ARVN operations.[29]

In mid-1966, when the helicopters of No. 9 Squadron arrived to support the task force, the RAAF Transport Flight Vietnam of Caribous, first committed in 1964, was redesignated as No. 35 Squadron. The Caribous were integrated into the American airlift program for Southeast Asia: from 1966 they were under the operational control of the US Seventh Air Force.[30] The Canberra bombers and personnel of No. 2 Squadron, who arrived 'in country' in March–April 1967, were also placed under the operational control of the US Seventh Air Force, serving with the 35th Tactical Fighter Wing at the large US air base at Phan Rang, about 250 kilometres northeast of Saigon. The government's decision in December 1966 to commit a third squadron raised the RAAF commitment to the largest number of aircraft and personnel that the service had deployed on operations since the Second World War.[31]

DEATH OF A PRIME MINISTER

For the first year of Holt's prime ministership, his enthusiastic support for the war he had inherited from Menzies was received almost entirely positively, winning electoral support at home and a powerful friend in the White House. In 1967, his second year, international and domestic political events turned against him. On 17 December, while relaxing with friends at Cheviot Beach, near Portsea in Victoria, he went swimming in rough waters and never emerged. The extraordinary circumstances of his death caused widespread shock. A memorial service was attended by political leaders and dignitaries including Prince Charles, President Johnson, British Prime Minister Harold Wilson, General Thieu of South Vietnam, President Ferdinand Marcos of the Philippines, and President Park Chung-hee of South Korea.[32]

Holt was unlucky to have become Prime Minister when he did. He was not well equipped to handle major questions of foreign policy and his personal endorsement of the Vietnam commitment showed more naive enthusiasm than prudent foresight. He had a genuine, if vague, vision of an Australian future in a prosperous and secure Asia that later Prime Ministers would be happy to claim, and he worked energetically to communicate that prospect to the Australian people by his visits to Asia and his rejection of racism. But that vision was overshadowed by

Australia's involvement in a war, the outcome of which was increasingly uncertain and against which significant dissent was appearing. It was not Holt alone but the whole Australian government who had failed to foresee developments not only in Southeast Asia but also in Britain and the United States which would cast doubt upon the wisdom of Australia's established policies. In late 1967 the government faced a range of challenges to which its traditional responses were inadequate but to which it could find no new solutions. Holt's death introduced another element of uncertainty into an increasingly turbulent phase of Australian and global politics.

— EIGHT —

THE TURNING-POINT 1968-69

The period from the beginning of 1968 to mid-1969 was in many respects the turning-point of the Vietnam War. Not only was it the high point of worldwide protest and debate but it also marked a turning-point in the crucial battlefield of American public opinion and, as a result, American policy. Caught between competing pressures, the Australian government was in a state of policy paralysis, unable to decide whether to stay on its established course or to seek a way out. In Vietnam itself, the Australian military commitment reached its peak and the task force was engaged in some of the biggest operations of the war. At this critical time Australia lacked the exceptionally astute, experienced, confident and united leadership that was needed in its political, military and diplomatic affairs.

THE REVOLUTIONS OF 1968[1]

In 1968 rebellions, revolutions and riots broke out all round the world, epitomising the 'Vietnam era' in the minds of many, on either side of the barricades. The Vietnam War, or simply 'Vietnam', was now more than a conflict or an event. Even in countries not involved in the war, like France, Germany and Japan, it had become a symbol of numerous conflicts: between capitalism and socialism, between established order and revolution, between the new nations of Asia, Africa and Latin America and the old powers of Europe and North America, between war and peace, between youth and their elders, between students and university authorities, between movements for liberation (both national liberation and personal liberation) and the authoritarianism of the old order.

Demonstrations against the war, and all that it was taken to represent, became more violent, polarising opinion in many Western countries. Much of the protest was centred on universities, where some leaders of student rebellions became household names around the world. Some prominent academics in major American universities lent their support to the students. In May student riots in Paris almost brought down the government, until the communists helped re-establish the traditional order. As this indicated, many of the student revolutionaries outflanked the old-style communists on the left. Mao Zedong and the Cuban revolutionary Che Guevara were among the heroes of the new left movements. The Soviet Union faced its own crisis when it used tanks to crush the 'Prague spring', an attempt by the leaders in Czechoslovakia to create a more liberal form of communism. In the United States, the assassinations of the civil rights leader Martin Luther King and of Robert Kennedy, who was campaigning for the presidency on an anti-war platform, prompted major riots in several cities. Established governments struggled as they sought to reassert law and order without appearing repressive or alienating the middle ground. Everything that happened in 1968 and 1969 has to be seen in the context of a world seemingly full of revolution and rebellion.

THE TET OFFENSIVE AND ITS IMPACT[2]

In late 1967 the United States authorities were aware that the enemy was gathering his forces for a major offensive. President Johnson personally warned the Australian Cabinet of this prospect when he attended the memorial service for Harold Holt in December. The military leadership in Vietnam believed that the offensive would be concentrated on the northern provinces of South Vietnam, where a major battle was already taking place at Khe Sanh, as well as Saigon and the nearby American base at Bien Hoa and Long Binh. In fact, the leadership in Hanoi had decided, after vigorous debate, to embark on a 'general offensive, general uprising'. Viet Cong forces, supported by the PAVN, would launch assaults on almost every major town and city throughout South Vietnam, intending to provoke a popular uprising throughout the country. The PAVN and the PLAF had grown in strength, despite the American strategy of attrition, and Hanoi was confident of striking a decisive blow, possibly bringing an end to the war.

The offensive was timed to coincide with the ceasefire declared for the New Year holiday known as Tet. The Tet offensive began on 31 January 1968, although some units acted prematurely the previous day. There was no popular uprising. After the initial shock, ARVN and United States forces reacted promptly and effectively. They quickly rebuffed the assaults in most South Vietnamese cities, but intense fighting continued in Saigon until mid-February and in Hue until late February. The communist forces suffered extremely heavy casualties, especially the Viet Cong units, which led most of the assaults. After the Tet offensive, most of the major fighting on the communist side would be conducted by the main force units of the PAVN.[3]

Although the Tet offensive was a military failure, it proved to be a turning-point in American public opinion.[4] Exaggerated reports of Viet

Cong successes appeared in the American media, both print and electronic. In particular, much was made of the fact that members of one PLAF unit entered the grounds of the United States Embassy in Saigon. They did not enter any major building and were quickly eliminated, but the symbolic effect of 'the Viet Cong in the American Embassy' was powerful, especially following Westmoreland's excessive claims of progress in preceding months. American television gave extensive coverage to the devastation caused by fighting in Saigon, especially the Chinese quarter, Cholon, and the bitter fighting around the old imperial citadel in Hue.

Senior members of the Johnson administration had already been losing confidence in the Vietnam commitment by the end of 1967. In July the Secretary of Defense, Robert McNamara, commissioned a highly classified historical study of American policy in Vietnam, based on Defense Department records, in order to understand how the United States could avoid such a policy failure in the future. His resignation was announced in November and took effect in February amid the intense debate over the Tet offensive. The Pentagon Papers, as the historical study came to be known, were handed to his successor, Clark Clifford, just before the 1968 election.

McNamara's resignation was overshadowed on 31 March when President Johnson announced that he would end the Rolling Thunder program of bombing North Vietnam in order to open the way to peace talks with Hanoi. To worldwide astonishment, he also announced that he would not stand for re-election in November. After a year marked by protests and riots, the Republican Richard Nixon won the election with a claim that he had a secret plan to end the war and to bring 'peace with honour'. Soon after taking office in January 1969 he initiated a policy of 'Vietnamisation', under which American forces would be gradually withdrawn and hand more of the combat role to the South Vietnamese. The first withdrawal of American troops was announced in June 1969, followed by another in September.

A MISSED OPPORTUNITY?[5]

The Tet offensive and the highly charged debates before the 1968 presidential election only underlined changes already evident in American political thinking. Both Democrats and Republicans observed the considerable changes in Southeast Asia since 1965. Many of the potential 'dominoes' of that time, such as Indonesia, Thailand, the Philippines, Malaysia and Singapore, were now more secure. The foundation in 1967 of the Association of Southeast Asian Nations (ASEAN) by these five nations indicated a greater willingness to cooperate. Most importantly, from Washington's perspective, the replacement of Sukarno by Suharto as President of Indonesia, the end to Confrontation and the virtual elimination of the PKI meant a transformation in regional politics. Nixon was one of the leading Americans who believed that the American stand in Vietnam had given the Indonesian generals the confidence to stand up to the communists in Indonesia in 1965: with the 'New Order' in place in Indonesia, much of the impetus behind the Vietnam commitment was reduced. Nixon and other leading Americans also indicated that they saw an opportunity to develop a more positive relationship with the People's Republic of China.

These signs of new American thinking should have indicated to Australian leaders not only that United States policy was susceptible to change but also that Australia had gained many of its strategic goals in committing forces to Vietnam. The changes in Indonesia, especially, had been fundamental to Australia's policy in the region. At the same time the American withdrawals created political pressure for Australia to follow suit. In August 1969, shortly after the first American withdrawal, a public opinion poll indicated that, for the first time, more Australians wanted the government to withdraw troops from Vietnam than wanted them to remain.

The Australian government was now constrained, however, by the way in which the Menzies and Holt governments had initiated, escalated and defended the commitment of Australian combat forces in 1965 and 1966. There had been no 'exit strategy': no limit had been placed on the duration or, until 1967, the size of the commitment. Having declared that Australia was acting from a concern for the security of South Vietnam as well as to ensure its own security and the strength of the American alliance, it would have been no easy matter to assert that, with the region more secure, Australia could withdraw and leave some 20 million people in South Vietnam to their fate. Political leaders had never clearly explained the importance of Indonesia to Australian policy, and so could not explain why the dramatic changes in Jakarta affected their attitude towards developments in Indochina. Moreover, uncertainties remained over the security of Malaysia and Singapore, and Britain was accelerating its withdrawal from the region. A principal element of Australian strategic policy was still under threat. Although it would have been extremely difficult, it is just possible that, if Australia had had united, skilful and authoritative leadership in its political, military and diplomatic agencies, a way might have been found to extricate the country, at least partially, from the Vietnam commitment, reducing the cost in lives, treasure and political harmony. This was not to be Australia's experience.

ANOTHER NEW PRIME MINISTER[6]

The turbulence that followed Holt's sudden death was in marked contrast to the predictability of his accession to the prime ministership. The leader of the Country Party and Deputy Prime Minister, John McEwen, who was sworn in as Prime Minister until the Liberal Party could elect a new leader, let it be known that his party would not serve under the deputy leader of the Liberal Party, William McMahon. The Liberals then elected John Gorton over Paul Hasluck and two other candidates. Although a Senator since 1950, Gorton had been in Cabinet for only two years. He had long taken a particular interest in foreign affairs and defence, but his views were not consistent with those of Menzies and the senior ministers. In his early years he expressed views popular with the vehement anti-communists on the right wing of the Liberal Party, such as WC Wentworth and Wilfrid Kent Hughes, especially on questions such as non-recognition of the People's Republic of China in Beijing and support for the Republic of China on Taiwan. He strongly supported the SEATO alliance and was enthusiastic about standardising Australia's military equipment with that of the United States. But Gorton was also concerned that the forward defence posture made Australia appear too subservient to both Britain and the United States, a favourite theme of the Labor Party, especially its left wing. Gorton did not approve of the forward defence practice of stationing Australian forces in Southeast Asia, preferring to have forces based in Australia that would be well equipped and prepared to fight in Southeast Asia, if necessary. He advocated the acquisition of missiles with nuclear warheads, so that Australia would not have to rely on its British and American allies to provide a nuclear deterrent.

Gorton's great respect for Menzies was not fully reciprocated, and his promotion was slow. After eight years as a backbench Senator, his first ministerial appointment came in 1958, when Menzies first divided the ministry into the Cabinet and an outer ministry. Gorton became the most junior of the non-Cabinet ministers as Minister for the Navy. He held the portfolio until 1963, becoming the longest serving minister in the history of the position. He was highly regarded in the navy for his active involvement and vigorous advocacy of the navy's interests, contributing substantially to the growth and modernisation of the fleet, but the RAN had little involvement in the Southeast Asian conflicts of the 1950s and 1960s, where the Australian commitment was carried out principally by the army with some air force support. When Menzies was both Prime Minister and Minister for External Affairs, Gorton was appointed Assistant Minister for External Affairs, but was allocated responsibilities, such as Antarctica, outside the department's central concerns. He also represented the Minister for External Affairs in the Senate, but he did not enter Cabinet or the Foreign Affairs and Defence Committee until the formation of the Holt government in 1966. Consequently he was not part of the group of senior ministers shaping policies towards Indonesia and Indochina, although he was called on to defend those policies in Parliament. In 1965, while still outside the Cabinet, he defended the decision to send the first battalion to Vietnam with distinctly less enthusiasm than his colleagues. In December 1966, soon after the election, he wrote privately to Holt to oppose any increase in the commitment, arguing that the electorate had supported some commitment but there was no need to increase it.

Gorton's sudden elevation therefore thrust him into responsibility for policies he had little part in shaping and, especially, for a war about which he had long held major reservations. The Tet offensive erupted within Gorton's first month as Prime Minister. On 2 February, without consulting Cabinet or the FAD Committee, Gorton announced that Australia would not increase its commitment to Vietnam beyond the current build-up to 8000 personnel. He was doing no more than making public Holt's advice to Johnson the previous October that the commitment of the third battalion put Australia 'at the full stretch of our present and planned military capacity', but Gorton's prompt and apparently unilateral statement indicated where his preferences lay. It appeared in the press on the same day as a photograph that had a profound impact on public opinion around the world, showing the Saigon police chief summarily executing a captured Viet Cong cadre.[7] Although Australian policy remained essentially unchanged, the combination of the Tet offensive and the new Prime Minister gave the Australian commitment to Vietnam a radically different tone from that associated with either Menzies or Holt.

GORTON ON FOREIGN AND DEFENCE POLICIES[8]

Gorton's relaxed and informal manner, his nationalism and his questioning of the forward defence posture gained popularity in the media and the electorate, but his centralist policies on domestic matters and his lukewarm endorsement of the foreign and defence policies he had inherited also created enemies on his own side of politics – within the coalition parties, among Liberal premiers in major states, and in the DLP. He alienated senior public servants by demoting the head of the Prime Minister's Department under Menzies and Holt, Sir John Bunting, and appointing CL (later Sir Lenox) Hewitt. He also relied heavily on an attractive young woman who was appointed his principal private secretary, Ainsley Gotto. His overt fondness for female company led to unfounded rumours about his relationship with Gotto.

Tensions soon emerged between the ministers and advisers who were reasserting the established policies of forward defence and Gorton's inclination towards a more assertive attitude to great power allies and a 'continental defence' or 'fortress Australia' approach to defence policy. Gorton's disdain for the Ministers for Defence and External Affairs, Fairhall and Hasluck, and their departments was obvious. When he first visited Washington as Prime Minister in May 1968, he was accompanied by only Hewitt and Gotto, with no minister or official from External Affairs or Defence. Although Hasluck and Fairhall remained in their portfolios until early 1969, when Hasluck was appointed Governor-General, and October 1969, when Fairhall retired from politics, colleagues and observers soon concluded that Gorton and Hewitt intended to control foreign and defence policies, as well as other major policies, in a presidential rather than a prime ministerial fashion. The appointment of a relatively junior minister with little expertise in foreign affairs, Gordon Freeth, to succeed Hasluck in External Affairs confirmed Gorton's opinion of the portfolio. The divisions over policy created what one newspaper called 'Defence dither'.[9] Gorton could see the weaknesses in the current policies but did not have the political authority or skill to chart a new course with the support of his colleagues. Uncertainty would remain a principal characteristic of the Australian government's policy for the next five years.

Adding to the uncertainty in Australian policy-making, the British government announced in early January that its withdrawal from 'east of Suez' would be more rapid than it had announced in mid-1967, arousing deep concern in Malaysia and Singapore. For the next several years, Britain, Australia, New Zealand, Malaysia and Singapore were engaged in diplomatic discussions over regional defence arrangements following the end of Confrontation and the British withdrawal. These discussions culminated in 1971 with the Five Power Defence Agreement (FPDA), but the path was long and difficult. Britain was determined to withdraw from the region despite the concerns of the four other countries. Malaysia and Singapore did not find cooperation in defence matters easy, and wanted the other three powers involved to ease the path to a new arrangement. Although Confrontation had been formally ended in 1966, some fears remained over Indonesian ambitions, and the Philippines renewed its claim to Sabah. Australia's longstanding unwillingness to be drawn into conflicts arising from communal tensions in Malaysia or the internal security of Singapore contributed substantially to Gorton's approach, especially after a major outbreak of communal violence in Malaysia in 1969. Gorton stated publicly at this time that Australian forces, which he had reluctantly agreed to keep stationed in Malaysia and Singapore, were for use only against 'external attack' on 'Malaya', distancing himself from defence of Sabah and Sarawak as well as from internal tensions. His statement was sharply criticised by the Malaysians.

These concerns strengthened the public uncertainty about the future of American policy in Vietnam, and indeed in the whole region. Australians continued to seek assurance that their policies towards Indonesia, Malaysia and Singapore were supported by the United States, with an assurance of ANZUS backing if required, but in a presidential election year, with Johnson a declared non-candidate and with the United States torn by social and political tensions, the future of American foreign policy was anything but clear. In his first visit to the White House Gorton did not establish a positive relationship with Johnson or Rusk, and he was only able to have brief conversations with the leading candidates for the presidency.

Soon after Richard Nixon took office in January 1969, having won the election on the promise to bring 'peace with honour' in Vietnam, he began to move towards withdrawal of some American troops, coupled with a policy of 'Vietnamisation' of the war effort. Since 1967 Nixon had indicated that America's allies would have to do more in their own defence if they were to expect support from the United States. Both sides of American politics had been delivering this message for some years, including to Australia, but after Nixon repeated it when commenting to reporters in Guam in July 1969, during a visit to several Asian countries, it became known as 'the Guam doctrine' and later 'the Nixon doctrine'. Combined with Nixon's known reluctance to become involved again in a land war in Asia, the Guam doctrine created considerable nervousness in the capitals of America's allies, not least Saigon and Canberra.[10]

When Gorton visited the White House again in 1969, he established a better relationship with Nixon than he had with Johnson the previous year. He said that Nixon had given him strong assurances of American support for its commitments under ANZUS and SEATO, particularly referring to the protection that ANZUS would offer to Australian troops in Malaysia and Singapore. His rapport with Nixon later helped to circumvent the repeated technical and financial problems encountered in the acquisition of the F-111 aircraft for the RAAF. Much of this good work was undermined, however, when, during a speech at a White House dinner, he said that 'wherever the United States is resisting aggression … we will go Waltzing Matilda with you'. He was evidently seeking both to assure his host of Australia's commitment to the alliance while striking a nationalist note for his domestic audience, but the phrase was treated with derision by the Australian media.¹¹

Gorton faced a profound dilemma over Vietnam policy, created to a large extent by the open-ended way in which Menzies and Holt had handled the commitment and its escalation. Like an increasing proportion of the electorate, Gorton wanted to find a way out of the commitment, but without damaging the alliance relationship with the United States (or losing the electoral preferences of the DLP). The beginning of American troop withdrawals created a further complication. The public clearly wanted to see a start to Australian withdrawals, in parallel with those of the United States, but the Nixon administration maintained pressure on the other 'troop-contributing countries', including Australia, to maintain their much smaller commitments at their existing levels. Moreover, the Australian military, especially its two most senior generals, Wilton and Daly, regarded the Australian task force, with its three battalions as well as tanks, artillery, engineers and other elements, as a balanced force. They opposed any partial reduction, such as the withdrawal of one battalion, which would reduce the task force's effectiveness and security.

Gorton's experience as an RAAF pilot during the Second World War and as a long-serving Minister for the Navy generated strong sympathy for the uniformed serviceman. He understood and strongly sympathised with the army's approach of 'one out, all out', rather than that of the ministers and civilian advisers in Defence and External Affairs, who saw the political benefits in a phased withdrawal. Much would depend on the scale and timing of American withdrawals, but Nixon would not give him any information on his own plans and hopes, which were withheld even from senior officials in Washington.[12]

AUSTRALIAN PROTEST[13]

Protests and demonstrations in Australia in 1968 and 1969 followed the pattern established in 1966 and 1967. Australian protesters adopted tactics and slogans from protesters around the world, often with a time-lag, more violent than before but generally a little more moderate than the most extreme models in Europe and North America, and with a distinctively Australian element. As world attention was focused on riots and confrontations in Paris, London, Washington, San Francisco and elsewhere in the Western world, Australian demonstrations became markedly more violent. Radicals infiltrated demonstrations and protests by non-violent groups such as clergy or Save Our Sons; they then provoked confrontation with the police and other authorities by throwing rocks, placing marbles or firecrackers under the feet of police horses, or occupying offices and buildings in 'sit-ins'. Their aim was to provoke physical confrontations with the police, especially in front of television cameras, which could be portrayed as 'police brutality', or to inspire legal or administrative actions by government, universities and other institutions that could be denounced as tyrannical or repressive. These tactics were denounced not only by governments and other institutions but also by many student leaders. Internal rivalries between Maoists, Trotskyites and numerous other left-wing groups divided the radicals as well as the more moderate groups, but their tactics did have some effect. Every demonstration that ended in conflict – and they were frequent in 1968 and 1969 – polarised opinions, driving conservatives towards stronger positions on 'law and order' and radicalising some moderate protesters.

While the radicals sought to undermine the institutions of a democratic, capitalist society, moderate protesters directed their attention to the war itself. Much attention was given to the weapons and tactics employed by the Americans, the South Vietnamese and their allies. Protesters continued to denounce the use of napalm. The huge media contingent in Vietnam devoted great attention to real and alleged atrocities. The Australian press, heavily dependent on American themes, followed the search for stories of massacre and atrocity.

In 1968 a book published by an American journalist referred to an alleged incident of 'water torture' by the Australian task force. In late 1966, as the task force was consolidating its position in Phuoc Tuy province, a platoon had captured a 23-year-old woman, To Thi Nau, a NLF cadre who had been operating an important Viet Cong radio. She was interrogated by a warrant officer at the task force base at Nui Dat before being handed over to the RVN authorities. During the interrogation, the warrant officer threatened to use 'the water treatment', forcing Nau to swallow about a cup of water before officers intervened. An investigation ordered by the task force commander found that the woman had not been physically hurt but that the interrogation had contravened approved procedures. The warrant officer was reprimanded and removed from interrogation tasks, which had not been part of his normal duties. His actions had been excessive and distasteful, but did not warrant description as water torture. The task force officers had quickly ended the improper action and ensured there was no repetition. When the story broke in the media in early 1968, the response by the new Prime Minister, Gorton, and the newest member of the ministry, the Minister for the Army, Phillip Lynch, was vacillating and ineffective, exacerbated by crudely flippant comments in Parliament. Their response, more than the incident itself, allowed the idea of Australians being involved in 'water torture' to take hold and to be cited for decades.[14]

Support for the war in Australia was also eroded by more soundly based criticisms, such as the number of Australian casualties caused by mines from the ill-conceived Dat Do minefield. Australians were also disturbed when they heard of Australian soldiers being involved in American-led operations outside Phuoc Tuy province: the general public shared the concern of military and political leaders over the heavy costs of the American tactics.

The greatest source of dissent, however, remained the system of selective conscription.[15] Defiance of the National Service Act, which was rare and generally regarded as aberrant in the early years, became more widespread. Anti-conscription groups continued the process that had begun with William White in 1966 of turning objectors to compulsory service into heroes and those who were punished for defiance into martyrs. One was John Zarb, who served ten months in Pentridge Prison in Melbourne because the Act did not recognise conscientious objection to a particular war. Another was Simon Townsend, whose persistent claims to be recognised as a conscientious objector on the grounds of pacifism were rejected by two magistrates and two judges. After he persisted in disobeying orders, he was sentenced by a court-martial to detention, and then to solitary confinement, at Holsworthy army base, near Sydney. There, like other offenders in military detention, he was restricted to a diet of bread and water, deprived of a mattress, and woken at half-hourly intervals during the night. This treatment was widely denounced.

The government handled these and other similar cases clumsily. Its attempts to amend the Act by increasing penalties for non-compliance and requiring universities and other institutions to disclose information about men eligible for the call-up led to the formation of a Committee in Defiance of the National Service Act. The CDNSA produced a

Statement of Defiance, supporting and encouraging young men not to register for national service and not to be coerced into a war that they believed to be immoral and unjust. To defy the National Service Act was itself a breach of the Crimes Act, but the thousands of signatories of the CDNSA Statement included leading members of both the moderate and militant wings of the protest movement, academics and politicians, the old left and the new left, professionals and working class, older clergy and young students. When the government declined to act against the signatories, members of the committee prosecuted each other; when defendants were found guilty and fined, the government again declined to act against those who refused to pay. By this tactic of self-prosecution, the CDNSA exposed the government's inability to punish large numbers of respectable citizens who declared that their consciences overruled its laws, and probably did more to undermine the government's authority than the militant students who provoked violent confrontations with police.

THE TASK FORCE 1968-69

In a considerable irony, public opinion was beginning to turn against the war just as the military commitment had reached its peak level of about 8000 personnel. Many of the initial problems, such as relations between army and air force, collaboration between infantry, artillery and armour, and the level of manpower and equipment assigned to signals and other technical needs, had been or were being resolved. The army recognised that the troop commitment had reached its peak, but had increasing confidence in its capacity and professionalism.

Nevertheless, tension remained between the competing demands on the force's limited resources, especially between pacification of villages and participation in operations against main force units, near or beyond the borders of Phuoc Tuy province. The army's leaders knew that there would never be sufficient resources, in troops and equipment, to meet all the demands placed on the force. Casualties from mines remained high, and the severe stress imposed on combat units was leading to morale problems and excessive consumption of alcohol. As first American, then Australian, attention turned to the challenges of 'Vietnamisation' and withdrawal, the task force began to feel the impact of serving in a conflict for which support was waning both in government and in the electorate.

THE TASK FORCE AND TET[16]

During 1968 and 1969 the principal emphasis in task force operations changed from pacification within Phuoc Tuy province to operations against the enemy's main force units, at and beyond the province borders. Although it did not foresee the scale and widespread nature of the Tet offensive, the American military command in January 1968 expected major attacks on Saigon and the nearby complex of United States and RVN military establishments at Bien Hoa and Long Binh. The air base at Bien Hoa was then the busiest airport in the world, while Long Binh housed a huge logistical base. The American command requested the task force to assist in the defence of the Bien Hoa–Long Binh complex, bringing Australian soldiers back to the area in which 1RAR had operated as part of the 173rd Airborne Brigade in 1965–66. This deployment outside the province of Phuoc Tuy was consistent with the terms of the United States–Australia military agreement, but initially caused some consternation in Canberra. Malcolm Fraser, the Minister for the Army, had repeatedly emphasised that the task force was committed to operating within Phuoc Tuy province. Army headquarters in Canberra finally approved the deployment, provided one of the three battalions remained at Nui Dat to ensure the security of Phuoc Tuy and the base itself.

The two battalions deployed on Operation Coburg for the defence of Bien Hoa–Long Binh, 2RAR and 7RAR, operated from two fire support bases, Fire Support Base (FSB) Andersen and FSB Harrison. Fire support bases, usually temporary constructions in enemy-dominated territory, were defended bases containing artillery batteries and usually the command post of an infantry battalion, located so that the artillery could support the infantry units operating in the surrounding area. This US Army concept would become an important feature of the Australian Army experience in Vietnam.

The two battalions deployed to Bien Hoa–Long Binh conducted reconnaissance-in-force operations in the last days of January, helping to disrupt the enemy plans. After the offensive started, while the world's attention was largely focused on the fighting in Saigon and Hue, the role of the Australians changed to that of intercepting enemy forces as they withdrew from the heavy fighting in Saigon. An entire enemy division passed by FSBs Andersen and Harrison – the Viet Cong 5th Division, including 274 and 275 Regiments with whom the Task Force had previously been in conflict in Phuoc Tuy province, including at the battle of Long Tan. The Australian battalions were involved in a number of engagements with their old foe.

Among the numerous operations conducted at this time was one carried out by C Company, 7RAR, which came to be known as the 'the battle of the bunkers'. Showing prodigious courage and skill in a three-day battle, the Australians assaulted and eventually captured a well-constructed and heavily defended bunker complex housing a large number of North Vietnamese Army soldiers. Unlike most of the major battles in which the Australian task force was involved, including Long Tan and others discussed later in this chapter, this engagement was initiated by the Australians. Because the action took place outside Phuoc Tuy province, with the attention of Australia and the rest of the world directed elsewhere, the men did not receive the awards that witnesses believed they deserved. Due recognition did not come until 2011, when a distinguished Australian novelist, Gerard Windsor, wrote *All Day*

Long the Noise of Battle, an evocative account of Australian soldiers in the Vietnam War.[17]

The Australian battalions committed to Operation Coburg continued their reconnaissance-in-force and other operations until the end of February. Their principal losses were suffered when the Viet Cong attacked FSB Andersen on 18 February, killing seven Australians and one American, and wounding 22 Australians and three Americans.

In Phuoc Tuy province itself, the enemy targets included the provincial capital, Ba Ria, and several smaller towns. The battalion that remained at Nui Dat, 3RAR, supported by the armoured personnel carriers of 3 Cavalry Regiment, played a major role in repelling the attack and driving another familiar enemy, the Viet Cong D445 Provincial Mobile Battalion, from Ba Ria. Despite their lack of training or experience in urban warfare, the Australians performed well. They clearly had the support of the local population in Ba Ria, but were not so warmly welcomed when they helped ARVN units to clear the smaller town of Long Dien.

In February political and military authorities in Australia confirmed that, while operations outside Phuoc Tuy province had always been envisaged, the task force would now have a 'wider combat role away from its operating base in Phuoc Tuy province'. This was based on the argument that the enemy's main force units had moved out of the province, leaving only D445 Provincial Mobile Battalion, which was regarded as significantly weaker, despite its attack on Ba Ria.

THE BATTLE OF CORAL-BALMORAL[18]

In the months after the Tet offensive, the Australian task force, under Brigadier Hughes, conducted cordon-and-search operations, as well as reconstruction work and civic action projects, to restore the security level in Phuoc Tuy province. In keeping with his more aggressive approach, Hughes undertook what the army's chief, Lieutenant General Daly, later described as an 'extraordinarily dangerous, difficult and costly' operation.[19] Operation Pinnaroo was directed at clearing Viet Cong bases in the Minh Dam Secret Zone in the Long Hai hills. Hughes committed two Australian battalions, armoured personnel carriers, tanks, artillery and engineers, with support from US Air Force B-52 bombers and American naval gunfire.

Opinions differ on the success of Operation Pinnaroo. The Australians penetrated the stronghold, destroyed a large number of bases and bunker systems, and seized or destroyed considerable amounts of weapons, munitions, stores and equipment, but at a high cost in casualties, many of which were caused by mines, probably lifted from the Australian minefield. The Australian troops were proud of what they achieved, but disappointed when the ARVN failed to consolidate the gains by providing sufficient troops to garrison the Long Hais and conduct aggressive operations in the area. The Viet Cong had suffered a major setback, but were able within weeks to return to their long-standing haven.

Operation Pinnaroo confirmed the widely held view that the costs of the Australian minefield outweighed whatever initial benefits it might have brought. Hughes started the process of trying to clear the minefield using the tanks. The first two methods that were attempted both failed, causing further casualties as well as severe damage to the tanks. The task force would have to live with the mounting costs of the minefield for years to come.

In April–May 1968 American, South Vietnamese, Australian, New Zealand and Thai forces combined in a major operation called Toan Thang (Complete Victory).[20] The original intention was to eliminate remaining enemy forces involved in the Tet offensive and to disrupt plans for a second offensive. The allied forces soon discovered that, while the Viet Cong had suffered heavy casualties during the Tet offensive, Hanoi had responded by raising the stakes. Not only were thousands of

PAVN troops sent to reinforce Viet Cong units but the PAVN had also infiltrated whole divisions. In early May the PAVN and PLAF launched a second offensive (sometimes referred to, somewhat misleadingly, as 'mini-Tet'), directed particularly at Saigon. The United States and the DRV were about to begin peace negotiations in Paris, and Hanoi evidently wished to portray Saigon as being under siege as negotiations began, just as Dien Bien Phu had been before the 1954 Geneva Conference. The civilian population of Saigon, in an apparent reprisal for its failure to respond to the expected popular uprising in February, was subjected to indiscriminate rocket attacks. The use of Soviet-supplied rockets against civilians and the widespread destruction of homes and buildings were described as 'barbarism' by the United Nations Secretary-General, U Thant, in his first criticism of the tactics employed by the PAVN and PLAF.[21]

The purpose of Operation Toan Thang was consequently changed to that of defence of Saigon and the Bien Hoa–Long Binh complex. The newly arrived Commander of the Australian Force Vietnam, Major General AL MacDonald, agreed with General Westmoreland's preference to use the Australian task force in conventional operations against the enemy's main force units in and around Saigon and Bien Hoa, rather than to employ them in pacification operations in Phuoc Tuy. This decision was confirmed by senior military and political authorities in Canberra.

As in February, the principal role of the task force was to operate from a series of fire support bases around Saigon and the Bien Hoa–Long Binh complex. The three infantry battalions were rotated so that at any one time two were engaged in operations in that region while the third attended to the security of the Nui Dat base. The RAR battalions were supported by artillery, armoured personnel carriers, engineers and tanks. For the first time the Australian Army was fighting against formed regiments of the North Vietnamese Army.

On 12 May, 1RAR, which had only recently arrived in-country, together with 3RAR and supporting units, occupied FSB Coral. The deployment was badly handled: reconnaissance had not been adequate; the assessment and distribution of intelligence on the enemy was seriously flawed; and neither the fly-in nor the establishment of the FSB and its defences was well coordinated. The Australians did not know that they were under close observation by the PAVN: the headquarters of the PAVN 7th Division was only a few kilometres distant. During the battalions' first night at Coral the PAVN mounted a major assault by several hundred well-trained, well-equipped and highly motivated troops, directed particularly at the artillery's howitzers and mortars. A combination of courage, skill, luck (the guns happened to be laid in the direction from which the attack was launched) and unorthodox tactics (including firing high explosive shells over open sights) enabled the soldiers to fight off the attack. The task force lost 11 soldiers killed and 28 wounded, including five killed and eight wounded from the mortar platoon, while the enemy lost 52 dead and one prisoner. Having learned a costly lesson, the task force improved its procedures in a form of deployment in which it had little previous experience.

Three days later the PAVN mounted another assault on FSB Coral, in which five Australian soldiers were killed and 19 wounded. At least 34 PAVN soldiers were known to be killed, and the bodies of others were removed from the battlefield. The Australians were deeply impressed by the determination and skills of the PAVN, whom they regarded as 'a race apart' from the local Viet Cong guerrillas in Phuoc Tuy.

Soon after this second attack, Brigadier Hughes took leave and his deputy, Colonel Donald Dunstan, came from Nui Dat to become acting commander of the task force. His first decision was to summon the tanks from Nui Dat to support the two battalions near Bien Hoa–Long Binh. The decision was courageous, as the enemy was known to have effective anti-tank weapons and tactics. For the first time since the Pacific campaign in the Second World War the Australian Army used tanks in close support of the infantry.

Dunstan's decision soon proved wise. 3RAR was ordered to move to another FSB, Balmoral, 4.5 kilometres north of Coral. On this occasion, the Australians knew that a PAVN regiment was located nearby. On the night of 25–26 May the PAVN mounted an assault on FSB Balmoral. The tanks contributed substantially to the defence of Balmoral, as they did in a subsequent attack on 28 May. The tanks also proved invaluable in operations outside the base, where the Australian infantry and armour were combined in operations against concealed bunkers.

The battles in and around FSBs Coral and Balmoral, for which the infantry, armoured and cavalry regiments involved were awarded the battle honour 'Coral–Balmoral', were among the most intense engagements of Australia's war in Vietnam. Australian units lost a total of 25 killed and nearly 100 wounded. They had inflicted heavy losses on the enemy, claiming more than 300 confirmed or probable kills as well as the destruction of enemy bases. These battles, even more than that at Long Tan, demonstrated that the war had changed in nature from that experienced by the first battalions in the task force in 1966 and 1967. The actions, which combined infantry and tanks against regular formations of the North Vietnamese Army, amounted to conventional warfare, radically different in nature from the counter-insurgency tactics in which Australian battalions were trained and which most commanders had sought to apply in Vietnam. The Australian battalions had, in effect, formed part of a large mobile reserve operating in depth against major enemy formations under direct American command – just what Westmoreland had long sought and what Wilton had tried to avoid.

TASK FORCE OPERATIONS FROM JULY 1968 TO DECEMBER 1969[22]

Having been seriously bloodied in the February and May offensives, the Viet Cong reverted to an earlier stage of insurgency in order to rebuild their positions in the rural areas. Security in Phuoc Tuy had deteriorated while the task force was operating out of the province, and much of its attention was directed towards recovering the position, especially in villages that had long been sympathetic to the insurgents. In mid-1968, when General Westmoreland left the position of commander of US forces in Vietnam to become the army's chief of staff in Washington, his successor, General Creighton Abrams, announced a new strategic approach known as 'One War', under which priority was to be given to pacification over main force operations. Ever since then, military historians and strategists have debated the respective merits of the strategies associated with Westmoreland and Abrams. The contrast, however, was far from absolute. The Australian task force came under the overall operational direction of the commander of II Field Force Vietnam (II FFV), responsible for the military direction of III Corps. Lieutenant General Julian Ewell, the commander of II FFV, while giving lip service to the directions from Abrams, remained a strong advocate of the strategy of attrition, as measured by the body count. Like Westmoreland in earlier years, Ewell pressed the Australians to give priority to aggressive actions designed to improve the kill ratio. This pressure created tensions with Australian task force commanders and difficulties for military and political leaders in Australia, where there was political criticism of the rising level of casualties. The public had been encouraged to believe that the Australians would operate only within Phuoc Tuy province, with an emphasis on pacification and civic action, rather than operating in close combination with American forces, which accepted casualty levels unacceptable in Australia.

From mid-1968 until the withdrawal of the task force in late 1971, the relative priority to be given to pacification and main force operations was a continuing source of contention, not only between Australian and American commanders but also between Australian officers. Each tactical approach had its advocates and its critics, with the balance of argument varying according to the state of the war, the changes in American strategic direction and its implementation and, not least, the strength and operational approach of the PAVN and PLAF forces. The commanders of the Australian Force Vietnam in 1967 and 1968, Major Generals Vincent and MacDonald, thought the task force was well suited to forward operations. Brigadier CMI 'Sandy' Pearson, who succeeded Hughes as task force commander in October 1968, continued his predecessor's approach for several months, mounting large-scale, reconnaissance-in-force operations at and beyond the borders of Phuoc Tuy province. Then, from May 1969, partly in response to General Abrams' revised strategy, he redirected the task force towards pacification in Phuoc Tuy province. Not all of his battalion commanders shared his view. Lieutenant Colonel Colin Khan (who later changed the spelling of his name to Kahn), who commanded 5RAR in its second tour, thought his principal aim was 'to kill the enemy, to destroy the main force fighting power'; until that was done, pacification was 'a waste of time'.[23] It was a different view from that taken by Lieutenant Colonel Warr, the commander of 5RAR in its first tour, as noted in Chapter 7.

While these debates among and between the Australian and American military commanders were taking place, the Australian task force continued to be heavily engaged in all its designated roles: pacification operations in Phuoc Tuy province; main force operations both in and beyond Phuoc Tuy; security operations around the Nui Dat base and along the major routes in Phuoc Tuy; civic action; and training the RVN forces. The only constant was that the task force, even with three battalions, tanks, artillery, engineers and other support units, never had sufficient resources to undertake all its expected tasks. Severe stress was placed on all ranks, from the task force commander to the private soldier. Many members of combat units spent more than 300 days of a one-year tour on operations 'outside the wire', and even when 'behind the wire' in Nui Dat total security could not be assumed.

THE BATTLE OF BINH BA[24]

In June 1969, while the task force was engaged in a major operation in Phuoc Tuy, two armoured vehicles were unexpectedly fired on from the village of Binh Ba. The village was known to be under communist domination, but at the time it was thought to house two PAVN platoons. In fact, an entire PAVN battalion was located there. The task force responded by deploying an under-strength infantry company, a troop of tanks and a troop of armoured personnel carriers. They received support from artillery and RAAF helicopter gunships, as well as an ARVN unit. What followed was a major battle in a substantial village, one of the few examples of Australian involvement in urban warfare in Vietnam other than the Ba Ria operation during the Tet offensive. The tanks, and the lessons the Australians had rapidly learned about collaboration between infantry and armour, proved invaluable. The PAVN lost about 99 killed in action, but a number of Vietnamese civilians were also killed. Some years later the incident was reported as an Australian atrocity. The Australians, who were responding to an unexpected provocation from the PAVN in the village, had received authorisation from the relevant RVN officials to engage the enemy, after civilians had been warned to leave.

By the middle of 1969 war correspondents were reporting critically on the casualty rate in the task force, especially on the number caused by mines believed to have been lifted from the Dat Do minefield. In May, June and July 1969, mines caused about half of the 270 casualties, including 31 soldiers killed, suffered by the task force. One explosion had virtually wiped out a platoon of 27 soldiers, killing three and leaving only four uninjured. Efforts by political and military leaders to deflect the criticism had little credibility. Attempts over two years to clear the minefield had only caused further casualties. In July the task force engineers improvised 'mine-killers' by fixing offset rollers to the rear of armoured personnel carriers fitted with additional armour plates.

This method proved relatively successful, but it took until 1970 before the minefield was declared to have been cleared.[25]

RAN AND RAAF COMMITMENTS 1968-69

While 1968 and 1969 saw some of the heaviest demands on the task force, including the major battles mentioned above, they also witnessed increasingly intense involvement for the RAN and RAAF units. When the government decided in October 1967 to commit a third battalion to the task force, it also doubled the number of Iroquois helicopters allocated to No. 9 Squadron from eight to 16. This commitment was met by purchasing a new and more capable model of Iroquois, so that the squadron's lift capacity was effectively quadrupled. In 1968 the RAAF contingent began developing its own version of helicopter gunships, dubbed 'Bushrangers', which became operational from 1969. To assist the RAAF to meet the demand for pilots, the New Zealand government increased its commitment of RNZAF pilots from one to four; in addition, eight RAN helicopter pilots also served with the RAAF squadron in 1968–69.[26] They operated separately from the pilots of the RAN Helicopter Flight Vietnam with the US Army's 135th Assault Helicopter Company, which in November 1968 moved its base from Camp Blackhorse to Bear Cat, 32 kilometres northeast of Saigon. These pilots flew an extraordinarily high number of sorties to support US, ARVN, Australian and Thai units.[27] The Caribous of No. 35 Squadron, which earned an enviable reputation for efficiency, increased the proportion of its missions in direct support of the Australian task force, although not to the extent that the army commanders would have liked.[28] The RAN clearance divers met intense and varied demands, as did the destroyers on the gun-line in the Gulf of Tonkin. The generally good relations between US and Australian forces were shaken by a 'friendly fire' incident in June 1968, when HMAS *Hobart*, on its second deployment, was mistakenly attacked by two US Air Force aircraft, killing two crew members, wounding several others, and causing extensive damage.[29] Although the Canberra bombers of No. 2 Squadron were regarded as obsolescent, their slow, level and low-altitude flying led to remarkably accurate bombing in comparison with the US dive-bombers.[30]

THE 1969 ELECTION[31]

Gorton considered calling an early general election in 1968, when his initial popularity would probably have won him a comfortable victory, but was dissuaded by opposition from the DLP and other electoral calculations. When the election was held in October 1969, the government's huge majority from the 1966 election no longer seemed impregnable. Public opinion was turning against the war, and especially against conscription. While much attention was given to the poll in August 1969 that indicated, for the first time, that more Australians wanted the government to withdraw troops from Vietnam than wanted them to remain, fewer noted a poll that suggested the commitment would have retained considerable support if it required only regular troops.

After President Nixon had begun to withdraw American troops and announced the 'Guam doctrine', the commitment of the United States to Southeast Asia was uncertain. The government had been vacillating over policy and seemed simply to hope that the war would end, without being able to say how or when. In his last months as Defence Minister, Fairhall was reported to have said that the war was 'inevitably moving towards an unpredictable end at an indefinite date'.[32] The

Liberal-Country Party coalition went to the election with foreign policies that echoed those of the Menzies and Holt governments in deference to the strength of conservative forces within the coalition and the DLP, but with a Prime Minister who was known to be uncomfortable with these views. Gorton promised to retain the national service system so that the army could maintain its nine-battalion strength. Defending the Vietnam commitment he said that Australia would not unilaterally withdraw its troops, but if the United States continued to reduce its military commitment he would ensure that Australia's forces were 'phased into' the American withdrawal. Somewhat contradictorily, he told an interviewer that, when the time came for withdrawal, Australia's three battalions would come home together, because a gradual withdrawal, one battalion at a time, would endanger the force. Gorton also promised to retain its military commitments in Malaysia and Singapore.

Since becoming leader of the Labor Party in 1967, Gough Whitlam had achieved considerable success in reforming the party's structures and policies, bringing it from the humiliating defeat of 1966 to give it a chance of victory that had seemed highly unlikely until shortly before the election. His Program, as he proudly called it, placed less emphasis on foreign policy than on social policy, appealing in particular to the rapidly growing outer suburbs of Sydney and Melbourne. After becoming leader, he maintained his approach of opposing the war, but with much less emotion than his predecessor, Calwell, or his left-wing colleagues, such as Dr Jim Cairns, Tom Uren and Clyde Cameron. He continued to emphasise the 'unwinnability' rather than the immorality of the war and to distance himself from the violent and extreme tactics of the militant left, while ensuring the support of all sectors of society who were opposed to, or simply weary of, the seemingly interminable war.

In late January 1968 Whitlam visited a number of Southeast Asian countries, including Vietnam, where he was subjected to intense pressure from the American military to accept their optimistic assessments of progress. Cameron later claimed that Whitlam was about to announce a change to Labor policy on Vietnam, but the Tet offensive erupted before he could take any such action.[33] Whatever the truth of this assertion, after the Tet offensive Whitlam was able to denounce the government's vacillations and divisions while saying little about the policies of a future Labor government. Official Labor policy for the 1969 election was that a Labor government would inform the United States that Australian troops would be phased out of Vietnam, with no specific timetable. In his policy speech Whitlam went further, promising that all Australian troops would be out of Vietnam by June 1970. Many observers thought this was unnecessarily precise, but it won support from those on the left who had doubted the strength of his opposition to the war.

Whitlam succeeded in neutralising the government's natural advantages of continuing prosperity and full employment during a minerals boom and the electorate's longstanding support for forward defence. His program of social and economic reforms, his courageous reorganisation of the party's structures, and his superiority as a campaigner, all in marked contrast to Gorton's leadership, came extremely close to achieving a remarkable victory. After a swing to Labor of 7.1 per cent, the government gained less than 50 per cent of the two-party preferred vote and its majority was cut from 39 to seven. It was effectively saved by DLP preferences in four Victorian seats. The swing in public opinion against the Vietnam War and conscription seemed only to strengthen the anti-communist views, and the electoral strength, of the DLP. Gordon Freeth's loss of his seat, after he had antagonised the DLP by a speech he had made in his brief tenure as Minister for External Affairs, only underlined the importance of this electoral consideration.

This was, in retrospect, a most unfortunate result. The electorate had neither unequivocally endorsed nor clearly rejected the policies that had sent Australian service personnel to a controversial war. Both sides of politics were seeking to end Australia's involvement, but the government's freedom of manoeuvre was constrained by the crucial importance of a party with about 10 per cent of the vote. The result ensured another three years of increasing division and uncertainty on the conservative side of politics.

— NINE —

SOCIAL DISSENT, POLITICAL DIVISION AND MILITARY WITHDRAWAL 1969–72

After his narrow election victory, Gorton reconstructed the Cabinet, appointing William McMahon as Minister for External Affairs and Malcolm Fraser as Minister for Defence. Australian policy and politics for the next three years would be dominated by the rivalries and ambitions of these three men.

McMahon was a skilful politician, but was mistrusted by many of his colleagues, not least for his close relations with the media empire of Sir Frank Packer, especially the journalist Alan Reid. Although a long-standing member of the FAD Committee, he was not noted for any particular contribution to foreign or defence policies, except in terms of their domestic political implications. McMahon achieved some of the diplomats' longstanding goals, including changing the name of the portfolio from External Affairs to Foreign Affairs and having responsibility for relations with the United Kingdom transferred from the Prime Minister to the Minister for Foreign Affairs. Moving McMahon from the Treasury to External Affairs was designed to reduce his influence, for Gorton continued to exclude the department and its minister from a major role in policy-making. McMahon became the willing focus for those in the parliamentary Liberal Party who were seeking to undermine Gorton's leadership.

Fraser was making a rapid rise in Liberal ranks. After ten years on the backbenches, he had been appointed to the low-ranking portfolio of Minister for the Army by Holt, then to the Cabinet as Minister for Education and Science in Gorton's first ministry. In Defence he quickly gained a reputation as an ambitious, forceful and interventionist minister, exerting more central control over the services and their ministers than his predecessors. Soon after taking the post he appointed Sir Arthur (1914–2001) Tange as secretary and permanent head of the department. Perhaps the most forceful public servant of his day, Tange had his own ideas, developed in his 11 years as head of External Affairs, on what Defence needed in order to become a better coordinated and more effective department. Fraser and Tange made a formidable combination as they set about imposing their will on a cumbersome and complex Defence bureaucracy.[1]

During the 18 months after Fraser's appointment as Minister for Defence, tensions developed in his relations with the army and with Gorton. While he was one of the few ministers willing and able to give a strong and well-argued defence of the Vietnam commitment, he liked to emphasise those aspects that were more acceptable to the electorate. As Minister for the Army he had developed a particular interest in the task force's civic action program in Phuoc Tuy province, but he suspected that the army did not share his enthusiasm. He also sought to have the army establish one of its proposed new task forces in Western Australia, a direction the army thought was based more on political than on military considerations. His interventions created tension with the Minister for the Army, Andrew Peacock, widely seen as a potential leader of the Liberal Party, and with the army's chief, Lieutenant General Daly. His relations with Gorton also soured during 1970, with the two men having a sharp difference of opinion on whether to call out the Pacific Islands Regiment in response to a political crisis in Papua New Guinea.

Divisions within the governing parties over Vietnam policy contributed to the personal tensions between groups of ministers, adding to the growing dissatisfaction with Gorton within the Liberal and Country parties. To add to Gorton's woes, at a half-Senate election in November 1970 the DLP gained its best result ever, winning more than 11 per cent of the vote and gaining seats while both the Liberal–Country Party coalition government and the Labor Party opposition lost seats. The DLP's strength reduced the government's freedom of manoeuvre, especially on matters that could be interpreted as weakness towards communism.

THE FIRST AUSTRALIAN WITHDRAWAL

After the October 1969 election, the conflicting pressures on the government over troop withdrawals mounted.[2] Fraser, supported by civilian officials in Defence and External Affairs, pressed his military advisers to end their opposition to the withdrawal of one of the three battalions in the task force. The military chiefs, led by Generals Wilton and Daly, maintained their stance. Although Gorton had said in his policy speech that Australia would be 'phased into' any further American withdrawal program, he had generally supported the army's 'one out, all out' approach, and had said that a proposal by Whitlam not to replace a battalion at the end of its tour would endanger the remaining two battalions. Much depended on Nixon's intentions, but the president did not share them with senior officials in Washington other than his national security adviser, Henry Kissinger, let alone with allied governments.

In December Gorton sent a personal message to Nixon asking for high-level discussions, hinting at a personal meeting between the two of them, so that Australian withdrawals could be based on joint planning rather than on Australian reactions at short notice to American announcements. The response came not from Nixon but from Marshall Green, a senior State Department official, who said that officials from both countries could begin talks about troop strengths. He did not express total opposition to Australian withdrawals, and even hinted that reduced strength could be offset by an increase in aid, such as the provision of better housing for the South Vietnamese forces. The Australians were disappointed and did not take up this opening. Days later, when Nixon announced a further reduction of 50 000 American troops, Gorton stated that some Australian troops would be withdrawn at the time of the next major American withdrawal. It was embarrassingly obvious that Australia was reacting to American announcements of which it had no prior notice.

Over the succeeding weeks the 'graduated withdrawal' approach favoured by Fraser and officials in External Affairs and Defence prevailed over the 'one out, all out' approach preferred by the chiefs and, until the last minute, by Gorton. In March Cabinet decided that the first Australian withdrawal would take place in November, when 8RAR would end its tour and not be replaced. Announcement of the decision would be withheld until April, allowing time for negotiations with the United States, South Vietnamese and New Zealand governments. As the combat role was wound down, Australia would expand its program for training South Vietnamese troops. During talks in Washington, Fraser was given no clear guidance on American plans for further withdrawals. The government was therefore surprised and embarrassed, once again, when Nixon announced on 20 April the withdrawal of a further 150 000 American troops. In a press statement and a hastily prepared speech to Parliament, Gorton announced that 8RAR would not be replaced in November and that Australia's training program for the South Vietnamese forces would be increased. He strongly defended the Vietnam policy along traditional lines and presented the withdrawal as demonstration of the success of Vietnamisation. Whitlam responded vigorously, asserting what was all too obvious — that the government was reacting not to the situation in South Vietnam but to the efforts of the United States government to extricate itself from what it now regarded as a tragic mistake.

THE FIRST MORATORIUM[3]

The impact of the anti-war movement in the United States had been blunted by the first withdrawals ordered by President Nixon, but in late 1969 the movement gathered its forces for a series of major demonstrations, especially a 'Moratorium' on 15 October. In American parlance, 'moratorium' usually meant an authorised delay in the payment of a debt, but the American anti-war movement adopted it to indicate a refusal to accept 'business as usual' as long as the war continued, while avoiding the negative connotations of 'strike'. The response in cities and towns across the United States far exceeded expectations, with hundreds of thousands, perhaps millions, of citizens attending anti-war rallies.

The concept of a major demonstration against the war, under the title of a Moratorium, was taken up by the protest movement in Australia. The initiative was taken by the long-established anti-war and anti-conscription groups whom the militants of the new left derided as 'peaceaucrats'. The organisational effort was intensive and extensive. State-based committees set up community groups based in workplaces, localities, university campuses, professions and trade unions. To the dismay of some authorities, school students were also involved. In the months leading to the first Moratorium in Australia, on 8 May 1970, the moderates and the militants tussled over the aims and tactics of the movement. For the most part, the moderates were able to retain control, but with some concessions to the militants over tactics. Conservative groups throughout the country, and some anti-war liberals, were seriously concerned at the potential for violence. Whitlam and other Labor leaders were careful not to endorse the Moratorium and to distance themselves from any action with the potential for violence. Dr Cairns, by contrast, became a principal spokesman for the Moratorium movement, exercising his considerable influence in favour of non-violent tactics.

Much of the emotional drive behind the Moratorium came from highly publicised events in the American war. In November 1969 news broke of what became known as the My Lai massacre. In March 1968 a company of American soldiers had killed between 350 and 500 civilians, including old men, women and children, in a hamlet known as My Lai 4. The savage killings had been accompanied by rapes and other brutalities. The impact of the story was increased by horrific photographs, which the Australian Moratorium organisers used extensively in their publicity material.

In March 1970 the Cambodian government of Prince Norodom Sihanouk was deposed in a coup led by the Prime Minister, General Lon Nol. Sihanouk had tried to maintain a balance between the Americans and the Vietnamese communists, who had established base areas in the east of Cambodia. Since 1969 the Americans had conducted a clandestine bombing campaign against these sanctuaries, but had not intervened with ground forces. On 30 April Nixon announced a joint American and South Vietnamese incursion into Cambodia, intended to clear the sanctuaries and destroy the communist operational headquarters there. Following news that American military involvement in Laos had been more extensive than Congress or the public had realised, the Cambodian incursion aroused protests on many university campuses, frequently violent and destructive. At Kent State University in Ohio, National Guardsmen opened fire on a student protest without orders and without warning, killing four young demonstrators.

Around the world these events, coming days before the Moratorium marches, raised the emotional commitment of anti-war protests. In the weeks leading to the Australian Moratorium, protesters made few references to the task force in Phuoc Tuy or even to conscription: the protest was against involvement in what was portrayed as an exceptionally brutal and futile war. The high point of the Moratorium movement was a march leading to a mass sit-down in Bourke Street, Melbourne, on 8 May 1970 by a crowd of about 70 000. The tone was set by Dr Cairns, who spoke of being 'opposed to violence, opposed to hate, opposed to every motive that has produced this terrible war'.⁴ The organisers had done their work well: about 400 Moratorium marshals, working with police who showed admirable restraint, ensured that no militants were able to break away and occupy a building or smash windows. After tension had built for weeks, the peaceful sit-down in Bourke Street by tens of thousands of citizens was cathartic. One reporter said that Melbourne had been:

> taken over with good humor, with laughter, with dignity and without violence. If that huge crowd had marched in America there would have been tear gas and National Guardsmen with masks and bayonets. If that crowd had marched in a banana republic there would have been tanks and anti-aircraft guns and yet another President. But Melbourne made you proud to be an Australian yesterday. Because it showed that in this country we can still make democracy work by turning out in the streets to exercise the right of dissent.⁵

The first Australian Moratorium was Dr Cairns' finest hour and the high point of success for the anti-war movement, but its long-term impact was less certain. Further demonstrations, including a second Moratorium in September, were characterised by violent confrontations between police and protesters and by dissension between the moderate and radical wings of the protest movement. While conscious that they were losing the middle ground of political opinion, the supporters of the Vietnam commitment saw no reason to change their minds. Whatever his private thoughts may have been, Gorton continued to endorse the war, saying that the government's policy was determined at the ballot box, not on the streets. Given the government's extremely slender victory at the election, it was not an entirely convincing response. From this time on, the conservative side of politics spoke less about the war itself and more about the perceived threat to 'law and order' from the tactics of the militants.

TASK FORCE OPERATIONS 1969-70

The fifth task force commander, Brigadier SP Weir, served from September 1969 to May 1970.[6] Described by one of the six battalion commanders who served under him as 'tough, hard, harsh and abrasive',[7] he soon changed the task force's priority away from pacification operations around the populated areas to operations to seek and destroy Viet Cong main force concentrations and bases in the more remote parts of the province. When it appeared that the main force elements had been driven from the province, Weir directed the task force's efforts towards the local guerrilla forces in the more populated areas. In the nine months of his command, the task force conducted 21 major operations, often of 30 days each, of which 14 were reconnaissance-and-ambush and five were reconnaissance-in-force (an alternative term for 'search-and-destroy' operations). Although the task force had three battalions throughout his tour, Weir operated under the constant threat of a partial withdrawal: the official announcement of the reduction to two battalions came in the last weeks of his time in Vietnam. The commander of II FFV, Lieutenant General Ewell, continued to press the Australians for aggressive action to achieve a high body count, while Weir had been warned by Daly to keep the casualty rate down, especially from mines and accidents. The toll from mines, generally believed to have come from the Dat Do minefield, remained high throughout 1969 and 1970. The severe stress of these competing demands on his limited resources told heavily on Weir, whose outbursts of rage led senior officers to question his fitness for his task.[8] The stress of the long and arduous operations also took its toll on those under his command.

By mid-1970, much appeared to have been achieved. Enemy action had been greatly reduced; roads and bridges built under the civic action program were opening up commerce; and the task force was making some headway in training the ARVN 18th Division. On the face of it, conditions seemed favourable to the program of 'Vietnamisation', under which the South Vietnamese would take over increasing responsibility. Nevertheless, the Viet Cong infrastructure in the villages was still firmly entrenched and able to control much of the province, at least by night. The Minh Dam Secret Zone in the Long Hai hills remained a safe haven for the guerrillas.

In these respects Phuoc Tuy was typical of much of South Vietnam. Despite the failure of the offensives of 1968 Le Duan, who had been Secretary-General of the communist party in Hanoi since 1960 and who had been the dominant figure in the politburo even before Ho Chi Minh's death on 2 September 1969, had not changed his goals. The Viet Cong, still recuperating from their heavy losses in 1968, resorted once more to small-scale guerrilla warfare, aimed at causing American and allied casualties that would increase the pressure for further troop withdrawals. Meanwhile, the PAVN built up its conventional forces in North Vietnam, with modern weapons including Soviet long-range artillery and T-54 tanks, and developed its logistic supply routes through Laos and Cambodia in preparation for a major conventional assault. The ARVN had been built up to one of the largest and best-equipped armies in the world, but it suffered from poor training and leadership, corruption among the senior commanders, high desertion rates, and confused command and logistic structures. The Australian commanders held grave doubts that the ARVN units could withstand an attack from the PAVN without the continuing support of the American and allied forces.

In this atmosphere Weir's successor as task force commander, Brigadier WG 'Bill' Henderson, adopted a different style of command and concept of operations.[9] In place of the large reconnaissance-in-force operations, which had often led to costly actions against enemy bunker systems, Henderson concentrated on local pacification and population security. In particular, he encouraged the tactic of 'close ambushing' around the villages, which had been developed by 8RAR under Lieutenant Colonel Kevin O'Neill. Unlike Weir, Henderson had good relations with his staff and devolved more authority to the battalion commanders. After 8RAR departed, the two remaining battalions were each given a separate area of responsibility, within which they could develop links with the local Vietnamese officials. Unlike Hughes and Weir, Henderson believed that the primary role of the SAS squadron should be reconnaissance; to obtain information on the enemy rather than carry out 'hit and run' actions designed to achieve a high body count. In this respect change came slowly. By one account, it was only under Henderson's successor that the SAS began providing information on which the task force could base major operations.[10]

As 8RAR departed in October 1970, Henderson told the press: 'Withdrawal will merely mean that we will have to work very much harder than at the moment, which is already pretty hard'. It was a simple statement of fact. Two battalions (further reduced by the withdrawal of one of the two New Zealand rifle companies) had to patrol the area, about two-thirds of Phuoc Tuy province, that had previously been covered by three. The units sent on patrols were reduced in size and stayed longer. Some rifle companies spent 60 days 'outside the wire' almost without respite. Base and administrative troops were used for local defence. Despite the claims being made for 'Vietnamisation', the South Vietnamese forces were not ready to take up the load. Henderson's comments nevertheless created a political controversy. Gorton, Peacock and army spokesmen made confusing and contradictory statements on whether the role of the task force had been changed. The brief controversy gave another weapon to the critics of the commitment, as they denounced 'the hypocrisy and dishonesty' of the government's 'ever-changing rationale for a military presence in Vietnam'.[11]

The threat and then the reality of the partial withdrawal of troops contributed to a perceptible decline in morale in the force. During 1970 there had also been a noticeable increase in incidents at Nui Dat related to boredom and frustration in combat units as well as among those with duties at the base or at Vung Tau. The feeling grew among the soldiers that the community in Australia knew and cared little about what they were doing: all the media coverage was about the Moratorium marches and other protests against the war. Although not as severe as in the American forces, disillusion about involvement in a war that was losing popular support undermined morale and discipline. In the United States, a group of Vietnam Veterans Against the War organised a major protest. One of their principal organisers, John Kerry, asked: 'How do you ask a man to be the last man to die for a mistake?' Something of the same feeling, less organised and less clearly articulated, was circulating among the Australian troops.[12]

Soldiers felt even stronger frustration and anger over the deaths and injuries caused by mines from what some were now cynically calling 'the Dat Do mine store'. The distress caused by mine casualties was felt acutely not only by the infantrymen but also by the crews of the armoured vehicles, including the tanks but most especially the armoured personnel carriers. The threat posed by mines, and the sight of the injuries they caused, had an enduring impact on the minds of private soldiers and their commanders.[13]

In the American forces, abuse of marijuana, heroin and other illicit drugs became a major problem. For the Australian forces in Nui Dat and Vung Tau, the drug of choice was alcohol. Excessive consumption of alcohol had been a major concern for the army hierarchy for several years, but no satisfactory solution was found. The quantities of beer consumed at the canteens were prodigious. A limit of two cans per man per day was imposed, but it was easily circumvented and the ration was cumulative, so that a soldier could return from a demanding 20-day patrol carrying a heavy load in enervating heat and be entitled to 40 cans.[14]

In 1970 the combination of deteriorating morale and easy access to alcohol led to 'a steady stream of injuries from accidental weapon discharges, self-inflicted wounds and even suicide attempts'.[15] On Christmas Day 1970, the medical staff at Nui Dat encountered 'an epidemic' of injuries from alcohol-related fights and accidents. That evening a private, very drunk, fired shots into a sergeants' mess, killing two and seriously wounding a third. This was the third fatal incident of 'fragging' in the Australian force between 1967 and 1971; the two previous occasions had caused the deaths of two officers. A common factor in all fatal or serious incidents was 'excessive and uncontrolled drinking' in Nui Dat and Vung Tau.

THE SECOND WITHDRAWAL, THE CIVIC ACTION CRISIS AND A NEW PRIME MINISTER[16]

After the first withdrawal of Australian troops was announced in early 1970 and put into effect at the end of the year, the crucial question surrounding the Vietnam commitment was the rate of withdrawal. The government had to find the right balance: if the rate were too slow, it would prompt further dissent and protests; if it were too fast, it could precipitate an embarrassing deterioration in South Vietnam's military position. There was little enthusiasm left for the commitment. Even longstanding supporters of the war were looking to end the agony, while a series of incidents at home and abroad served to increase the government's embarrassment. The Liberal–Country Party coalition, which had committed combat troops to the war in 1965 and had received a strong electoral endorsement in 1966, was now tired, divided and increasingly out of touch. Many of its supporters wanted an end to a war that had become a huge liability, but withdrawals had to be coordinated with the American administration, which was secretive about its plans and responding to its own domestic political pressures. The task force was obliged to maintain a high level of operations, while coping with the additional strains imposed by the withdrawal of some of its forces, the likelihood of further withdrawals, and the growing sense that it no longer had the support of the government or the people.

Early in 1971 the Minister for Defence, Malcolm Fraser, told Cabinet that President Nixon was expected to announce another American troop withdrawal in April. Cabinet accepted Fraser's recommendation that, before being seen once again to be reacting to American decisions, Australia should announce the withdrawal of about 1000 men. The task force would retain its two battalions but lose the tank squadron and other combat and support elements, a total of about 650 men. The navy would withdraw 45 men serving with an American helicopter company and the six-man clearance diving team, while the air force would bring back the squadron of Canberra bombers (with 280 men) and part of the squadron of Caribou transport aircraft (with 44 men). The total Australian commitment, which had been around 8000 at its peak between 1968 and 1970, would now be down to around 6000.

This decision had been endorsed by Cabinet but not announced, pending discussions with the Americans and the South Vietnamese, when a minor administrative matter in Vietnam triggered a major political explosion in Canberra. Preparing for the possibility that the entire task force might be withdrawn at short notice, the Australian military staff in Saigon issued guidelines that discouraged new civic action projects that might have to be abandoned in the event of a withdrawal. The document was leaked to an Australian Broadcasting Commission (ABC) journalist and reported in terms that suggested that the army was abandoning its civic action program. The story ignited the smouldering tensions between Fraser and the army and between Fraser and Gorton. Fraser had for some time given briefings to journalists, leading to unattributed stories critical of the army's handling of civic action in Vietnam. Following the ABC report from Saigon, more such stories appeared, leading to a media furore, with attention centring on Fraser, Gorton and the army's chief, Daly. The affair culminated when Fraser resigned from Cabinet, making a statement to Parliament on 9 March denouncing Gorton as unfit to be Prime Minister. On the following day, at a meeting of the parliamentary Liberal Party, a vote of confidence in Gorton was tied. Knowing his position was untenable, Gorton exercised a casting vote against himself and vacated the leadership. His longstanding rival, William McMahon, won the leadership and therefore became Prime Minister. (John McEwen, who had vetoed McMahon's appointment as Prime Minister after Holt's death, had resigned from politics a few weeks earlier, and the Country Party by this time regarded McMahon as at least preferable to Gorton.) In another extraordinary turn, Gorton then stood for and won the position of deputy leader of the Liberal Party. Exercising the deputy leader's privilege of choosing his portfolio, he became Minister of Defence, the position that Fraser had just resigned. McMahon reshuffled the Cabinet, removing or demoting many of Gorton's supporters, including Leslie Bury, who was moved from the Treasury to Foreign Affairs with the Cabinet ranking of eleventh. With Gorton in Defence, Bury in Foreign Affairs and Fraser on the backbench, the McMahon government had few prospects of giving clear and coordinated direction to foreign and defence policy.

In one of his first major statements as Prime Minister, McMahon announced the withdrawal of about 1000 men, which had been decided when Gorton had been Prime Minister. As Minister for Defence, Gorton undertook the proposed consultations with Vietnamese and American authorities in Saigon. They accepted the Australian decision, while Gorton promised that the two battalions in the task force would remain at least until the end of the year.

THE PENTAGON PAPERS[17]

McMahon's announcement served its intended political purpose, reducing the domestic pressure on the Australian government after Nixon made his expected announcement of a further withdrawal of American forces. It also reduced the impact of the protest movement, which organised a third Moratorium in the form of a series of demonstrations in April, May and June. By this time the factional tensions within the movement, especially between the moderate and radical wings, were increasingly obvious. The moderates were able to retain control over the Maoists, Trotskyites and others on the far left, but only by adopting more radical aims and tactics than those they had previously countenanced. Moreover, an increasing proportion of the energy of the more constructive protesters, both reformers and radicals, was directed away from the war and conscription towards other causes, especially a new wave of feminism.

In June 1971 political debate in the United States was dominated by the publication of the Pentagon Papers, the study that, as noted in Chapter 8, had been commissioned by Robert McNamara in 1967 and presented to his successor as Secretary of Defense, Clark Clifford, in 1968. One of the officials working on the project, Daniel Ellsberg, leaked the 47 volumes, including 3000 pages of analysis and 4000 pages of documents, to the *New York Times*, which began to publish extracts in June. The Nixon administration's attempts to prevent publication were overruled by a special sitting of the Supreme Court. Ellsberg's concern, and the theme of much of the controversy in the United States, was that successive administrations in Washington had deceived the American people by publicly asserting that the war had been going well when they knew that the political and military position of the Republic of Vietnam was close to terminal. Much of the debate in the United States was focused on the wisdom of the Vietnam policies pursued by the Kennedy and Johnson administrations, the veracity of their public statements, and the right of the press to print classified documents on major questions of national security.

In Australia the Opposition and the media concentrated overwhelmingly on a single, limited issue – whether the Menzies government had deceived the Australian people over the request that it claimed to have received from the Saigon government at the time of the commitment of the first battalion of Australian combat troops in 1965. In Washington this matter had been handled by the State Department and the White House rather than the Pentagon, but one document in the Pentagon Papers implied that the Americans had generated the request from the RVN government for an Australian battalion. This rekindled the concerns expressed by some critics of the commitment in 1965. In response, the government was able to point to several requests for assistance from RVN governments in the preceding years, as well as the authority of the RVN Prime Minister in April 1965 to say that Australia was 'in receipt of a request' from Saigon. Moreover, Menzies' public statements had made it abundantly clear that the commitment had been made in the context of the Australian–American alliance. Menzies emerged reluctantly from retirement to deny that he had lied to Parliament in announcing the commitment. Gorton said that he was surprised that so much attention was given to legal and diplomatic issues rather than the fundamental question of whether the commitment was in Australia's national interests: the comment was disregarded. McMahon unwisely reminded the public that he was the only member of the 1965 FAD Committee still in active political life. While Menzies' denial was generally accepted, the media debate served only to create more pressure for the withdrawal of Australian troops and to diminish McMahon's authority.

In mid-1971, even before the publication of the Pentagon Papers, McMahon told senior officials that he wanted 'new thought' to be given to both the Vietnam commitment and the national service scheme.[18] After consulting allies, the Defence Committee recommended a program, to be announced in October 1971, which envisaged that the task force's remaining two battalions would be relieved without replacement in February and May 1972. By August 1972, almost all troops would be out of Vietnam, except for the Training Team and possibly a civic action unit. While presented in the context of the military security of Phuoc Tuy and South Vietnam, the withdrawal program was obviously framed with close attention to political pressures from both allies and the Australian electorate. It would have kept the promise to Saigon and Washington not to withdraw before the end of 1971, while enabling McMahon to minimise the impact of Vietnam on the election due by the end of 1972.

Before this timetable for Australian withdrawal could be implemented, it was overtaken by remarkable and unexpected events. In July 1971 Whitlam visited the People's Republic of China, where he was publicly received by Premier Zhou Enlai. To undertake this mission was a considerable gamble for an Opposition leader, but Whitlam had reason to think that Australia was falling behind other Western nations by its rigid adherence to the policy of non-recognition of the government in Beijing. Canada's establishment of diplomatic relations with Beijing in 1970 was threatening Australia's lucrative wheat exports to China. A number of other countries had followed Canada's example, others were known to be moving in that direction, and there were indications that even the United States and China were seeking a new and more positive relationship. Nevertheless, McMahon denounced Whitlam's initiative, telling a Liberal Party meeting that it was 'incredible that at a time when Australian soldiers are still engaged in Vietnam, the leader of the Labor Party is becoming a spokesman for those against whom we are fighting'.[19] Four days later, Nixon shocked the world when he announced that he had accepted an invitation to visit China. It emerged that his influential national security adviser, Henry Kissinger, had been in China at the same time as Whitlam, negotiating the new opening. Once again, McMahon had been embarrassed, while Whitlam appeared to be in touch with the tide of international affairs. Even though McMahon had shown his speech to the Americans before delivery, he had been given no hint of the Nixon–Kissinger initiative.

McMahon's association of China with 'those against whom we are fighting' was an echo of the ill-advised statement by Menzies in 1965 that the commitment in Vietnam was intended to counter 'a thrust by Communist China between the Indian and Pacific Oceans'. Whatever Australians and Americans had believed at that time, it was no longer relevant to thinking in Washington. Nixon and Kissinger had long indicated that they regarded Hanoi, not Beijing, as the enemy in Vietnam. But the McMahon government evidently decided that the 'Nixon shock' might well be followed by further withdrawals of American forces from Vietnam, and that Australia should accelerate its withdrawal accordingly. Days after the Nixon announcement, the government decided that the two battalions of the task force would be withdrawn in October and December 1971, contrary to the assurances given to American and South Vietnamese authorities earlier in the year. On 18 August, the fifth anniversary of the battle of Long Tan, McMahon announced that all remaining combat forces would be withdrawn from Vietnam, and most would be 'home in Australia by Christmas'. The RVN authorities had not been consulted and were given only two days' notice.

As Minister for Defence, Gorton made several public statements indicating his preference for a strategic policy based on continental defence rather than forward defence. When he took the same approach in Cabinet, he received no support. With the need for American support and stability in Southeast Asia in mind, ministers wanted to adhere to forward defence as long as possible, regarding continental defence, and especially 'fortress Australia', as financially and politically undesirable. In August Gorton published the first in a series of newspaper articles in response to a book by the journalist Alan Reid. McMahon regarded the article as a breach of Cabinet solidarity: he sacked Gorton and installed David Fairbairn, a long-time critic of Gorton, as Minister for Defence. A few days earlier he had sacked Bury from Foreign Affairs and replaced him with Nigel Bowen.[20] Fraser was brought back to the Cabinet, but as Minister for Education and Science. For the first time in several years, the Prime Minister, Foreign Minister and Defence Minister were of one mind, but they were not a conspicuously successful team. When McMahon made the expected visit to the White House, he could claim few achievements and his speech at the formal dinner was reported as unduly long and embarrassingly fulsome. Fortunately for McMahon, more attention was given to the daring dress worn by his glamorous wife.

The government agreed at this time to train Cambodian forces in camps in Phuoc Tuy province. This was consistent with the stated change of emphasis away from combat operations to training and advisory roles, but the decision and its announcement were ineptly handled. McMahon was mocked as much by the Gorton supporters in the Liberal Party as by the media and the Opposition. One of his Liberal Party critics, James Killen, described the government's performance as 'a grand imperial display of bungling'.[21] McMahon's reputation for incompetence overshadowed diplomatic achievements for which he might otherwise have gained some credit, such as the successful conclusion of the Five Power Defence Agreement after long and difficult negotiations with Malaysia, Singapore, Britain and New Zealand.

By this time the protest movement was descending into further bitter divisions between radicals and reformists. With the imminent withdrawal of Australian troops, most of the moderate reformers felt their work had been done. The new left pressed for radical changes to Australian society, but with little support. As in the early days of the war, anti-war protests were smaller but more violent.

As part of his 'new thought' on the war and conscription, designed to strengthen the government's position before the 1972 election, McMahon announced that national servicemen would serve 18 months, not two years. This was too little to counter the increasing unpopularity of the scheme. Even the highly respected Governor of New South Wales, Sir Roden Cutler VC, questioned its relevance. Considerable media attention was given to some episodes in which draft resisters managed to avoid arrest and embarrass the authorities trying to enforce the National Service Act. To the government's frustration, these incidents drew far more attention than the fact that those who actively avoided the draft were far outnumbered by those who had volunteered to undertake national service. In 1970–71, for example, nearly 500 men had volunteered for national service after being balloted out or granted indefinite deferment, and another 255 had volunteered at the age of 18 years and nine months under a provision of the Act that was seldom publicised. By contrast, only 62 men had failed to report for service. A year later, the Minister for Labour and National Service reported that 442 men had volunteered for national service, while 65 had failed to report without due cause.[22]

OPERATING UNDER A WITHDRAWAL 1971-72[23]

For the task force, 1971 was exceptionally stressful. Having been reduced to two battalions since the end of 1970, it was still required to maintain a highly demanding level of operations. The soldiers' task was made more hazardous when the Centurion tanks were withdrawn in June and July in accordance with the government's decision in March. These were replaced with 'fire support vehicles', a more heavily armoured version of the armoured personnel carriers, but these were unsatisfactory substitutes. They frequently became bogged or lost their tracks, and their guns caused severe noise and blast problems for their drivers. The infantrymen greatly regretted the absence of tanks and the inadequacies of the fire support vehicles when encountering the enemy's reinforced and well-disguised bunker systems.[24]

In late 1970 and early 1971 there had been few signs of enemy activity in Phuoc Tuy, but in March and April main force elements returned to their base areas in the north of the province and just across the border in Long Khanh province. In the view of the last commander of the task force, Brigadier Bruce McDonald, the close ambushing and other pacification operations that his predecessor, Brigadier Henderson, had conducted in and around the main populated areas had been effective. McDonald redirected the task force's efforts towards targeting the main force units reasserting themselves around the northern borders of Phuoc Tuy.[25] This required the last two battalions to serve in the task force, 3RAR and 4RAR/NZ (ANZAC), to carry out a heavy program of aggressive patrols without the support of tanks and with units that were under-strength because of illness, injuries, leave, and the withdrawal of individual national servicemen who had completed their required time. The field strength of some rifle companies in 3RAR, for example, fell from 125 to 85 men; one company had been on operations for 60 days before it was able to take leave.[26]

In September, after McMahon had announced the withdrawal of all combat forces before Christmas, 4RAR/NZ conducted Operation Ivanhoe against an NVA main force regiment, which resulted in 'the battle of Nui Le'. With the support of massive artillery and air support, the ANZAC battalion and a South Vietnamese unit assaulted a major bunker position. In a manner reminiscent of some of the encounters earlier in the Australian experience, the enemy did not withdraw as had been expected but counter-attacked. One Australian company came close to being overrun. Five soldiers of 4RAR/NZ, including four national servicemen, were killed, and 30 were wounded, including at least 19 national servicemen, one New Zealander and four members of the APC crews. This costly operation, coming so close to the withdrawal of all combat troops and after official assurances that Phuoc Tuy was secure, was strongly criticised in Australia. As in the early years of the commitment, the public did not expect Australian soldiers to be involved in large and costly conventional operations at or beyond the borders of Phuoc Tuy province.

The army itself was not convinced of the value of such operations. While McDonald argued that enemy main forces had been engaged and ejected when they tried to enter Phuoc Tuy, the last Commander of the Australian Force Vietnam, Major General Donald Dunstan, thought that the operations had been 'rather futile' and the task force would have been better advised to concentrate on building up the South Vietnamese forces in and around the population centres. Dunstan was probably right: the communists were rebuilding their forces and awaiting the withdrawal of Australian and other allied forces in preparation for a major offensive in 1972. By chasing the main force elements, rather than concentrating on the security of population centres, the Australians may have fallen into an enemy trap.[27]

INCREASING THE ADVISORY ROLE 1971-72[28]

The policy of 'Vietnamisation' coupled the withdrawal of American, Australian and other combat forces with an increased effort to train and develop the South Vietnamese forces so that they could stand on their own. The first announcement of the withdrawal of some Australian forces, announced by Gorton in April 1970, stated that Australia would contribute a number of Mobile Advisory and Training Teams (MATTs), to work with the Regional Force (RF) and Popular Force (PF) units, and that consideration was being given to building a training centre for territorial forces on the part of the Nui Dat base to be vacated by the battalion that was not being replaced. This idea had been raised by Malcolm Fraser during his discussions with Vietnamese authorities before the announcement of the first withdrawal. Fraser knew that an advisory role was more acceptable to the Australian public than large-scale, and often costly, operations away from the task force base. In 1970 and 1971, as the task force adjusted from three battalions to two, the Australian force placed an increasing effort into working with the South Vietnamese units. Combined operations were mounted with RF companies; a training centre, known as the Jungle Warfare Training Centre (JWTC), was established at Nui Dat; and 15 MATTs were established. To make this possible the AATTV was doubled in size to 200 men, including corporals as well as officers and warrant officers. Instead of operating across South Vietnam giving operational advice to ARVN and Special Forces units, AATTV members were concentrated in Phuoc Tuy province to establish the MATTs and instruct at the JWTC.

Many of the soldiers felt that these efforts, however well intentioned, were a misplaced use of the AATTV's skills and experience, designed to meet the political needs of the Australian and South Vietnamese governments rather than the demands of the military situation.

The commander of the AATTV in 1970, Lieutenant Colonel RDF Lloyd, believed that there were already enough training centres in South Vietnam. The real need, in his view, was for the Australian advisory effort to be upgraded but integrated into the American structures. The Australians saw little point in training South Vietnamese forces in Australian techniques that they were unlikely to use in operations. They believed that the training of the Regional Force units, who were poorly motivated and reluctant to leave their bases to engage with the enemy, had at best a marginal effect on their standards. The pressure to create 15 MATTs in Phuoc Tuy was also misplaced: there were so many teams that, as one AATTV member put it, the province was saturated and the MATTs were more static than mobile.[29]

Matters were only slightly improved when the RF and PF forces attending the centre were replaced by the regular soldiers of the ARVN. Over two years, about 1500 South Vietnamese soldiers were trained by the Australians. Nui Dat was found to be unsuitable and the Australian effort was relocated to a previously established training centre at Van Kiep, near Ba Ria. In 1971–72 the AATTV was also allocated to train Cambodian soldiers of the Forces Armées Nationales Khmers (FANK) at training centres in Phuoc Tuy. Despite their efforts, the standards of these units remained alarmingly low. Initially, many were 'boy soldiers', barely in their teens, until public pressure in Australia ended their inclusion. By the time this commitment ended in November 1972, the Australians feared for the future of the untrained boys.[30]

THE WITHDRAWAL OF RAN AND RAAF FORCES

The RAN and RAAF units serving outside Phuoc Tuy province were also affected by 'Vietnamisation' and the impending allied withdrawal.

For the most part, there was little reduction in the intensity of their operations, but they were more frequently required to serve in support of ARVN units. The RAN helicopter pilots, for example, flew numerous missions in support of several ARVN divisions until the last contingent of the RANHFV was withdrawn in June 1971.[31] The RAN clearance divers also maintained a heavy workload until shortly before their withdrawal in April–May 1971.[32] The last of the RAN destroyers on the gun-line in the Gulf of Tonkin, HMAS *Brisbane*, did not end its tour until October 1971. In mid-1971 it had provided naval gunfire support to the 1st ARVN Division, one of the ARVN's most competent formations, but for the most part *Brisbane* and its sister ships had supported US Army and Marine units.[33] The Canberra bombers of RAAF's No. 2 Squadron continued to provide accurate bombing support to South Vietnamese as well as American forces. The squadron suffered no losses until November 1970 and March 1971, in large measure because the government directed that its operations be confined to South Vietnam. Contrary to some later claims, historian Chris Coulthard-Clark concluded that any interventions into North Vietnamese or Laotian airspace were unintended accidents.[34] As part of the graduated withdrawal of Australian forces, the strength of No. 35 Squadron of Caribous was reduced in June 1971 from seven aircraft to four. The last of the Caribous departed in February 1972, more than seven years after the arrival of the RTFV in August 1964.[35]

THE EASTER OFFENSIVE

While the public and the media were absorbed in domestic political controversies in 1972, few Australians noticed a pronounced change in the nature of the war itself. In March 1972 the North Vietnamese mounted what became known as 'the Easter offensive' against the south, the first since the Tet offensive of 1968. The Viet Cong of the mid-1960s had been severely weakened in the Tet offensive and subsequent operations: the communists' greatest strength now lay with the main force elements of the PAVN, which was one of the largest armies in the world. For years, Australians, Americans and others had debated whether the conflict in Vietnam was essentially a southern rebellion or an assault instigated and implemented by the north. The Easter offensive was clearly a conventional invasion of the south by the north, but few in Australia noticed or cared. With most American and allied ground forces now withdrawn, the offensive made major advances, until President Nixon ordered an increased level of air attacks against the north. He also took the highly controversial decision to mine the entrances to Haiphong and other ports in North Vietnam to restrict the entry of supplies, especially from the Soviet Union.

The offensive was eventually defeated by the ARVN, but only with the aid of massive American air support and a strategic error by General Giap, who attempted to achieve victory on three separate fronts. In Phuoc Tuy province the residual Australian force of about 150 soldiers, including about 60 advisers training South Vietnamese and Cambodian forces, could do little but watch the generally poor performance of the ARVN and FANK units. The army felt that the Australian force had outlived its usefulness, but the government insisted that no plans even be prepared for its withdrawal. The Australian commitment had become a token military presence, intended to encourage the United States to continue the air and logistic support without which the Republic of Vietnam could not survive.

— : —

After the McMahon government's numerous mistakes and embarrassments, especially in foreign affairs, the 1972 election result was surprising not so much for the Labor victory as for its narrow margin. Even after 23 consecutive years in office and their association with the longest and most controversial war of the 20th century, the conservative parties retained substantial support. McMahon's reiteration of traditional policies and attitudes, together with an irresponsibly generous 1972 budget, proved more successful than many expected. The conservative parties won seats in Western Australia and South Australia, but the swing towards Labor in the expanding suburbs of the major cities on the eastern seaboard gave it an overall majority of nine in the House of Representatives. The Labor campaign slogan, 'It's Time', captured the mood of enough Australians to bring the party out of the political wilderness.

— TEN —

THE WHITLAM GOVERNMENT AND THE END OF THE VIETNAM WAR 1972-75

The Whitlam Labor government that was elected in December 1972 and re-elected in May 1974 is often remembered as exemplifying how a reformist government should not perform. Its tenure started with a rapid flurry of decisions, both symbolic and substantive, in its earliest days and ended in a major political and constitutional crisis, culminating in November 1975 with the first ever dismissal of an elected government by the Governor-General. During those three years there seemed to be an endless series of scandals and controversies. The government's major flaws were twofold. One was structural: the indiscipline, inexperience and excessive enthusiasm of ministers and their close associates were exacerbated by the decision that all 27 ministers would sit in Cabinet, with no outer ministry, and that Cabinet could be overruled by Caucus. The other concerned economic policy. The government's handling of the economy was particularly inept, as Whitlam and many of his ministers were reluctant to acknowledge that 'the Program' developed before the 1969 election, at the end of the long post-war boom, could no longer be afforded after the 1973 'oil shock', when producers in the Middle East raised their prices sharply, and amid the 'stagflation' – the combination of stagnant growth and inflation – that afflicted all Western economies in the 1970s. The scandals and turmoil of these three years have tended to obscure the fact that the Whitlam government introduced many overdue reforms, especially in foreign and defence policies, which would be preserved by later governments of all political persuasions.

THE SUSPENSION OF CONSCRIPTION, THE WITHDRAWAL OF THE AATTV[1]

The Vietnam War and conscription were not prominent in the 1972 election campaign. The McMahon government had largely defused these issues by withdrawing all Australian forces, apart from the AATTV, all of whom were regulars. Only a relatively small number of voters identified Vietnam and conscription as their principal motive for voting for the first Labor government in 23 years. For several years, however, the war and the associated system of selective national service had contributed heavily to the growing sense that the conservative coalition parties were out of touch with international affairs and that it was time to entrust Labor with government. It was therefore important symbolically that the new government should take immediate action on the remaining vestiges of both policies.

The appointment of the full ministry could not take place until the counting of votes had been completed. In the meantime Whitlam created a 'duumvirate', allocating all portfolios to himself and his deputy, Lance Barnard (excluding even the party's leader and deputy leader in the Senate). Among the first of many administrative actions announced by the duumvirate in its two weeks' duration was an immediate and dramatic end to the national service scheme. Whitlam and Barnard announced that there would be no further call-up, that all national servicemen who wished to leave the army could do so immediately, and that those who had joined the Citizens' Military Force in order to avoid conscription could leave without penalty. Seven men in prison for evading conscription were immediately freed and all pending prosecutions for evading, defying or disrupting the system were dropped. The 2200 men who had been selected in the last ballot and who were scheduled to be called up in January were free of their obligations.

These administrative actions effectively suspended the working of the National Service Act, but did not repeal it. Leaving the Act in place gave the government a firm statutory basis for the payment of those national servicemen who elected to stay in the army. It also enabled any future government to reinstate a form of national service if it chose to do so. Plans made in late 1975 to repeal the National Service Act and to consider compensation were casualties of the crisis that brought the government down in November.

After the withdrawal of the task force in 1971, the McMahon government left a small residual force in Vietnam, largely members of the AATTV who were engaged in training South Vietnamese and Cambodian soldiers, together with some headquarters staff. By the time of the Australian election, the training commitments were winding down, and the few remaining Australian troops were awaiting the outcome of the Paris peace negotiations, involving the United States, the DRV, the RVN and the Provisional Revolutionary Government (PRG) established by the communists as the alternative government in South Vietnam. Plans were prepared for various contingencies, including an orderly withdrawal after a ceasefire had been negotiated. All plans and expectations were abruptly overtaken by the decision of the Whitlam–Barnard duumvirate on 7 December, announced on 11 December, that all troops, other than a platoon to guard the Australian Embassy in Saigon, were to leave by 18 December. The troops had to organise their departure in what the last commander of the residual force described as 'a screaming hurry'.² Many felt it was a dishonourable and unprofessional way to end the commitment, and sensed that the Americans and South Vietnamese, especially President Thieu, were shocked and disappointed that the Australians were leaving in such haste at a crucial time in the ceasefire negotiations, when a show of solidarity would have been especially appreciated.

Because Vietnam had not been a declared war, the government could not declare that the war was over. Instead it directed that the Governor-General issue a formal proclamation on 11 January 1973 of the cessation of hostilities in Vietnam by Australian forces. The fact that the Governor-General was Sir Paul Hasluck, who as Minister for External Affairs from 1964 to 1969 had been a principal architect of the commitment, gave the proclamation an additional irony.³

The speed and dramatic flourish of these actions fulfilled Whitlam's wish to demonstrate that new politicians with new ideas were now in office, but they served to sharpen rather than to heal the divisions of the 'Vietnam era'. Opponents of the war and of conscription, especially the families and friends of those who were freed from prison or exempted from prosecution, were euphoric. By contrast, supporters of the commitment, and many servicemen who had responded to the directions of the government that had sent them to Vietnam, felt that the extremely hasty withdrawal before the war was formally over was less than honourable.

THE 'CHRISTMAS BOMBING' AND THE NEAR RUPTURE IN AUSTRALIA– US RELATIONS⁴

Whitlam was Minister for Foreign Affairs as well as Prime Minister for 11 months, and retained personal control over foreign policy even after he appointed Senator Don Willesee to the portfolio. His aims, developed over many years, were reformist rather than radical. He sought to portray Australia as an independent ally rather than an uncritical follower of London or Washington. Coolness towards Moscow, Beijing and Hanoi would thaw, as foreign policy would change from stubborn resistance to communist expansion to what he called 'the intelligent anticipation of change', while defence policy would shift from forward defence to the 'logic and independence' of continental defence. At the same time, he intended to maintain Australia's traditional alliances with Britain and the United States, and to retain the American defence installations in Australia.[5]

Changing the balance between alliance and independence in this way would have been a challenging task at any time, but it was made exceptionally difficult by the course of the Vietnam War in the government's first weeks. The negotiations in Paris had taken a positive turn in October, encouraging Kissinger to declare that peace is 'at hand'. A few days later, Nixon was re-elected in a landslide win over the anti-war Democrat candidate, Senator George McGovern. In early December the Hanoi government raised new difficulties. Nixon ordered the bombing of military targets in the Hanoi–Haiphong area. Over 11 days, from 18 to 29 December except for Christmas Day, American aircraft dropped more bombs over this area than they had over all Indochina in the previous three years. In early January the DRV negotiators adopted a more positive stance, and on 23 January representatives of the United States, the DRV, the RVN and the PRG initialled a peace agreement that brought a ceasefire.

In a manner reminiscent of the Tet offensive, the United States seemed to have won a military battle but lost the public relations war. The bombing was largely confined to military and industrial targets, with relatively few civilian casualties by the standards of the war, but 'the Christmas bombing' was reported around the world as if civilian areas of

Hanoi had been 'carpet-bombed' with mindless barbarity. The Swedish government compared Nixon's administration to Hitler's. Opinion in the United States Congress turned even more strongly against the war.

In Australia several left-wing ministers in the new government spoke as if they were still leaders of the protest movement. Dr Cairns, the Minister for Trade and Industry and third-ranking member of the government, called the bombing 'the most brutal, undiscriminating slaughter of defenceless men, women and children in living memory'; Tom Uren, Minister for Urban and Regional Development, condemned Nixon's and Kissinger's 'mentality of thuggery'; and Clyde Cameron, the Minister for Labour, called the bombing the most monstrous act in human history and the policy of maniacs. The militant maritime unions, the Waterside Workers' Federation and the Seamen's Union, which had been constrained by the ACTU for most of the war, threatened to disrupt trade between Australia and the United States.

Amid the global clamour, Whitlam tried to reassert his control over foreign policy and to confront the issue in a more statesmanlike manner. He sent a personal letter to Nixon that praised Kissinger and the American negotiators for their patience and resolve and expressed his desire to cooperate with Washington on a wide range of matters, but said that the breakdown in the peace negotiations had been a bitter blow and questioned 'most earnestly' whether bombing would bring the North Vietnamese back to the negotiating table. Whitlam said that he intended to approach heads of government in the Asia–Pacific region (he had Indonesia and Japan in mind) to seek a joint statement appealing to both Hanoi and Washington to resume serious negotiations.

Nixon reacted with outrage and fury. As Kissinger explained to the Australian Embassy in Washington, the Americans did not care to be placed on the same level as the North Vietnamese by a longstanding ally.[6] It seemed that before the election neither the Labor Party nor the

American Embassy in Canberra had prepared Washington for a new government that sought simultaneously to take a more independent stance and to retain much of the substance of the defence relationship. The vitriolic comments by left-wing ministers poisoned the atmosphere.

Nixon declined to answer Whitlam's letter. He let it be known that he regarded Australia and Sweden as his least favoured Western governments and that Australia should regard the security guarantees under the ANZUS treaty as being in jeopardy. The Australian–American relationship was closer to a rupture than at any time since the signing of the ANZUS treaty.

The details and the full extent of the tension between the Nixon administration and the Whitlam government were kept to official channels. Whitlam reprimanded the ministers for speaking outside their responsibilities; with the help of the ACTU president, Bob Hawke, he ensured that the maritime unions called off their bans on American shipping; and, while letting it be known that he had written to Nixon, he kept his promise not to reveal the text. Nevertheless, it took months of diplomatic effort before Whitlam was permitted to call on Nixon, in July 1973, in an atmosphere markedly cooler than that of any previous Australian Prime Minister's visit to the White House.

In the subsequent months, Labor's left wing continued to criticise Australia's hosting of the defence facilities, while the United States intelligence agencies became increasingly suspicious of Australia's reliability as a loyal ally, especially when Cairns became Deputy Prime Minister following the government's re-election in May 1974. As part of a general review of the Australian–American relationship, Nixon ordered the CIA to consider whether the joint facilities should be relocated to another country, but by this time Nixon was becoming mired in the 'Watergate affair', which led to his resignation in August. Whitlam's visit to his successor, President Gerald Ford, in October took place in a more cordial atmosphere.[7]

RECOGNITION OF THE DEMOCRATIC REPUBLIC OF VIETNAM[8]

One of the decisions announced dramatically in the early weeks of the Whitlam government was the recognition of the People's Republic of China in Beijing as the government of China. While this was a major turning-point in Australia's relations with the world, it was not a bold innovation as Whitlam's visit in 1971 as Leader of the Opposition had been. After the global shock of Nixon's opening to China, many Western countries were taking the same course. More radical was Whitlam's determination to recognise the DRV government in Hanoi. It was not easy to do so while maintaining diplomatic relations with the RVN government in Saigon, since the DRV and the RVN each claimed to be the sole legitimate government of all Vietnam. The Australian negotiator finally accepted the DRV insistence that the announcement should refer to 'reciprocal recognition', on the understanding that the Australian government would, if challenged, say that it recognised the DRV with respect to the north and the RVN with respect to the south. The negotiations were quickly concluded in February 1973 and the Australian Embassy in Hanoi was opened under a *chargé d'affaires* in July.

While moving promptly to recognise the DRV, the Whitlam government resisted pressure from the Labor Party's left wing to recognise the PRG, the alternative government in the south established by the NLF, which had been a party to the peace agreement of January 1973. The terms of that agreement left the PRG in effective control of much of South Vietnam, and its ministers campaigned effectively in Western countries, including Australia, to be recognised as the legitimate authority in the south, rather than President Thieu's RVN government in Saigon. At the Labor Party's 1975 federal conference in Terrigal in New South Wales, which became notorious for the erratic personal and political behaviour of several Labor leaders, a resolution committing the government to recognise the PRG was passed, then replaced by one that would have authorised the establishment of a PRG information office in Australia, a traditional way of allowing discreet, quasi-diplomatic dealings with a controversial regime.

The Labor left also called for the removal of the Australian forces stationed in Malaysia and Singapore under the Five Power Defence Agreement (FPDA). Although these forces were welcomed by the Malaysian and Singaporean governments, some on the left saw them as manifestations of the forward defence policy which, in their view, was totally discredited by the Vietnam experience. Lee Kuan Yew, who had been regarded as a hero by socialists in his early years, was now seen by the left as an ideological enemy. Whitlam and Barnard announced that Australia would continue to honour its commitment to the FPDA, but they reduced the level of the naval, military and air forces stationed in Malaysia and Singapore.

FROM 'FORWARD DEFENCE' TO 'THE SELF-RELIANT DEFENCE OF AUSTRALIA'[9]

One of Whitlam's principal aims was to reduce the emphasis on military aspects of Australia's relations with the world and to place more on diplomatic measures. His close personal involvement in foreign policy, including votes in the United Nations, was not matched in defence, which he delegated to Barnard. With little fanfare, however, Whitlam gave important support to major reforms in strategic policy and defence structures, which were broadly associated with the reaction against policies associated with Vietnam. Whitlam and Barnard commissioned the Secretary of the Defence Department, Sir Arthur Tange, to prepare and implement a major reorganisation of Australian defence. The five departments of the Defence group, including separate departments for each of the navy, army and air force, were brought into a single, enlarged Defence Department. The boards of senior officers that had governed each of the services were abolished, along with the positions of Minister for the Navy, Army and Air. The three armed services, while retaining their separate identities and uniforms, were brought into a single Australian Defence Force. Reforms along these lines had been recommended by a high-level committee in 1959, but the Liberal–Country Party governments of Menzies and his successors had declined to grasp the nettle, knowing what opposition this reform would provoke from uniformed members of the three services and their civilian supporters.

The 'Tange reforms' in defence, which provoked considerable controversy, were accompanied by reforms designed to increase the capacity of the Defence Department to advise the government on strategic and broad defence policies. Whitlam supported the proposal to establish an Australian Defence Force Academy, in which officers of all three services would learn to work together and would receive a 'broad and liberal education', deepening their understanding of the region and the world in which they would be called on to serve. Tange had long felt, from his time as Secretary of the Department of External Affairs in the ten years before the Vietnam commitment, that the Defence Department, including both civilian and the uniformed members, had too little capacity to give advice to government on what Tange called 'higher defence policy'. Many advisers in and around the public service shared Whitlam's and Barnard's view that there must be a new emphasis in Australian strategic and defence policies. Dependence on allies was to be reduced in favour of a much greater degree of 'self-reliance' in Australian defence, while forward defence was to be replaced by a strategy based on 'the defence of Australia', meaning the Australian continent and its approaches.

These were indeed controversial reforms, which provoked heated debate in political and defence circles. Statements by Whitlam and Barnard to the effect that Australia faced no direct military threat for the next 15 years were vigorously challenged. The establishment of the Australian Defence Force Academy encountered repeated rebuffs before its creation in the early 1980s. Serving and retired officers expressed outrage, especially in the army, which could see that the new approaches were likely to favour the navy and air force. The extent to which Australia could be truly self-reliant in defence, and the degree to which the three services could cooperate with each other rather than with the sister services of Australia's traditional allies, would be tested, debated and refined in the coming years, but the essential structures of the defence reorganisation would remain in place under Labor and conservative coalition governments in subsequent decades.

THE FALL OF SAIGON 1975[10]

The peace agreement of January 1973 allowed units of the PAVN to remain in South Vietnam, giving the PRG effective control of large areas. The agreement provided for a reconciliation process between the RVN and the PRG, but this proved impossible to effect. Nixon promised American support for the RVN if the north should repeat its 1972 attempt to invade the south, but after Nixon had left office in disgrace his successor, Gerald Ford, could not persuade Congress to back the anti-communist cause. In January 1975 Hanoi began what it later called 'the Ho Chi Minh campaign', a broadly based attack using tanks supplied by both China and the Soviet Union. It soon became clear that, without any American support, the RVN would not be able to withstand this fourth assault, as it had those of 1965, 1968 and 1972. The PAVN rapidly cut through the northern and central provinces of South Vietnam, reaching the outskirts of Saigon by early April. The fall of Saigon was imminent, and with it the demise of the anti-communist cause in the former French colonies of Indochina.

Like its predecessors in 1968 and 1972, the 1975 offensive did not prompt popular uprisings in favour of the DRV and the PRG. Instead hundreds of thousands of Vietnamese fled from the communists. The flood of refugees first poured south as the communists quickly overran cities in the northern and central provinces of South Vietnam, then tried to leave Vietnam by any means available, starting with any civilian or military aircraft. Soon they clambered onto boats, often far from seaworthy, which took them on hazardous voyages to places such as Malaysia and Singapore, from whence they hoped to find safe haven in Australia and other Western countries. The enduring images of the end of the war were of Vietnamese clinging desperately to the skids of an American helicopter leaving a building in central Saigon in late April, and of a North Vietnamese tank crashing through the gates of the presidential palace in Saigon on 30 April, the last day of the RVN.

In March and April the Australian government came under increasing pressure to assist the torrent of Vietnamese seeking to flee from the victorious communists. Like other Western embassies, the Australian Embassy in Saigon was besieged by thousands seeking refuge in Australia. Some had particular claims. The ambassador, Geoffrey Price, was especially concerned for the embassy's Vietnamese staff and their dependants, as well as for those who had served other Australian interests or agencies. Pleas came from RVN diplomats in Canberra and elsewhere. Vietnamese and Cambodian students already in Australia sought to remain and to bring out their families. The media, especially in the United States and Australia, gave extensive coverage to the fate of the thousands of babies and small children in Saigon's orphanages, of whom there were many Australians seeking to become adoptive parents.

Intense and emotional debate over humanitarian assistance brought the Vietnam War back to prominence in Australia. Although Whitlam was, as so often in his prime ministership, travelling overseas, it was he rather than the Foreign Minister, Don Willesee, or the Immigration Minister, Clyde Cameron, who remained in control of Australian policy. Whitlam, whose moderate attitudes had incurred the suspicion of many on the left in the early years of the war, now agreed with those like Cairns and Cameron who argued that Hanoi's imminent victory proved that the communist cause was legitimate and that to fear a communist massacre or ill-treatment of the defeated was to accept the propaganda of Saigon and Washington.

Whitlam knew that public opinion in Australia was divided on the prospect of mass immigration from Indochina. He also shared the view, strong on the Labor left, that Vietnamese refugees were likely to be as vehemently anti-communist as those 'new Australians' who had come in the 1940s and 1950s from the Baltic states and other eastern European countries forcibly incorporated into the Soviet Union, and who were usually strong supporters of the conservative parties in Australia. In reacting to the pressures of March–April 1975, Whitlam placed the establishment of a good relationship with the new regime ahead of concerns for the fate of the South Vietnamese, even those who had worked closely with the Australians. After protests by Hanoi, RAAF aircraft rendering assistance in South Vietnam were ordered not to carry refugees, whether ARVN soldiers or civilians, and were confined to transporting emergency relief supplies. In adopting a highly restrictive attitude to the pleas from diplomats and others seeking admission to Australia, Whitlam repeatedly urged officials not to mistrust the assurances from the DRV and PRG that the people of South Vietnam had nothing to fear from their new rulers.

The fate of Vietnamese orphans aroused strong emotions and divided opinions. When Whitlam ordered that some be found and returned to Australia, Price felt that he was being instructed to carry out a 'baby-hunt' for Australian domestic political purposes, when there were many more pressing claims for admission to Australia. Eventually, two plane-loads of orphans were flown to Australia. On the day that the first flew out, a US Air Force Galaxy aircraft, destined for the United States, crashed soon after taking off from Tan Son Nhut airport, Saigon, killing some 200 people including 143 orphans and two Australian civilian welfare workers who had volunteered to escort them.

Amid the chaos of the fall of South Vietnam and the controversies over refugees and orphans, another loss passed almost unnoticed. In March 1975 the *chargé d'affaires* at the Australian Embassy in Hanoi, Graham Lewis, flew to Vientiane to meet the new ambassador who was about to take up his post. Lewis then took an Air Vietnam flight to Saigon. The plane flew over Pleiku in the central highlands, where a major battle was taking place. The plane disappeared, with the loss of all aboard. It had probably been mistaken, by one side or the other, as a military aircraft and shot down by a missile. In the last months of the war, a diplomat was added to the seven civilians (four journalists, the two women welfare workers and an entertainer) and 521 service personnel who lost their lives in the Vietnam War.

Before the Australian Embassy closed on 25 April, the 60th anniversary of Australia's most famous military campaign, 3667 adult Vietnamese had applied to come to Australia, of whom 342 were approved and only 76 actually made the journey. Among those left behind were Vietnamese members of the embassy staff. Whitlam's attitude to Vietnamese refugees in these last days was seen as dishonourable and shameful by many in his own party. It was strongly denounced by Malcolm Fraser, the recently elected leader of the Liberal Party and

Leader of the Opposition, who said that Australia should accept large numbers of Vietnamese refugees. He would live up to that promise as Prime Minister from 1976 to 1983.

Throughout this time Whitlam claimed that he was adopting an even-handed and balanced attitude towards the contesting governments in Hanoi and Saigon. This was a fair summary of instructions he sent to the two Australian embassies in March: it was not true of cabled instructions sent on 2 April, which were far more sympathetic to Hanoi than to Saigon. Whitlam's primary concern was clearly to ensure that, when Hanoi achieved its goal of a united Vietnam under communist rule, it would not look unfavourably on Australia as a former enemy.

The cables were leaked to the press and published on 29 April, the day before Saigon fell. In that atmosphere, they did much to undermine the government's authority and even, in the eyes of some critics, its legitimacy. The *Sydney Morning Herald* editorial asserted that the 'cables affair' was 'the gravest political scandal since Federation' and concluded that: 'A Government which cannot be trusted, which abuses its power and its command of secrecy, forfeits its right to govern. It should be brought down'.[11] This editorial carried more significance than most such expressions of opinion. As the Whitlam government was becoming mired in a succession of scandals and crises, mostly associated with an attempt to secure an overseas loan from unorthodox sources, Fraser had promised that the conservative parties would use their Senate majority to refuse Supply only if the government's actions were 'reprehensible'. The presentation of the 'cables affair' in these terms was hugely significant.

Whitlam's handling of the last days of the Vietnam War thus contributed to the atmosphere in which, in the ensuing months, the conservative parties under Fraser's leadership would take steps that would lead to the dismissal of the Whitlam government by the Governor-General on 11 November. Between 1972 and 1975 the Vietnam War was no longer the dominant issue it had been in Australian politics in the late 1960s, but it contributed substantially both to the heady and hubristic euphoria when the Whitlam government was elected and to the atmosphere of dishonour and political polarisation that surrounded its highly controversial demise.

— ELEVEN —

LESSONS, LEGACIES AND LEGENDS

In Australia, as in many other countries, the Vietnam War had an extraordinarily long and profound effect on many areas of political and social life. A debate on 'the lessons of Vietnam' had begun early in the war and continued for decades afterwards. In the United States, many struggled to explain how the greatest superpower the world had ever seen could be humiliated by a relatively small Third World country. Australians followed the debate and conducted their own version, often mirroring some of the major trends but with less intensity and with some distinctly Australian variations. The Vietnam War and the Vietnam era also generated numerous legends, some with a substantial basis in fact, some quite mythical. As with so many aspects of the Vietnam War, many of the lessons, the legacies and the legends have been, and in some cases still are, vigorously contested. This chapter will touch lightly on some of lasting importance: strategic and defence policy, with a particular focus on the American alliance; foreign policy, especially with respect to Southeast Asia; operational methods in counter-insurgency operations; conscription; and the post-war experience of Vietnam veterans.

Although all these areas of debate have their own distinctive features, a common pattern can also be discerned. In the immediate aftermath of the fall of Saigon, the Vietnam War was often portrayed as an abject failure. Anything that could be linked to the war, its personnel or its policies was discredited. Any intervention by the United States to counter an insurgency or radical movement beyond its shores, or any request from the United States to an ally to join it in a counter-insurgency campaign, was immediately challenged as 'another Vietnam', meaning another costly and counter-productive quagmire. Anything associated, however remotely, with Vietnam – the name of the country becoming shorthand for the war and the era – was treated as tainted or fundamentally flawed. In Australia, the Vietnam War was taken as different and separate from the ANZAC tradition. It was regarded as at best a strategic mistake, at worst an immoral commitment, reflecting discredit on anyone and anything associated with it, including those who served there as well as those responsible for sending them.

Allegations and accusations along these lines endured for years. Reverberations were still evident well into the 21st century, when commitments by the United States and its allies in Iraq and Afghanistan were said to be 'another Vietnam'. By this time, however, some major reassessments had taken place in attitudes to the Vietnam War and to its lessons and legacies. In the United States and Australia, as some of the literal and metaphorical wounds of the war slowly healed, some of the more sweeping denunciations of 'the Vietnam era' were seen to have been exaggerated. Some strong supporters and vigorous critics remained, but for the most part opinions for and against the war approached, if not a consensus, then at least a more moderate division in the middle ground. By the early 21st century, Australia's Vietnam experience had, to a substantial degree, been reintegrated into the mainstream of Australia's political, military, diplomatic and social history.

DEFENCE AND STRATEGIC POLICY

In the 1970s and 1980s a vigorous debate on Australian strategic policies took place based on the assumption that, as one of the major participants put it, 'seventy years of tradition in defence thinking seemed to have been trashed by the outcome of the Vietnam War'.[1] Forward defence was seen as a disastrous failure. The fall of Saigon had led to communist governments in Laos and Cambodia but not to the fall of further 'dominoes' beyond the Mekong River. The tradition of relying on allies, especially the United States and Britain – which Menzies had famously called 'our great and powerful friends' – was also discredited. The despatch of forces overseas to cement these alliances had failed in its purpose, for Australia had failed to keep the United States and Britain engaged in Southeast Asia. Britain was proceeding to withdraw its forces east of Suez, and the United States conducted a major drawdown of its forces in Southeast Asia. Instead of a successful joint exercise, Australia had associated itself with the United States in what was widely perceived as one of the greatest disasters in American foreign policy. The place of the American alliance in Australian strategy was under question as never before.[2]

After the Vietnam War – indeed, well before it had ended – the left argued that the alliance linked Australia to American arrogance, immorality and incompetence. Some on the right argued that the failure to stand by South Vietnam after 1973 showed that the United States was not a reliable ally. The prestige and authority of the United States were further undermined by the ignominious resignation of President Nixon in 1974 and the humiliating crisis over Americans held hostage in Iran in 1979–81. President Ford, who was in the White House when Saigon fell, lost office at the 1976 election, but his successor, Jimmy Carter, fared no better, failing to gain re-election in 1980. Congressional committees revealed that American intelligence and security agencies, most famously the CIA, had intervened illegally in the politics of friendly as well as hostile countries. This struck a particular chord in Australia, where many on the left believed that the CIA had played an underhand part in the Governor-General's dismissal of the Whitlam government in November 1975.

The reaction in Australia against Vietnam was accompanied by a pronounced trend in popular culture and popular history, which became more assertively nationalistic and anti-imperial. Two popular feature films, *Breaker Morant* (1980) and *Gallipoli* (1981), were set in the South African War and the 1914–18 war respectively, but they could be seen as reading one of 'the lessons of Vietnam' into those conflicts – the costly folly of Australian involvement in distant wars on behalf of an imperial mentor.

In Australia the focus of attention was the 'joint facilities', such as Pine Gap, Nurrungar and North-West Cape, often referred to as 'American bases'. These had been welcomed, indeed eagerly sought, by the Menzies government in the late 1950s and early 1960s as a means of ensuring that the United States would see a strong interest in guaranteeing Australia's security. The government at that time accepted the likelihood that they made Australian territory a Soviet target in any nuclear exchange if the Cold War turned hot.

After 1975, Australia's willingness to send expeditionary forces to conflicts some distance from its shores was portrayed by critics not as an acceptable price for strategic insurance, nor as a defence of common values, but as an indecent inclination to take part in 'other people's wars'. Many assumed that Australia's involvement in the Vietnam War had been at the instigation of, and under pressure from, the United States. The idea that Australia had been pressing to become involved, that it had been 'looking for a way in and not a way out' as Menzies put it in April 1965, took some time to be recognised. In any case the 'Guam doctrine' or 'Nixon doctrine' had already made it clear that the United States would expect its allies, especially those in the Asia–Pacific region, to rely more on their own resources and less on those of the United States. Having lost 58 000 lives in Vietnam, the American public was in no mood to defend those countries who seemed eager to 'fight to the last American'. A broad consensus emerged that Australia's strategic posture should turn away from dependence on allies in favour of a greater degree of 'self-reliance', while forward defence and the despatch of expeditionary forces were to be replaced by a strategy based on 'the defence of Australia', a concentration on the continent and its approaches. These concepts were under discussion in the early 1970s, and were promoted during the Whitlam years, emerging as the basis of the first Defence White Paper, brought down in 1976, the first year of the Fraser coalition government.

In the 1980s President Ronald Reagan brought a new mood of optimism and confidence to the United States. Part of this was a rejection of the post-Vietnam reaction. Reagan declared that Vietnam had been 'a noble cause' undermined by flawed strategy and tactics. Events in Vietnam and Cambodia, to be discussed later in this chapter, helped to reinforce this perception. At the same time Australian policy-makers began to appreciate the potential cost of 'self-reliance' in defence and pointed to the valuable peacetime benefits that Australia gained, as a close ally, from access to American defence science, technology and intelligence. Following a report on defence capability by consultant and former Defence official Paul Dibb in 1986 and a White Paper prepared under Minister for Defence Kim Beazley in 1987, the guiding principle for Australia's strategic posture was modified to become 'the self-reliant defence of Australia in an alliance context'.

Consequently, the government led by Bob Hawke from 1983 to 1991, with Beazley as Minister for Defence and Bill Hayden as Foreign Minister, worked vigorously and effectively to restore the American alliance to a leading place in Australian foreign and defence policies, but on a new basis. Their principal opponents in this endeavour were the left wing of their own party and some elements further to the left, such as the Nuclear Disarmament Party, which won a Senate seat in 1984. Amid a renewed outbreak of Cold War tensions, the left argued that the 'US bases' exposed Australia to serious danger of nuclear war. Hawke and his ministers countered this by arguing that the joint facilities contributed to deterrence of nuclear war and to the monitoring of arms control agreements by providing timely information on missile launches and nuclear tests. They were therefore an instrument for maintaining peace, not merely for making war. The government took steps to ensure that they were more truly 'joint facilities' rather than American establishments on Australian soil. Hawke also made skilful use of his party's high regard for John Curtin, the Prime Minister who had famously 'turned to America' in the darkest days of the 1939–45 war, to show that alliance with the United States was fully compatible with Labor tradition.

Hawke and Beazley convinced their party that the American alliance was in Australia's interests, provided it was on the basis of a genuinely reciprocal exchange of views, information and responsibilities and not merely a matter of a subservient Canberra following Washington 'all the way'. A Republican administration in the United States and a Labor government in Australia thus re-established the alliance, putting many of the negative associations of the Vietnam legacy behind them. After the United States led a coalition of nations, including Australia, in a successful operation to counter Iraqi aggression against Kuwait in 1990–91, President George HW Bush said that the United States had 'kicked the Vietnam syndrome'. Much the same could be said of Australia.

The negative associations of the Vietnam commitment had not completely disappeared. After the terrorist attacks in the United States on 11 September 2001, Prime Minister John Howard invoked the ANZUS treaty for the first time in its 50-year history and subsequently committed Australian forces to the two theatres of the 'war on terror',

Iraq and Afghanistan. In both cases, critics frequently made comparisons with Vietnam, implying that the United States and its allies were again becoming involved in a quagmire. There were similarities – the tendency of the Western powers to see local politics in global terms, to underestimate the importance of sectarian and ethnic rivalries, and to overestimate the capacity of American military power to conduct counter-insurgency and to effect regime change – but there were also important differences.

The Iraq commitment of 2003 – which Garry Woodard among others compared with Vietnam[3] – had some marked differences from the Australian perspective. Iraq could not be said to be 'in our region'; nor had Australia been pressing the United States to intervene there in its own interests. But Howard demonstrated how the lessons and legacies of the Vietnam War were perceived by an Australian Prime Minister determined to reinforce the strength of the American alliance by supporting a controversial foreign commitment. Under Howard's leadership, Australian forces were committed quickly and left after a specified time without becoming entangled in the problems of protracted conflict or contentious post-war administration; Australia committed relatively small numbers of well-trained troops, all of whom were volunteers; the Australians operated separately from the American forces, being given a role in an area where they had a large degree of operational autonomy; Australian officers were placed in the chain of command; the exposure to risk was such that Australia suffered no battle fatalities. Australia had less direct interest in Iraq in 2003 than in Vietnam in 1965, but the government did not pay a political price for involvement in an unpopular war alongside our principal ally.

By the early 21st century both sides of politics reaffirmed the alliance and deprecated comparisons with Vietnam. A coalition government committed forces to both Iraq and Afghanistan, and a Labor government continued to support the Afghanistan commitment as it dragged on even longer than the Vietnam War. In 2011 a new Labor Prime Minister, making her first official visit to the White House, not only proclaimed her admiration for the United States in fulsome terms but also announced a substantial Australian contribution to a new Vietnam Veterans' Education Centre in Washington. Few in the 1970s or 1980s would have imagined that a Labor Prime Minister would be so eager to remind Americans that, in Australia, they had a loyal ally in the most controversial war of the 20th century. Vietnam had been integrated into the history of the Australian–American alliance. The 'insurance policy' argument seemed to have gained at least some degree of retrospective vindication, albeit at a heavy cost.

DOMINOES

The other main argument behind the commitment was the 'domino theory'. This also was taken to be discredited, even risible, immediately after 1975, when only Laos and Cambodia became communist: their fates had always been closely linked to that of Vietnam. A large part of the post-Vietnam reaction was the idea that Australia's relationship with Asia had to change from one dominated by security concerns over 'falling dominoes'. The rejection of the 'Vietnam era' was evident in Whitlam's early proclamations that he wished to establish 'an Australia which will be less militarily oriented and not open to suggestions of racism', that he sought 'further initiatives to be directed towards peace and progress in the Asian and Pacific region to which Australia belongs', and that he did not see Southeast Asia 'as a frontier where we might fight nameless Asian enemies as far north of our own shores as possible'.[4]

In *Facing North*, a major publication on Australia's relations with Asia over the 20th century, the chapter on the Southeast Asian conflicts is followed by a chapter called 'Reorientation'.[5] The Whitlam and Fraser governments saw a major reorientation of Australia's relations with Asia away from a heavy emphasis on defence and towards trade, migration and other more positive aspects. These governments picked up ideas that had been voiced before 1975. Holt, for example, spoke of the next century as 'the century of Asia'. But in the post-Vietnam environment, ideas that had been subordinated amid the actual and feared conflicts in Southeast Asia were able to flourish. As the authors of 'Reorientation' put it, those who led the discussion of Australia's 'Asian future' in the late 1970s and early 1980s:

> rejected attitudes towards Asia that were premised on the need to retain stronger Western influence, even dominance, expressing rather a willingness to build relations directly with Asian countries on a basis of equality. [They also] … replaced an insular and homogeneous notion of Australian society and identity with a culturally and racially pluralist one.[6]

These ideas were manifested in a number of different ways and with different styles. The Whitlam government undertook numerous diplomatic initiatives to establish better relations with Asian countries, both communist and non-communist, and made numerous policy changes on colonial, racial and human rights issues. Many of these changes were consolidated by Malcolm Fraser's coalition government (1975–83), whose policies on immigration, international relations and multicultural affairs, especially on relations with Asian countries and people of Asian origin, were markedly different from those of both sides of politics in the 1950s and early 1960s.

Establishing a peaceful and constructive relationship with all the countries of Southeast Asia – both Indochina and the ASEAN members – was to prove no easy matter. In Vietnam, the victorious communists in Hanoi lost no time in not only uniting the two halves of the country but also imposing a harsh, neo-Stalinist system on what was renamed in 1976 the Socialist Republic of Vietnam. Collectivised agriculture and forced industrialisation were imposed, impoverishing the country and requiring financial support from Hanoi's model and mentor, the Soviet Union. More than 300 000 citizens of the former RVN were placed in 're-education camps' and relocated to 'new economic zones'. All ARVN war cemeteries were destroyed: not only were the rulers of the former regime dismissed as 'puppets' but any memorial to the hundreds of thousands, perhaps quarter of a million, ARVN soldiers who had died to defend it was also erased. Even active members of the National Liberation Front and the Provisional Revolutionary Government in the south were dismissed as irrelevant to the new regime: the victory, they were told, had been won by the communists in Hanoi, whose accomplices in the south could now be dismissed or even punished if they showed disappointment. Hundreds of thousands of Vietnamese fled the rigidly ideological and vindictively repressive regime in any way possible, mostly in unseaworthy boats.

These developments, although reported in the West, were overshadowed by concurrent developments in Cambodia, where the Khmer Rouge who came to power in 1975 represented a different, and even crueller, form of communism. Reports soon emerged of a genocidal regime, which caused about 2 million deaths in imposing an extreme form of Maoist communism. In 1978–79 the Vietnamese invaded Cambodia and imposed a new government. The Chinese, who backed the Khmer Rouge, were infuriated and invaded Vietnam in 1979 to 'teach the Vietnamese a lesson'. This conflict, sometimes known as the Third Indochina War, was more costly than either side has usually been willing to admit. The unfortunate Cambodians, having been caught between the North Vietnamese and the Americans in one war, were now pawns in a power struggle between China on the one hand and Vietnam, backed by the Soviet Union, on the other.

Australian governments faced considerable challenges in shaping an independent and creative policy towards Indochina amid the conflicts involving the contesting Cambodian regimes, the ASEAN countries, Vietnam, China, the United States and the Soviet Union. In the 1980s and early 1990s, the Foreign Ministers of the Hawke and Keating governments, Bill Hayden and Gareth Evans, undertook active diplomatic roles in the region, culminating in a major multilateral effort under United Nations auspices to effect a peaceful transition to a new, peaceful settlement in Cambodia. Australia's major contribution to the Cambodian settlement of the early 1990s illustrated how far Australian defence and foreign policy had come since 1975. Australians, notably Evans and the diplomats in his department, played an active and constructive role in regional diplomacy, acting independently of the United States and achieving results that the global superpower could not itself have achieved. The role of an Australian soldier, Lieutenant General John Sanderson, as head of the military mission backing the United Nations authority in Cambodia, exemplified the political and diplomatic skills now expected of Australian military leaders. Australia's creative diplomacy in Southeast Asia owed much to the close relationship that successive governments established with Indonesia, despite public concern over the authoritarian nature of the Suharto government and Indonesia's invasion and occupation of East Timor in 1975.

These developments in Indochina and their ramifications throughout Southeast Asia cast some retrospective light on Australia's commitment to Vietnam. They demonstrated that to see developments in Indochina as simply a struggle between communist and anti-communist blocs had been to dangerously over-simplify. Both supporters and critics of the Second Indochina War in Australia had underestimated the extent and importance of national and regional rivalries in the Indochina peninsula. The rivalry between China and Vietnam, and their competition for hegemony in the region, was as relevant in the late 20th century as it had been in previous centuries. Some argued that the Third Indochina War pointed to the lost opportunity to use Vietnam as a buffer against

China, instead of treating Vietnam as a Chinese ally and instrument. By the second decade of the 21st century, the United States and Vietnam were establishing a rapprochement, clearly based on mutual apprehensions of the rise of China. Whether such a rapprochement could have been achieved in the 1960s, in the context of the Sino–Soviet split and Mao's adventurism, is another matter, but the China–Vietnam relationship and the triangular relationship of the two with the Soviet Union were certainly more complex than many understood in the 1960s. At the same time, the post-1975 developments in Indochina also discredited communism in general and Vietnamese communism in particular. The Maoists and other militant critics of the war who had called for 'victory to the Viet Cong' were shown to have been, at best, extraordinarily naive about the nature of the conflict and the combatants.

In the longer view one form of the domino theory gained a degree of credibility. This was the argument that intervention by the United States and its allies, including Australia, had served a useful purpose by delaying the fall of the RVN by ten years, from 1965 to 1975. As noted in Chapter 6, this argument had been voiced in Australia as early as 1966: after the war, its most prominent advocate was Lee Kuan Yew, Prime Minister of one of the principal potential dominoes, Singapore. As Lee and others pointed out, between 1965 and 1975 numerous changes in Southeast Asia affected the regional impact of Hanoi's victory. Thailand, which had faced an insurgency in the region closest to the border with Laos, was now able to resist insurgencies; Malaysia and Singapore had not only survived but thrived; Indonesia was now firmly under the control of the anti-communist 'New Order' regime of Suharto.

No one can say exactly what would have happened in the region if Saigon had in fact fallen in 1965, but it is highly probable that the consequences would have been severe. In particular, it is impossible to say definitively whether the Indonesian generals would have had the confidence to act against the PKI after 30 September 1965 if the United States had not been standing firm in Vietnam. Their actions were driven principally by Indonesia's internal politics, but it is plausible to argue that the stance of the United States and its allies contributed to one of the most important turning-points in recent Southeast Asian history, and therefore on Australia's strategic environment. From this point of view, the commitment had served a useful regional purpose.

Many of these gains, however, were already apparent by 1968–69. The New Order regime of Suharto, although seen as uncertain in 1966–67, was firmly establishing itself by the end of the decade. ASEAN was formed in 1967, giving a welcome appearance of regional solidarity in the non-communist countries of the region. When seen from this perspective, the tragedy was not so much the original commitment but its open-ended nature. As Gorton, especially, found, it was much harder to get out of a commitment than to get into it. Having entered the commitment in an open-ended way, having escalated it against increasing domestic opposition, and having declared that it was acting in the interests of the South Vietnamese people, any government that tried to withdraw in the late 1960s would have been accused of betraying those it was supposedly defending.

Although it would have been extremely difficult, if Australia had pursued a determined and skilful diplomacy from 1968 onwards, based on an exit strategy laid down when forces were committed, it might have been possible to reduce the costs of the commitment in lives, treasure, political capital and social harmony, while gaining many of its strategic benefits. One of the major lessons of Vietnam was the need not only for much greater prudence in entering any commitment but also for 'an exit strategy' when embarking on any such commitment. With half a century's hindsight, the 'domino theory' arguments gain at least some element of credibility; but, as with the 'insurance policy', at a cost that was unnecessarily high.

OPERATIONAL METHODS

An important casualty of the widespread rejection of anything associated with the Vietnam War was a long delay in the discussion and analysis of the operational methods, abilities and effectiveness of the various forces committed by Australia. The 60 000 Australians who served, representing a range of units from all three armed services, and the many others who supported them during a decade-long commitment, had an extraordinarily diverse range of experiences. Recollections and published accounts often focused on major battles, particularly Long Tan, which were not typical of the experience of the infantry battalions of the task force, let alone the other units who served. The courage and skill of those who served at Long Tan and in other major battles certainly deserved recognition, but so did the service and sacrifice of many others in less well-known capacities.

For many years, recollections and reflections on the major themes of Australia's military experience – such as cooperation with United States, New Zealand and South Vietnamese forces, collaboration within and between the three services, and relations with the Vietnamese people – contained ambiguities and unresolved contradictions. Critical appraisals of American tactics of attrition and use of firepower, for example, competed with gratitude for the generous, courageous and effective support often provided by US artillery, helicopters, fixed-wing aircraft and logistic units.

Generally positive recollections of the integration of New Zealand infantrymen, helicopter pilots and other personnel into Australian units were sometimes overshadowed by tensions over 'friendly fire' incidents. Soldiers, diplomats and other officials had mixed memories of their South Vietnamese counterparts, as accounts of courage, decency and effectiveness conflicted with those of incompetence, cowardice and corruption. Examples of unspectacular but vitally important cooperation between the services were sometimes overshadowed by outbursts of inter-service rivalry.

A particularly important omission was the lack of serious consideration of the Australian approach to counter-insurgency operations. From the arrival of 1RAR at Bien Hoa in 1965, through the intense campaigns of the late 1960s to the withdrawal of forces in the early 1970s, Australians debated the competing merits of pacification operations and operations against main force units. Some argued that the tactics that Australian units, especially the RAR battalions and the SAS squadrons, had developed and practised in the Malayan Emergency and Confrontation were equally applicable in Vietnam. Others contended that the nature of the war and the scale of the political and military challenge in Vietnam were so different that other approaches had to be learned and applied. For many years, the emotions associated with the Vietnam War would make it difficult to conduct a dispassionate assessment of these issues and the effectiveness of Australian approaches. Those who served in Vietnam deserved better, and Australia would have benefited when faced with new counter-insurgency campaigns in the early 21st century.

CONSCRIPTION

As noted in Chapter 10, the Whitlam government suspended but did not repeal the National Service Act. It therefore remains open to any future government to reintroduce some form of compulsory national service, but one major legacy of the Vietnam era is a total change in public attitudes to conscription. This is perhaps the protest movement's most significant legacy, more enduring than opposition to overseas military commitments or to the American alliance.

One objection to the national service scheme of 1965–72 was its rejection of the principle of conscientious objection to a particular war. Applicants for exemption on these grounds had to prove that they conscientiously objected to all wars. In the 1960s and 1970s many magistrates seemed to take the view that only adherents to certain small religious denominations could be regarded as genuine conscientious objectors. The law on this matter was changed in the 1990s. When Michael Tate became Minister for Justice in the Hawke government, he drafted a bill to allow selective conscientious objection to a particular war. It was opposed by the conservative coalition parties, and the Defence Department feared its potential impact on the service of regulars as well as national servicemen. Consideration of the bill was delayed for many reasons, including the Australian commitment to the Gulf war prompted by Iraq's invasion of Kuwait, but Tate's bill was finally passed in 1992. Tate was a devout Catholic, who entered the priesthood after his retirement from politics.

More importantly, the protest movement of the Vietnam era may well have brought about the end to the longstanding debate over compulsory military service overseas. The distinction established in the 1903 Defence Act between compulsory training and service at home but only voluntary service abroad had been a source of contention and controversy in two world wars, but had evidently been rendered obsolete by the Vietnam experience. When a retired Chief of the Defence Force, Admiral Chris Barrie, floated the idea of national service in 2006, having in mind provisions quite different from those applying in 1965–72, Howard immediately made it clear that he had no intention of reintroducing any form of conscription for service in Iraq, Afghanistan or anywhere else. With demanding commitments in many parts of the world, the Australian Defence Force in the early 21st century was often severely strained, requiring regular troops and reserves to serve multiple tours of duty, but conscription has always been ruled out. The fact that many in the army regarded the selective system of 1965–72 as a welcome boost to quality as well as numbers has had little impact. Today, unlike the Australia of the 1950s and early 1960s, the principle of voluntary military service is entrenched at every level, from school cadet units to front-line troops.

THE VETERANS' EXPERIENCE

A major legacy of the Vietnam War, still highly sensitive, concerns the impact on those who served, and by extension on their friends and families. This is a complex story, in which at least three major strands can be discerned: the reception given to the veterans by government agencies, such as the army, the Department of Veterans' Affairs (as the former Department of Repatriation had been renamed) and the Repatriation Commission, by ex-service organisations, and by the wider Australian community; the impacts, both direct and indirect, of post-traumatic stress on the post-war health of veterans; and the impact of a number of herbicides and other toxic chemicals, generally known collectively as Agent Orange. While much has been written on various elements of these controversies, including numerous official reports on the scientific, legal and medical aspects, there is no independent scholarly study comparable in nature to an official war history that chronicles and analyses the post-war experience of Vietnam veterans. The *Official History of Australia's Involvement in Southeast Asian Conflicts 1948–1975* included an essay of one aspect of this story which itself became part of an ongoing controversy. What follows is a short and impressionistic summary of a long and complex subject.[7]

Even before the Vietnam War had ended, there was evidence of serious problems affecting the repatriation of service personnel to Australia, their re-entry into civil society and their rehabilitation from physical and mental ailments. Some experienced outright hostility, facing accusations that they had burned villages and killed children. Others found that cool indifference could be no less confronting: families, friends, workmates and the general community neither understood nor wanted to understand what the veterans had experienced. Many stories circulated of Vietnam veterans being told by veterans of earlier conflicts in Returned Service League sub-branches that they had not been in 'a real war'. The army, it was claimed, had brought soldiers back secretively in order to avoid protests. The Department of Veterans' Affairs and the Repatriation Commission were accused of failing to offer Vietnam veterans the understanding and support that they deserved. Resentment was felt particularly keenly by some national servicemen, who felt that they had been conscripted to serve in an unpopular war while those of the same age had prospered in security and peace. Some of those who fought in the later years of the war felt especially disillusioned, being obliged to risk life and limb in a war that had lost the support of the government and people. Where lives and limbs were lost to mines that had been removed from the Dat Do minefield, the pain was especially cruel. Others who remained committed to the war felt that the manner of the withdrawal was dishonourable. The sense of having fought in a losing cause, which some but certainly not all felt was an unworthy one, was common. Some veterans complained that, instead of being given the heroes' welcome that they deserved, as upholders of the ANZAC tradition established by their forefathers in two world wars, they had been betrayed by the government's military and civilian agencies, by the established ex-service organisations, and by the whole community.

Many of these stories may have been exaggerated or imported from American experience, but there had clearly been some serious failures in the repatriation procedures, caused as much by what was not done as by what was done. Many veterans had been welcomed home. Of the 16 battalions who served one-year tours, 15 received welcome-home marches, with the last being as welcoming as the first. Those who returned on HMAS *Sydney*, the 'Vung Tau ferry', had the benefit of a relatively slow trip home, with the opportunity to 'decompress' and prepare to be reintegrated into either civilian or regular service life. National servicemen, however, were discharged as soon as their two years' service was complete, even if that was only days before their unit was due to return. Like all those in units other than the infantry battalions and artillery batteries, they were flown back by chartered Qantas jets. Some found themselves departing Nui Dat one morning, flying back to Sydney where they arrived that night, to be given one night's accommodation and a train ticket to their home address, possibly interstate, with no debriefing or offers of continuing assistance. The absence of positive support or comprehension of the difficulties of reintegration into a totally different environment created a vacuum in which stories of hostile incidents could multiply and the sense of abandonment and disorientation could fester.

Some veterans, profoundly disappointed with the response of the authorities and the RSL to the evidence of physical and mental ailments, formed the Vietnam Veterans Association of Australia (VVAA). They particularly pressed two matters which in their minds were closely related. The first was the need for a counselling service specifically for Vietnam veterans, to minister to the number of cases of post-traumatic stress disorder (PTSD, now known as post-traumatic stress or PTS). Symptoms of PTSD commonly included 'flashbacks, nightmares, anxiety, rage and depression, often associated with alcohol and drug dependence' and the social effects included 'divorce and family breakdown, crime, violence, vagrancy, and even suicide'.[8] Considerable publicity was given to these problems, until it became common to associate Vietnam veterans with serious mental problems.

The VVAA also took up the assertion, developed in the United States, that many if not all of the ailments suffered by veterans and their families, including cancers, miscarriages and birth defects, as well as the typical manifestations of PTSD, were caused by the toxic herbicides sprayed by the US Air Force to defoliate jungles and destroy Viet Cong food sources. The name given to one of these herbicides, Agent Orange, came to be used collectively for them all. These campaigns, and the linking of PTSD with Agent Orange, reinforced the idea that Vietnam was an especially evil war. Vietnam, it seemed, was not only strategically unwise if not immoral in its purpose and in the methods used against the enemy; it also inflicted horrible ailments on those who fought for the United States and its allies, and on their offspring.

The VVAA's campaign aroused controversy not only in the agencies against which it was directed but also among veterans. Many, probably the majority of the 60 000 who served, had reintegrated well into society; a number, including national servicemen, some of whom had become officers, achieved notable success. Some objected to the implication that all Vietnam veterans were likely to be damaged and unstable. Many, believing that they had served honourably and well, wanted not to be singled out from the ANZAC tradition but to be incorporated into it. More veterans joined the RSL than joined the VVAA; more again joined neither.

The VVAA members proved effective lobbyists. Their first campaign bore fruit when the Vietnam Veterans Counselling Service was established and opened its first offices in 1982. Since then it has treated thousands of veterans, evidently with considerable success. Over time its exclusive concentration on veterans of the Vietnam War, a longstanding source of concern to the RSL, has changed. PTSD, from which more than 14 000 Vietnam veterans are now officially recognised as suffering, is generally seen as a close relative to the post-war traumas suffered by veterans of wars since ancient times, commonly known by terms such as 'shell shock' or 'combat neurosis' after the two world wars. The relevance of the counselling service to veterans of more recent campaigns was recognised in the early years of the 21st century. In 2007 the Vietnam

Veterans Counselling Service was officially renamed the VVCS – Veterans and Veterans Families Counselling Service. Its application to the veterans of all conflicts was thus recognised, while the retention of the acronym acknowledged the role of Vietnam veterans in its creation.

The campaign over Agent Orange encountered greater problems.[9] The evidence that many Vietnam veterans were suffering from a wide range of ailments was powerful, but it was extremely difficult to prove, by scientifically reputable standards, that the extensive range of diseases of mind and body encountered by veterans and their offspring had been caused by exposure to the herbicides sprayed in Vietnam. The VVAA succeeded in having a Royal Commission appointed in 1983 to investigate their claims. Two years later the Royal Commissioner, Justice Phillip Evatt, brought down a report of nine volumes and 2760 pages. To the bitter disappointment of the VVAA and its supporters, he pronounced Agent Orange to be 'not guilty' of the assertions made against it. Evatt evidently took the view later expressed more bluntly by one of the scientific advisers to the Royal Commission, who said that '… most of the problems that worried the veterans after the Vietnam War weren't due to Agent Orange: they were just due to it being a bloody awful war'.[10] The outcome appeared to vindicate the fears of the RSL that holding a Royal Commission on the Agent Orange question would limit rather than expand the ability of veterans to receive appropriate compensation.

The controversy that surrounded Evatt's uncompromising conclusion and the populist way in which it was expressed obscured some important points.[11] Evatt, like others before and since, pointed to post-traumatic stress, alcohol and smoking as major contributors to the veterans' problems, but amid the furore the government quietly rejected his recommendation that veterans should be compensated for ailments related to these causes. Evatt noted, in the body of the report but not in his summary, that there did appear to be a link between the toxic chemicals and some cancers. The VVAA also pointed out that he had criticised the Repatriation Commission's interpretation and application of the standard of proof required under the legislation, the so-called 'reverse onus of proof', which required the authorities to disprove a veteran's claim for compensation. The question of the standard of proof to be applied to such claims was a major source of contention between the repatriation authorities and the VVAA. Evatt had hoped that his report would assuage the fears of veterans and their families concerning the toxic chemicals while turning attention to the major sources of the real problems encountered by many veterans, but it only exacerbated the conflict between the activist veterans and the repatriation authorities.

Amid the continuing conflict over the standard of proof and the continuing arguments over toxic chemicals, many veterans made successful claims for disability pensions, including the 'totally and permanently incapacitated' (TPI) pension introduced after the 1914–18 war. By 2009 nearly 32 000 Vietnam veterans were receiving disability pensions, with more than 19 000 classified as TPI, of whom more than 14 000 were suffering from PTSD.[12] Many regarded a TPI pension as having been fully earned by stressful service in an unpopular war that had left them with physical or mental damage: some complained that the stipend was small and they were prohibited from working. Other veterans wondered whether the reputation of all veterans was damaged by the emphasis of those fighting the Agent Orange cause on the extent of physical and mental damage.

A degree of resolution of these vexed issues was achieved in the mid-1990s. A major scientific report and some policy changes in the United States opened the way for a greater degree of compensation to Vietnam veterans for many of the ailments that had been linked to toxic chemicals. In Australia the Veterans' Compensation Review Committee, established by Minister for Veterans' Affairs Senator John Faulkner and chaired by Professor Peter Baume, brought down in 1994 a report entitled *A Fair Go*, which sought to establish a 'balance between fairness to veterans (adequate compensation), fairness to taxpayers (protection of revenue), and fairness to other recipients of community support (relativities between payments)'.[13] The government subsequently introduced major amendments to the Veterans' Affairs legislation, which among other things established a Repatriation Medical Authority (RMA). Since then the leading medical practitioners on the RMA have established detailed Statements of Operating Principles, creating a consistent if complex framework within which claims by veterans for compensation for particular ailments are assessed. Most ex-service organisations, including the RSL and the VVAA, work within this system, but one group of veterans formed a separate organisation, the Vietnam Veterans Federation of Australia (VVFA), which has maintained the confrontational attitude towards repatriation and other authorities associated with the early days of the VVAA.[14]

In the meantime, veterans' organisations and governments had taken several measures to reassure Vietnam veterans that their service was honoured equally with those of earlier wars. In 1987 veterans' organisations arranged the 'Vietnam Forces National Reunion and Welcome Home March' in Sydney. More than 25 000 veterans were cheered by about 60 000 spectators in the march, which many veterans attested put to rest many of the negative aspects of their return to Australia. Five years later the Australian Vietnam Forces National Memorial was opened on Anzac Parade in Canberra, an unequivocal sign that the Vietnam War was now incorporated into the ANZAC tradition. By the turn of the century, 'Vietnam veteran' was a term of respect, most clearly demonstrated by public reactions to the appointments of Major General Peter Cosgrove as head of the international force in East Timor in 1999, of former national serviceman Tim Fischer as leader of the National Party and Deputy Prime Minister, and of Major General Mike Jeffery as Governor-General in 2003.

By the second decade of the 21st century, the mental health of veterans was widely recognised as a major problem for authorities to address. Far from being neglected, it was the subject of research and policy advice by many organisations. The potential problem foreseen for Iraq and Afghanistan veterans was that the system was so complex and structured that appropriate recognition, especially for stress-related ailments, could be unfairly delayed. Nevertheless, the Vietnam veterans had succeeded in placing the issue at the centre of debate. The attention given to the welfare of service personnel and their families during and after overseas service is greatly different from that applied during and after the Vietnam War.

SOME FINAL REFLECTIONS

The story told in the preceding chapters is of a government that faced a complex strategic situation in a region of immediate relevance to Australian security. During the 1950s the Menzies government developed a set of responses to the challenges of decolonisation and the Cold War in Southeast Asia. Forward defence was not simply a matter of 'fighting the enemy up there before we have to fight them here'. It struck a sensible balance between relationships with powerful but distant allies and those with the new nations of its region, and between the nation's financial and military resources and its commitments. The commitment to Malaya in the 1950s and other potential commitments were widely debated within the policy-making structures, in diplomatic channels and in public discourse. With a mixture of good management and good fortune, the government was more often than not successful – successful militarily, successful in its international relations, and successful in gaining domestic political support.

By the late 1950s and especially the early 1960s, a substantial part of the skill and sensitivity in management had gone. By 1964–65 the government was facing twin crises, with its two principal allies giving priority to two different theatres of conflict. One, Confrontation, was handled with considerable skill both diplomatically and militarily. Even as Australians and Indonesians were engaged in combat, diplomatic and aid relations were continued, while soldiers from each country attended staff colleges in the other.

The other conflict, in Vietnam, was handled quite differently. It was a far greater challenge, but the intellectual effort put into understanding its political and military dimensions, and the political and diplomatic skill employed in assessing the appropriate Australian responses, were paradoxically far less. Policy debates and consultation were narrowed when they most needed to be broadened; in the mind of Menzies and of those few to whom he entrusted crucial decisions and discussions, the complexities of the challenge were simplified. Menzies listened only to those who he knew agreed with him, and excluded knowledgeable advisers who recommended caution. As far as can be discerned from his statements and actions, Menzies believed that in making the commitment he was simply repeating a winning formula that would achieve military success in Southeast Asia, strengthen the alliance with the United States, and divide the Labor Party's right and left wings.

The fault lay not simply in the fact that Australia was committed to a conflict but in the imprudent and overconfident way in which Australian forces were committed, putting blind faith in the ability of American military power to overcome the perceived threat without giving careful attention to the nature of the challenge, the clarity of the political aim, the adequacy of the military strategy, or the ability of the Australian forces to apply their preferred tactics. As a result, the soldiers and others who served in Vietnam encountered a conflict for which they were not adequately prepared, while the public was drawn into a divisive issue that had profound consequences on many areas of Australian life. When the costs of the commitment began to bear heavily on Australian governments from late 1967 onwards, they found it impossible to disentangle themselves because of the incautious way in which the initial commitments had been made and escalated under the Menzies and Holt governments.

The servicemen acquitted themselves as well as could have been expected given the circumstances into which they were thrust. Because of the flawed nature of the RVN government and the strength of the position that the communists had gained by the time Australian forces – not to mention the vastly greater American forces – arrived, it is highly unlikely that any meaningful 'victory' could have been achieved. The allied forces in fact achieved all that could have been achieved: they delayed the communist victory by ten years, from 1965 to 1975, and in so doing they greatly reduced the impact on the other potential 'dominoes'. The strategic position facing Australia, as well as countries such as Thailand, Malaysia, Indonesia and Singapore, was much better in 1975 than it would have been if the RVN had fallen in 1965. The real tragedy is that many of those gains had already been achieved by around 1968 or 1969. If Australia, and more especially the United States, had found a way to depart the war around that time, all the countries involved in the war would have paid a smaller cost in blood and treasure, as well as environmental and social dislocation. Unrealistic definitions of 'victory', as much as the lack of clear political and military strategies, lay behind the disruption and dislocation caused by the war and the associated national service system.

Could it have been different? Much depends, of course, on how far one wishes to wind back the clock, or how many changes of personnel or political circumstance one posits. Woodard has suggested that Australian forces might not have been committed in 1965 if Barwick, instead of Hasluck, had still been Minister for External Affairs at that time.[15] That seems a little remote, given the determination of Menzies to press the commitment forward with all the authority that he possessed. It is conceivable, however, that Barwick, or another minister, might have challenged Menzies and those close to him sufficiently to temper the commitment and to ensure that it was less open-ended in both size and duration. Such a difference in 1965 would have made it easier to seek an honourable exit in, say, 1968 or 1969. It is also possible to imagine a different Australian Prime Minister taking a similar view to that of the New Zealand Prime Minister, Keith Holyoake, who was most reluctant to send forces to Vietnam. If the Australian, New Zealand and British Prime Ministers together had argued that they were playing a full part in ensuring stability in Southeast Asia by their involvement in countering Indonesia's Confrontation of Malaysia, perhaps they might have convinced an American administration to exempt them from service in Vietnam: but given the determination of President Johnson and his senior officials to enlist the support of allies in the region, with Australia and New Zealand at the head of the list, this may also be a long bow to draw.

With the benefit of half a century's hindsight, some of the old arguments take on different nuances. Vietnam was not an example of fighting 'other people's wars'; in the minds of Menzies and his principal advisers, it was a matter of getting the United States to fight a war for Australian security. Paying a premium for Australia's strategic insurance with the United States was not of itself wrong, but should have been handled with a great deal more care. The comparison with the way in which John Howard handled the Iraq commitment in 2003 is illustrative. Before 2003 Australian policy-makers had not held long-standing concerns about Iraq, as they had about Indochina before 1965, so the latter commitment was much more heavily based on concern for the alliance. But the manner in which the commitment was handled ensured that Howard did not pay the political price for Iraq that Menzies' successors did for Vietnam.

Both the insurance policy and the domino theory arguments for the Vietnam War commitment have gained a degree of vindication by events and policies over the subsequent 50 years. Australia did gain some of its strategic objectives from the service and sacrifice of those who were committed there, but the costs were unnecessarily high. When future Australian governments contemplate any more-or-less comparable commitments, they would be wise to remember how politicians, diplomats and military leaders in the 1950s and 1960s handled Australia's involvement in the Malayan Emergency and Confrontation as well as the commitment to the Vietnam War. Any future overseas commitment need not be 'another Vietnam', provided it is accompanied by careful and consultative decision-making, energetic and independent diplomacy, and skilful military leadership.

APPENDIX 1
AUSTRALIAN ARMY DEPLOYMENT IN VIETNAM 1962–73

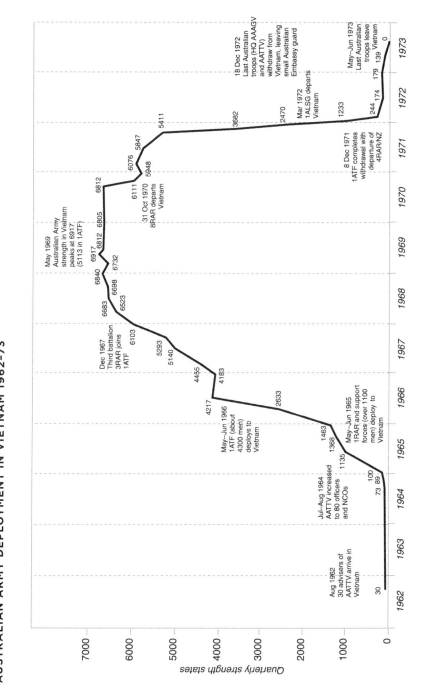

From *Fighting to the Finish: The Australian Army and the Vietnam War 1968–1975*, AWM, 2012

APPENDIX 2
AUSTRALIAN CHAIN OF COMMAND AND BATTALION DEPLOYMENT IN VIETNAM 1962–73

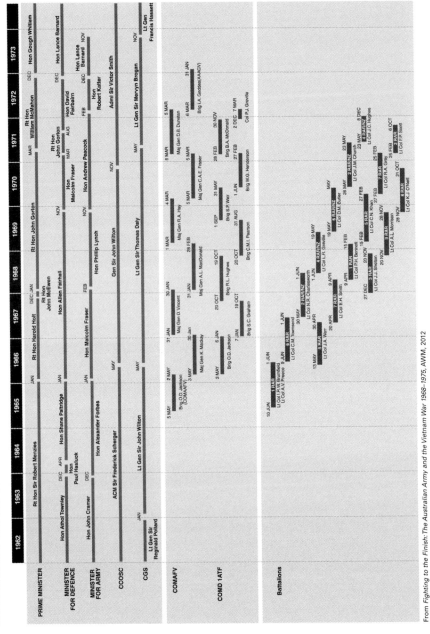

From *Fighting to the Finish: The Australian Army and the Vietnam War 1968–1975*, AWM, 2012

APPENDIX 3
PERSONS NAMED

The following list refers to the individuals named more than once in the text, with the positions held at the time to which reference is made.

Abdul Rahman Putra, Tunku
Malayan, later Malaysian, politician: first Prime Minister of Malaya, 1957–63, and of Malaysia, 1963–70.

Abrams, General Creighton
US army officer: Deputy to Commander of US Military Assistance Command Vietnam (COMUSMACV), 1967–68; Commander of US Military Assistance Command Vietnam (COMUSMACV), 1968–72.

Anderson, David
Australian diplomat: ambassador to the Republic of Vietnam, 1964–66.

Bao Dai
Vietnamese politician: deposed as Emperor by the Viet Minh, 1945; reinstated by France as Head of State of the Associated State of Vietnam, 1949; removed from power by Ngo Dinh Diem in referendum, 1955.

Barnard, Lance
Australian politician (ALP): Deputy Leader of the Labor Party and of the Opposition, 1967–72; Deputy Prime Minister, 1972–74; Minister for Defence, 1972–75.

Barwick, Sir Garfield
Australian politician (Liberal): Minister for External Affairs, 1961–64 (Acting Minister on occasions, 1959–61).

Beazley, Kim C
Australian politician (ALP): Minister for Defence, 1984–90.

Bevin, Ernest
UK politician (Labour): Foreign Secretary, 1945–51.

Bunting, Sir John
Australian public servant: Secretary of the Prime Minister's Department, 1959–68; Secretary of the Department of the Cabinet Office, 1968–71; Secretary of the Department of the Prime Minister and Cabinet, 1971–74.

Burton, Dr JW
Australian public servant: Secretary of the Department of External Affairs, 1947–50.

Cairns, Dr JF 'Jim'
Australian politician (ALP): leader of anti-war and anti-conscription protest movement in 1960s and early 1970s; Minister for Overseas Trade and for Secondary Industry, 1972–74; Deputy Prime Minister and Treasurer, 1974–75; Minister for the Environment, 1975.

Calwell, Arthur
Australian politician (ALP): Leader of the Labor Party and of the Opposition, 1960–67.

Cameron, Clyde
Australian politician (ALP): active in campaigns against the Vietnam War and conscription; Minister for Labour, 1972–74; Minister for Labour and Immigration, 1974–75.

Casey, RG
Australian politician (Liberal): Minister for External Affairs, 1951–60.

Chifley, JB 'Ben'
Australian politician (ALP): Prime Minister, 1945–49.

Chin Peng
Malayan communist leader: Secretary-General of the MCP from 1947; leader of the MCP throughout the Malayan Emergency.

Churchill, Sir Winston
UK politician (Conservative): Prime Minister, 1951–55.

Clifford, Clark
US lawyer and politician (Democrat): adviser to Presidents Truman, Kennedy and Johnson; Chairman Foreign Intelligence Advisory Board, 1963–68; Secretary of Defense, 1968–69.

Critchley, TK
Australian diplomat: High Commissioner to Malaya, 1957–63; to Malaysia, 1963–65.

Daly, Lieutenant General Sir Thomas
Australian army officer: Chief of General Staff, 1966–71.

De Gaulle, Charles
French army officer and politician: President of France, 1958–69.

Dedman, JJ
Australian politician (ALP): Minister for Defence, 1946–49.

Dulles, John Foster
US politician (Republican): Secretary of State, 1953–59.

Dunstan, Donald
Australian army officer: Deputy Commander (acting commander May 1968) 1st Australian Task Force, 1968–69 (Colonel); Commander Australian Force Vietnam (COMAFV), 1971–72 (Major General).

Eden, Sir Anthony
UK politician (Conservative): Foreign Secretary, 1951–55.

Eisenhower, Dwight D
US politician (Republican): President, 1953–61.

Evans, Gareth
Australian politician (ALP): Minister for Foreign Affairs, 1988–96.

Evatt, Dr HV
Australian lawyer and politician (ALP): Minister for External Affairs, 1941–49; Leader of the Opposition, 1951–60.

Ewell, Lieutenant General Julian
US army officer: Commander II Field Force Vietnam, 1969–70.

Fairhall, Allen
Australian politician (Liberal): Minister for Defence, 1966–69.

Fraser, Malcolm
Australian politician (Liberal): Minister for the Army, 1966–68; Minister for Education and Science, 1968–69; Minister for Defence, 1969–71; Leader of the Liberal Party and of the Opposition, 1975; Prime Minister, 1975–83.

Freeth, Gordon
Australian politician (Liberal): Minister for External Affairs, 1969.

Gorton, John
Australian politician (Liberal): Senator, 1950–68; MHR, 1968–71; Minister for the Navy, 1958–63; Minister Assisting the Minister for External Affairs, 1960–63; Prime Minister, 1968–71; Minister for Defence, March–August 1971.

Gotto, Ainsley
Australian official and entrepreneur: principal private secretary to John Gorton as Prime Minister and Minister for Defence, 1968–72.

Graham, Brigadier Stuart
Australian army officer: Commander 1st Australian Task Force, January to October 1967.

Harrison, Eric
Australian politician (Liberal): Minister for Defence, 1949–50; Resident Minister in London, 1950–51.

Hasluck, Paul
Australian politician (Liberal): Minister for External Affairs, 1964–69; Governor-General, 1969–74.

Hawke, RJL 'Bob'
Australian trade union official and politician (ALP): President, Australian Council of Trade Unions, 1969–79; Prime Minister, 1983–91.

Henderson, Brigadier WG
Australian army officer: Commander 1st Australian Task Force, 1970–71.

Hewitt, (Cyrus) Lenox
Australian public servant: Secretary of the Prime Minister's Department, 1968–71.

Ho Chi Minh
Vietnamese communist leader: President of the DRV, 1945–69; First Secretary of the Central Committee of the Communist Party, 1956–60.

Holt, Harold
Australian politician (Liberal): Treasurer, 1958–66; Prime Minister, 1966–67.

Holyoake, Keith
New Zealand politician (National): Prime Minister and Minister for External Affairs, 1960–72.

Hughes, Brigadier RL
Australian army officer: Commander 1st Australian Task Force, 1967–68.

Jackson, Brigadier OD
Australian army officer: Commander 1st Australian Task Force, 1966–67.

Johnson, Lyndon Baines
US politician (Democrat): Vice President, 1961–63; President, 1963–69.

Kennedy, John Fitzgerald
US politician (Democrat): President, 1961–63.

Kissinger, Henry
US academic and politician (Republican): national security adviser, 1969–75; Secretary of State, 1973–77.

Lai Tek
Secretary-General of Malayan Communist Party, 1939–47.

Le Duan
DRV politician: General Secretary of Central Committee of Communist Party of Vietnam, 1960–86.

Lee Kuan Yew
Singapore politician (People's Action Party): Prime Minister, 1959–90.

Letourneau, Jean
French politician: Minister for Relations with the Associated States, January to May 1953.

Lynch, Phillip
Australian politician (Liberal): Minister for the Army, 1968–69; Minister for Labour and National Service, 1971–72.

MacDonald, Major General AL
Australian army officer: Commander Australian Force Vietnam (COMAFV), 1968–69.

McDonald, Brigadier Bruce
Australian army officer: Commander 1st Australian Task Force, 1971.

MacDonald, Malcolm
UK official: Commissioner-General for Southeast Asia, 1948–55.

McEwen, John
Australian politician (Country Party): Leader of the Country Party, 1958–71; Minister for Trade and Industry, 1956–71; Prime Minister, December 1967 to January 1968; Deputy Prime Minister, 1968–71.

Mackay, Major General Ken
Australian army officer: Commander Australian Force Vietnam (COMAFV), 1966–67.

McMahon, William
Australian politician (Liberal): Minister for Labour and National Service, 1958–66; Treasurer, 1966–69; Minister for Foreign Affairs, 1969–71; Prime Minister, 1971–72.

McNamara, Robert S
US industrialist and politician (Democrat): Secretary of Defense, 1961–68.

Menzies, Sir Robert
Australian politician (Liberal): Prime Minister, 1939–41, 1949–66.

Mao Zedong (Mao Tse-tung)
Chinese communist leader: Chair of Central Committee and Politbureau, 1943–76; effective ruler of People's Republic of China, 1949–76.

Mountbatten, Admiral Lord Louis
UK naval officer: Supreme Allied Commander, Southeast Asia Command, 1943–46; UK Chief of Defence Staff and Chairman of Chiefs of Staff Committee, 1959–65.

Murdoch, Sir Keith
Australian journalist and newspaper magnate: Managing Director, Melbourne *Herald* and *Sun-News Pictorial*, 1939–49; Chairman of Directors, Herald and Weekly Times Ltd, 1942–52.

Nasution, Abdul Haris
Indonesian army officer: commander of division that suppressed communist rebellion at Madiun in 1948; narrowly escaped assassination in attempted coup of 30 September–1 October 1965.

Ngo Dinh Diem
RVN politician: President of RVN from 1955 until his assassination in November 1963.

Ngo Dinh Nhu
RVN politician: brother and adviser to Ngo Dinh Diem; assassinated November 1963.

Ngo Dinh Nhu, Madame
Wife of Ngo Dinh Nhu; effectively first lady of RVN.

Nguyen Cao Ky
RVN air force officer and politician: commander of RVN Air Force by 1960s; Prime Minister, 1965–67; Vice-President, 1967–71.

Nguyen Khanh
RVN army officer and politician: leader of government, January 1964 to February 1965.

Nguyen Van Thieu
RVN army officer and politician: Minister for Defence, 1964–65; Head of State, 1965–67; President, 1967–75.

Nixon, Richard M
US politician (Republican): Vice-President, 1953–61; President, 1969–74.

Paltridge, Senator Shane
Australian politician (Liberal): Minister for Defence, 1964–66.

Peacock, Andrew
Australian politician (Liberal): Minister for the Army, 1969–72.

Pearson, Brigadier CMI 'Sandy'
Australian army officer: Commander 1st Australian Task Force, 1968–69.

Petrov, Vladimir
Soviet official: intelligence officer in Soviet Embassy in Australia, defected 1954.

Phipps, Rear Admiral Sir Peter
New Zealand naval officer: Chief of Defence Staff, 1963–65.

Plimsoll, James
Australian diplomat: High Commissioner to India, 1962–65; Secretary of the Department of External Affairs (later Foreign Affairs), 1965–70; Ambassador to the United States, 1970–73.

Price, Geoffrey
Australian diplomat: ambassador to RVN, 1974–75.

Radford, Admiral Arthur
US naval officer: Chairman of Joint Chiefs of Staff, 1953–57.

Reid, Alan
Australian journalist and author.

Roosevelt, Franklin D
US politician (Democrat): President, 1933–45.

Rusk, Dean
US politician (Democrat): Secretary of State, 1961–69.

Santamaria, Bartholomew Augustine
Australian Catholic activist: President, Catholic Social Studies Movement, 1943–57; Director National Secretariat Catholic Action, 1947–54; founder and first President of National Civic Council, 1957.

Scherger, Sir Frederick
Australian air force officer: Air Officer Commanding (UK and Commonwealth) Far East Air Forces, Malaya, 1953–55 (Air Vice Marshal); Chairman of Chiefs of Staff Committee, 1961–66 (Air Chief Marshal).

Serong, Colonel FP 'Ted'
Australian army officer: Commander, Jungle Warfare Training Centre, Canungra, Qld, 1955–57; military adviser to government of Burma, 1957 and 1960–62; first commander of AATTV, 1965–68; adviser to Generals Harkins and Westmoreland as COMUSMACV.

Shann, Keith
Australian diplomat: ambassador to Indonesia, 1962–66.

Sharkey, Lawrence 'Lance'
Australian communist official: Secretary-General of Australian Communist Party, 1948–65.

Sharp, Admiral USG
US naval officer: Commander-in-Chief, US Pacific Command, 1964–68.

Shedden, Sir Frederick
Australian public servant: Secretary to Department of Defence, 1937–56.

Sihanouk, Prince Norodom
Cambodian monarch and politician: under a number of titles and offices, effective ruler of Cambodia, 1960–70.

Snedden, Billy
Australian politician (Liberal): Minister for Labour and National Service, 1969–71.

Spender, Sir Percy
Australian politician (Liberal): Minister for External Affairs, 1949–51.

Stalin, Joseph
Soviet politician: General Secretary of Communist Party of Soviet Union and effective ruler of USSR, 1924–53.

Subandrio
Indonesian politician: Foreign Minister, 1957–66.

Suharto
Indonesian general and politician: played a central role in the events of 30 September–1 October 1965; took effective power, 1966; Acting President, 1967–68; President, 1968–98.

Sukarno
Indonesian politician: proclaimed independence, 1945; achieved sovereignty, 1949; President, 1949–67; effectively removed from power, 1965.

Tange, Sir Arthur
Australian public servant: Secretary of Department of External Affairs, 1954–65; Secretary of Department of Defence, 1970–79.

Taylor, General Maxwell
US military officer and diplomat: military adviser to the US President, 1961–62; Chairman, Joint Chiefs of Staff, 1962–64; US ambassador to RVN, 1964–65; Special Consultant to the President, 1965–69; Chairman of Foreign Intelligence Advisory Board, 1968–69.

Townley, Athol
Australian politician (Liberal): Minister for Defence, 1958–63.

Truman, Harry S
US politician (Democrat): President, 1945–51.

Uren, Tom
Australian politician (ALP): active in campaigns against Vietnam War and conscription; Minister for Urban and Regional Development, 1972–75.

Vincent, Major General D 'Tim'
Australian army officer: Commander Australian Force Vietnam (COMAFV), 1967–68.

Vo Nguyen Giap
Vietnamese politician and military leader: Commander of PAVN at defeat of French at Dien Bien Phu, 1954; DRV Minister for Defence, 1955–76.

Waller, (John) Keith
Australian diplomat: First Assistant Secretary (in charge of Southeast Asia Division), Australian Department of External Affairs, 1962–64; Australian ambassador to US, 1964–70.

Warner, Denis Ashton
Australian correspondent in Asia; author of books on Vietnam War.

Weir, Brigadier Stuart
Australian army officer: Commander 1st Australian Task Force, 1969–70.

Westmoreland, General William
US army officer: Commander US Military Assistance Command Vietnam (COMUSMACV), 1964–68; Chief of Staff, US Army, 1968–72.

Whitlam, Edward Gough
Australian politician (ALP): Deputy Leader of the Labor Party and of the Opposition, 1960–67; Leader of the Labor Party and of the Opposition, 1967–72; Prime Minister, 1972–75.

White, William
Australian conscientious objector.

Willesee, Senator Donald
Australian politician (ALP): Minister for Foreign Affairs, 1973–75.

Wilson, Harold
UK politician (Labour): Prime Minister, 1964–70, 1974–76.

Wilton, John Gordon Noel
Australian army officer: Chief, Military Planning Office, SEATO, 1960–63 (Major General); Chief of General Staff, Australian Army, 1963–66 (Lieutenant General); Chairman of Chiefs of Staff Committee, 1966–70 (General).

Zhou Enlai (Chou En-lai)
Chinese politician: Premier of People's Republic of China, 1949–76; Foreign Minister, 1949–58.

NOTES

1 DECOLONISATION AND THE COLD WAR IN SOUTHEAST ASIA 1945–50

1 See Peter Edwards with Gregory Pemberton, *Crises and Commitments: The Politics and Diplomacy of Australia's Involvement in Southeast Asian Conflicts 1948–1965*, Allen & Unwin in association with the Australian War Memorial, Sydney, 1992, and the sources cited there, together with Christopher Bayly and Tim Harper, *Forgotten Wars: Freedom and Revolution in Southeast Asia*, Harvard University Press, Cambridge Mass., 2007; and Milton Osborne, *Southeast Asia: An Introductory History*, 10th edition, Allen & Unwin, Sydney, 2010.

2 AUSTRALIA AND SOUTHEAST ASIA 1945–53

1 Peter Edwards with Gregory Pemberton, *Crises and Commitments: The Politics and Diplomacy of Australia's Involvement in Southeast Asian Conflicts 1948–1965*, Allen & Unwin in association with the Australian War Memorial, Sydney, 1992, chs 1–7.
2 Edwards with Pemberton, *Crises and Commitments*, p. 12.
3 On the origins and early development of the Royal Australian Regiment, see David Horner and Jean Bou eds, *Duty First: A History of the Royal Australian Regiment*, Allen & Unwin, Sydney, 2008, chs 1–3.
4 Edwards with Pemberton, *Crises and Commitments*, p. 70.
5 Edwards with Pemberton, *Crises and Commitments*, p. 84.
6 Edwards with Pemberton, *Crises and Commitments*, p. 87.
7 Edwards with Pemberton, *Crises and Commitments*, pp. 94–95.
8 Peter Dennis and Jeffrey Grey, *Emergency and Confrontation: Australian Military Operations in*

Malaya and Borneo 1950–1966, Allen & Unwin in association with the Australian War Memorial, Sydney, 1996, Part I.
9 Dennis and Grey, *Emergency and Confrontation*, p. 33.
10 Edwards with Pemberton, *Crises and Commitments*, chs 7–9.
11 Edwards with Pemberton, *Crises and Commitments*, p. 110.
12 Edwards with Pemberton, *Crises and Commitments*, p. 113.

3 AUSTRALIA AND SOUTHEAST ASIA 1954-60

1 Peter Edwards with Gregory Pemberton, *Crises and Commitments: The Politics and Diplomacy of Australia's Involvement in Southeast Asian Conflicts 1948–1965*, Allen & Unwin in association with the Australian War Memorial, Sydney, 1992, ch. 8.
2 Edwards with Pemberton, *Crises and Commitments*, pp. 139–53.
3 Edwards with Pemberton, *Crises and Commitments*, pp. 153–59.
4 David Horner, *Strategic Command: General Sir John Wilton and Australia's Asian Wars*, Oxford University Press, Melbourne, 2005, ch. 13. See also Damien Fenton, *To Cage the Red Dragon: SEATO and the Defence of Southeast Asia 1955–1965*, NUS Press, Singapore, 2012.
5 See Edwards with Pemberton, *Crises and Commitments*, ch. 10.
6 Menzies, 20 April 1955, cited in Edwards with Pemberton, *Crises and Commitments*, p. 171.
7 Peter Dennis and Jeffrey Grey, *Emergency and Confrontation: Australian Military Operations in Malaya and Borneo 1950–1966*, Allen & Unwin in association with the Australian War Memorial, Sydney, 1996, Part I, 'The Malayan Emergency'.
8 Dennis and Grey, *Emergency and Confrontation*, p. 164.
9 See, for example, John Nagl, *Learning to Eat Soup with a Knife: Counterinsurgency Lessons from Malaya and Vietnam*, University of Chicago Press, Chicago, 2005.
10 Dennis and Grey, *Emergency and Confrontation*, p. 165.
11 Edwards with Pemberton, *Crises and Commitments*, pp. 192–200.
12 Edwards with Pemberton, *Crises and Commitments*, pp. 200–07.
13 Menzies, 4 April 1957, quoted in Edwards with Pemberton, *Crises and Commitments*, p. 205.
14 Edwards with Pemberton, *Crises and Commitments*, pp. 205–06; Peter Edwards, *Arthur Tange: Last of the Mandarins*, Allen & Unwin, Sydney, 2006, pp. 124–26.

4 THE CRISES OF THE EARLY 1960s

1 Peter Edwards with Gregory Pemberton, *Crises and Commitments: The Politics and Diplomacy of Australia's Involvement in Southeast Asian Conflicts 1948–1965*, Allen & Unwin in association with the Australian War Memorial, Sydney, 1992, ch. 12.
2 Garry Woodard, *Asian Alternatives: Australia's Vietnam Decision and Lessons on Going to War*, Melbourne University Publishing, Melbourne, 2004, ch. 2.
3 Menzies, 2 May 1961, quoted in Edwards with Pemberton, *Crises and Commitments*, pp. 223–24.
4 Edwards with Pemberton, *Crises and Commitments*, pp. 230–32.

5 Edwards with Pemberton, *Crises and Commitments*, pp. 232–33, 238–39.
6 Edwards with Pemberton, *Crises and Commitments*, ch. 13.
7 Denis Warner, *Herald*, 12 May 1962, quoted in Edwards with Pemberton, *Crises and Commitments*, p. 249.
8 Chris Coulthard-Clark, *The RAAF in Vietnam: Australian Air Involvement in the Vietnam War 1962–1975*, Allen & Unwin in association with the Australian War Memorial, Sydney, 1995, ch. 1.
9 Ian McNeill, *The Team: Australian Army Advisers in Vietnam 1962–1972*, University of Queensland Press in association with the Australian War Memorial, Brisbane, 1984.
10 A sympathetic biography is Anne Blair, *Ted Serong: The Life of an Australian Counter-Insurgency Expert*, Oxford University Press, Melbourne, 2002. See also Ashley Ekins with Ian McNeill, *Fighting to the Finish: The Australian Army and the Vietnam War, 1968–1975*, Allen & Unwin in association with the Australian War Memorial, Sydney, 2012, pp. 669, 679, 1061; and Jeffrey Grey, *A Soldier's Soldier: A Biography of Lieutenant-General Sir Thomas Daly*, Cambridge University Press, Melbourne 2013, pp. 128–29.
11 'Strategic Basis of Australian Defence Policy', 13 July 1962, and associated Cabinet papers, quoted in Edwards with Pemberton, *Crises and Commitments*, p. 248.
12 Edwards with Pemberton, *Crises and Commitments*, p. 254.
13 Edwards with Pemberton, *Crises and Commitments*, ch. 14.
14 Edwards with Pemberton, *Crises and Commitments*, pp. 269–72.
15 Alan Stephens, *The Royal Australian Air Force*, vol. II of *The Australian Centenary History of Defence*, Oxford University Press, Melbourne, 2001, pp. 285–88.
16 Menzies, 22 May 1963, quoted in Edwards with Pemberton, *Crises and Commitments*, p. 272.
17 Edwards with Pemberton, *Crises and Commitments*, pp. 255–70; Peter Dennis and Jeffrey Grey, *Emergency and Confrontation: Australian Military Operations in Malaya and Borneo 1950–1966*, Allen & Unwin in association with the Australian War Memorial, Sydney, 1996, chs 10–12.
18 Edwards with Pemberton, *Crises and Commitments*, pp. 280–81.
19 Edwards with Pemberton, *Crises and Commitments*, pp. 273–75.
20 Edwards with Pemberton, *Crises and Commitments*, p. 274; Coulthard-Clark, *RAAF in Vietnam*, pp. 29–30.
21 Edwards with Pemberton, *Crises and Commitments*, chs 15, 16.
22 Woodard, *Asian Alternatives*, ch. 16.

5 COMMITMENTS TO CONFRONTATION AND VIETNAM 1965

1 Peter Edwards with Gregory Pemberton, *Crises and Commitments: The Politics and Diplomacy of Australia's Involvement in Southeast Asian Conflicts 1948–1965*, Allen & Unwin in association with the Australian War Memorial, Sydney, 1992, ch. 17.
2 Edwards with Pemberton, *Crises and Commitments*, p. 335.
3 Hasluck, 19 January 1965, quoted in Edwards with Pemberton, *Crises and Commitments*, p. 342.

4 Marshall Green, 5 January 1965, quoted in Edwards with Pemberton, *Crises and Commitments*, p. 339.
5 Edwards with Pemberton, *Crises and Commitments*, pp. 335ff.
6 On the Australian decision-making in December 1964, see Edwards with Pemberton, *Crises and Commitments*, pp. 335ff., and Garry Woodard, *Asian Alternatives: Australia's Vietnam Decision and Lessons on Going to War*, Melbourne University Publishing, Melbourne, 2004, chs 10 and 11.
7 Edwards with Pemberton, *Crises and Commitments*, pp. 340–34; Peter Dennis and Jeffrey Grey, *Emergency and Confrontation: Australian Military Operations in Malaya and Borneo 1950–1966*, Allen & Unwin in association with the Australian War Memorial, Sydney, 1996, ch. 11; Jeffrey Grey, *Up Top: The Royal Australian Navy and Southeast Asian Conflicts 1955–1972*, Allen & Unwin in association with the Australian War Memorial, Sydney, 1998, ch. 3.
8 John McEwen, January 1965, quoted in Edwards with Pemberton, *Crises and Commitments*, p. 341.
9 Edwards with Pemberton, *Crises and Commitments*, ch. 18.
10 See Edwards with Pemberton, *Crises and Commitments*, pp. 358 and 489, n.29.
11 See Roberto Rabel, *New Zealand and the Vietnam War: Politics and Diplomacy*, Auckland University Press, Auckland, 2005, ch. 4.
12 Edwards with Pemberton, *Crises and Commitments*, pp. 361–62.
13 Edwards with Pemberton, *Crises and Commitments*, pp. 367ff.
14 Edwards with Pemberton, *Crises and Commitments*, pp. 363–75; Peter Edwards, *A Nation at War: Australian Politics, Society and Diplomacy during the Vietnam War 1965–1975*, Allen & Unwin in association with the Australian War Memorial, Sydney, 1997, ch. 2.
15 Edwards with Pemberton, *Crises and Commitments*, pp. 355–56, 363, 365–66.
16 Edwards with Pemberton, *Crises and Commitments*, pp. 372–74.
17 Edwards, *A Nation at War*, pp. 33–34.
18 Edwards, *A Nation at War*, p. 34.
19 Edwards, *A Nation at War*, ch. 2.
20 Edwards, *A Nation at War*, pp. 67–71.
21 Edwards, *A Nation at War*, pp. 77–85.
22 Dennis and Grey, *Emergency and Confrontation*, ch. 15.
23 Ian McNeill, *To Long Tan: The Australian Army and the Vietnam War 1950–1966*, Allen & Unwin in association with the Australian War Memorial, Sydney, 1993, pp. 13–15, 21–23; John Blaxland, *Organising an Army: The Australian Experience 1957–65*, Canberra, 1989; Dennis and Grey, *Emergency and Confrontation*, p. 218.
24 Dennis and Grey, *Emergency and Confrontation*, p. 281.
25 McNeill, *To Long Tan*, chs 4–7.
26 McNeill, *To Long Tan*, ch. 8.
27 Edwards, *A Nation at War*, pp. 56–62.
28 Edwards, *A Nation at War*, pp. 62–64.

6 THE TASK FORCE AND THE ELECTION 1966

1 Peter Edwards, *A Nation at War: Australian Politics, Society and Diplomacy during the Vietnam War 1965–1975*, Allen & Unwin in association with the Australian War Memorial, Sydney, 1997, ch. 4.

2. Peter Edwards with Gregory Pemberton, *Crises and Commitments: The Politics and Diplomacy of Australia's Involvement in Southeast Asian Conflicts 1948–1965*, Allen & Unwin in association with the Australian War Memorial, Sydney, 1992, p. 362.
3. Edwards, *A Nation at War*, p. 140, p. 405, n. 4.
4. Edwards, *A Nation at War*, pp. 140–41.
5. Edwards, *A Nation at War*, pp. 93–96.
6. Peter Dennis and Jeffrey Grey, *Emergency and Confrontation: Australian Military Operations in Malaya and Borneo 1950–1966*, Allen & Unwin in association with the Australian War Memorial, Sydney, 1996, ch. 16.
7. Edwards, *A Nation at War*, chs 5 and 6.
8. Edwards, *A Nation at War*, pp. 106–07.
9. TB Millar, *Australia's Defence*, Melbourne University Press, Melbourne, 1965, p. 187.
10. Ian McNeill, *To Long Tan: The Australian Army and the Vietnam War 1950–1966*, Allen & Unwin in association with the Australian War Memorial, Sydney, 1993, chs 8, 9 and 10.
11. McNeill, *To Long Tan*, chs 14, 15 and 16.
12. McNeill, *To Long Tan*, ch. 18.
13. McNeill, *To Long Tan*, pp. 430–33 at 431. On army–RAAF relations, see also Chris Coulthard-Clark, *The RAAF in Vietnam: Australian Air Involvement in the Vietnam War 1962–1975*, Allen & Unwin in association with the Australian War Memorial, Sydney, 1995, pp. 77–81, 140–44; Jeffrey Grey, *A Soldier's Soldier: A Biography of Lieutenant-General Sir Thomas Daly*, Cambridge University Press, Melbourne, 2013, pp. 148–52, 163–67.
14. McNeill, *To Long Tan*, pp. 427–30.
15. McNeill, *To Long Tan*, pp. 424–30.
16. Edwards, *A Nation at War*, pp. 111–18.
17. Edwards, *A Nation at War*, p. 112.
18. Edwards, *A Nation at War*, pp. 133–41.
19. Edwards, *A Nation at War*, pp. 133–41.

7 ESCALATION OF THE COMMITMENT, ESCALATION OF CONTROVERSY 1967

1. Peter Edwards, *A Nation at War: Australian Politics, Society and Diplomacy during the Vietnam War 1965–1975*, Allen & Unwin in association with the Australian War Memorial, Sydney, 1997, ch. 8. See also Tom Frame, *The Life and Death of Harold Holt*, Allen & Unwin in association with the National Archives of Australia, Sydney, 2005.
2. Edwards, *A Nation at War*, p. 162.
3. Ian McNeill and Ashley Ekins, *On the Offensive: The Australian Army in the Vietnam War 1967–1968*, Allen & Unwin in association with the Australian War Memorial, Sydney, 2003, ch. 1.
4. McNeill and Ekins, *On the Offensive*, p. 6.
5. Edwards, *A Nation at War*, ch. 7.
6. Edwards, *A Nation at War*, p. 147.
7. McNeill and Ekins, *On the Offensive*, p. 35.
8. McNeill and Ekins, *On the Offensive*, p. 63.
9. McNeill and Ekins, *On the Offensive*, p. 70.
10. McNeill and Ekins, *On the Offensive*, p. 115.
11. McNeill and Ekins, *On the Offensive*, pp. 127ff, 178–84; Ashley Ekins with

Ian McNeill, *Fighting to the Finish*, Allen & Unwin in association with the Australian War Memorial, Sydney, 2012, ch. 8. See also Greg Lockhart, *The Minefield: An Australian Tragedy in Vietnam*, Allen & Unwin, Sydney, 2007; Jeffrey Grey, *A Soldier's Soldier: A Biography of Lieutenant-General Sir Thomas Daly*, Cambridge University Press, Melbourne, 2013, pp. 168–70.

12 Ekins with McNeill, *Fighting to the Finish*, p. 273.
13 McNeill and Ekins, *On the Offensive*, p. 179.
14 Ekins with McNeill, *Fighting to the Finish*, pp. 268, 270.
15 Ekins with McNeill, *Fighting to the Finish*, p. 274.
16 Lockhart, *The Minefield*, p. xix.
17 Ekins with McNeill, *Fighting to the Finish*, pp. 270ff, especially p. 274.
18 Grey, *A Soldier's Soldier*, p. 170. See also David Horner, *Strategic Command: General Sir John Wilton and Australia's Asian Wars*, Oxford University Press, Melbourne, 2005, pp. 328–31.
19 McNeill and Ekins, *On the Offensive*, p. 222.
20 Edwards, *A Nation at War*, ch. 7; McNeill and Ekins, *On the Offensive*, pp. 245–50 at p. 246.
21 Edwards, *A Nation at War*, p. 155.
22 Edwards, *A Nation at War*, p. 156.
23 McNeill and Ekins, *On the Offensive*, pp. 162–4. See also the chart of chain of command and the battalion tours, Ekins with McNeill, *Fighting to the Finish*, p. 839.
24 McNeill and Ekins, *On the Offensive*, pp. 81–84.
25 McNeill and Ekins, *On the Offensive*, p. 39.
26 Jeffrey Grey, *Up Top: The Royal Australian Navy and Southeast Asian Conflicts 1955–1972*, Allen & Unwin in association with the Australian War Memorial, Sydney, 1998, ch. 5.
27 Grey, *Up Top*, ch. 6.
28 Grey, *Up Top*, ch. 8.
29 Grey, *Up Top*, ch. 7.
30 Chris Coulthard-Clark, *The RAAF in Vietnam: Australian Air Involvement in the Vietnam War 1962–1975*, Allen & Unwin in association with the Australian War Memorial, Sydney, 1995, chs 3 and 6.
31 Coulthard-Clark, *RAAF in Vietnam*, ch. 5.
32 Edwards, *A Nation at War*, pp. 173–76.

8 THE TURNING-POINT 1968–69

1 Peter Edwards, *A Nation at War: Australian Politics, Society and Diplomacy during the Vietnam War 1965–1975*, Allen & Unwin in association with the Australian War Memorial, Sydney, 1997, pp. 177–85.
2 Ian McNeill and Ashley Ekins, *On the Offensive: The Australian Army in the Vietnam War 1967–1968*, Allen & Unwin in association with the Australian War Memorial, Sydney, 2003, pp. 287ff; Edwards, *A Nation at War*, pp. 191–93.
3 McNeill and Ekins, *On the Offensive*, p. 311.
4 McNeill and Ekins, *On the Offensive*, pp. 315ff; Edwards, *A Nation at War*, p. 193.
5 Edwards, *A Nation at War*, ch. 9.
6 Edwards, *A Nation at War*, ch. 10. See also Ian Hancock, *John Gorton: He Did it His Way*, Hodder, Sydney, 2002.
7 Edwards, *A Nation at War*, p. 193.
8 Edwards, *A Nation at War*, ch. 10.
9 *Sydney Morning Herald*, 11 December

1968; quoted in Edwards, *A Nation at War*, p. 200.
10 Edwards, *A Nation at War*, p. 202.
11 Edwards, *A Nation at War*, p. 202.
12 Ashley Ekins with Ian McNeill, *Fighting to the Finish*, Allen & Unwin in association with the Australian War Memorial, Sydney, 2012, pp. 305–13; Edwards, *A Nation at War*, pp. 203–04.
13 Edwards, *A Nation at War*, ch. 11.
14 Ashley Ekins, ' "Not One Scintilla of Evidence"?: The Media, the Military and the Government in the Vietnam Water Torture Case', *Australian Journal of Politics and History*, vol. 42, no. 3, 1996, pp. 345–62; Edwards, *A Nation at War*, p. 208–11; Ian McNeill, *To Long Tan: The Australian Army and the Vietnam War 1950–1966*, Allen & Unwin in association with the Australian War Memorial, Sydney, 1993, pp. 395–98.
15 Edwards, *A Nation at War*, pp. 212–22.
16 McNeill and Ekins, *On the Offensive*, ch. 10.
17 Gerard Windsor, *All Day Long the Noise of Battle: An Australian Attack in Vietnam*, Pier 9, Sydney, 2011. See also McNeill and Ekins, *On the Offensive*, pp. 299–301.
18 McNeill and Ekins, *On the Offensive*, chs 12, 13.
19 McNeill and Ekins, *On the Offensive*, p. 341.
20 McNeill and Ekins, *On the Offensive*, chs 12, 13.
21 McNeill and Ekins, *On the Offensive*, p. 348.
22 Ekins with McNeill, *Fighting to the Finish*, chs 1, 2.
23 Ekins with McNeill, *Fighting to the Finish*, p. 391.
24 Ekins with McNeill, *Fighting to the Finish*, ch. 7.
25 Ekins with McNeill, *Fighting to the Finish*, ch. 8.
26 Chris Coulthard-Clark, *The RAAF in Vietnam: Australian Air Involvement in the Vietnam War 1962–1975*, Allen & Unwin in association with the Australian War Memorial, Sydney, 1995, chs 7 and 8.
27 Jeffrey Grey, *Up Top: The Royal Australian Navy and Southeast Asian Conflicts 1955–1972*, Allen & Unwin in association with the Australian War Memorial, Sydney, 1998, ch. 7.
28 Coulthard-Clark, *RAAF in Vietnam*, ch. 6.
29 Grey, *Up Top*, pp. 175–88.
30 Coulthard-Clark, *RAAF in Vietnam*, ch. 8.
31 Edwards, *A Nation at War*, pp. 233–35.
32 Edwards, *A Nation at War*, p. 233.
33 Clyde Cameron, *China, Communism and Coca-Cola*, Hill of Content, Melbourne, 1980, pp. 222–23.

9 SOCIAL DISSENT, POLITICAL DIVISION AND MILITARY WITHDRAWAL 1969–72

1 Peter Edwards, *Arthur Tange: Last of the Mandarins*, Allen & Unwin, Sydney, 2006, ch. 10.
2 Peter Edwards, *A Nation at War: Australian Politics, Society and Diplomacy during the Vietnam War 1965–1975*, Allen & Unwin in association with the Australian War Memorial, Sydney, 1997, pp. 236–45; Ashley Ekins with Ian McNeill, *Fighting to the Finish*, Allen & Unwin in association with the Australian War Memorial, Sydney, 2012, pp. 305–13.
3 Edwards, *A Nation at War*, pp, 245–75.
4 The following passage is based on

Edwards, *A Nation at War*, pp. 267–70. Sources are cited in Edwards, *A Nation at War*, p. 420, notes 1–3.
5 John Hamilton, *The Age*, 9 May 1970, cited in Edwards, *A Nation at War*, p. 270.
6 Ekins with McNeill, *Fighting to the Finish*, chs 10–12.
7 Major General RA Grey, quoted in Ekins with McNeill, *Fighting to the Finish*, p. 316.
8 Ekins with McNeill, *Fighting to the Finish*, p. 390.
9 Ekins with McNeill, *Fighting to the Finish*, chs 13–14.
10 Ekins with McNeill, *Fighting to the Finish*, p. 434.
11 Ekins with McNeill, *Fighting to the Finish*, pp. 473–75.
12 Ekins with McNeill, *Fighting to the Finish*, p. 487–88. Kerry is quoted on p. 488.
13 Ekins with McNeill, *Fighting to the Finish*, pp. 496–501.
14 Ekins with McNeill, *Fighting to the Finish*, pp. 353–56, 487–92.
15 The following passage is based on Ekins with McNeill, *Fighting to the Finish*, pp. 353–56, 487–90. The quotations are from pp. 487, 489 and 490.
16 Edwards, *A Nation at War*, pp. 292–97; Jeffrey Grey, *A Soldier's Soldier: A Biography of Lieutenant-General Sir Thomas Daly*, Cambridge University Press, Melbourne, 2013, ch. 7; Ian Hancock, *John Gorton: He Did it His Way*, Hodder, Sydney, 2002, p. 320; Edwards, *Arthur Tange*, pp. 187–90. See also the sources cited in Edwards, *A Nation at War*, p. 424, n. 5.
17 Edwards, *A Nation at War*, pp. 297–301.
18 Edwards, *A Nation at War*, pp. 302ff.
19 Edwards, *A Nation at War*, p. 303.
20 Edwards, *A Nation at War*, pp. 302, 305.
21 Edwards, *A Nation at War*, p. 307.
22 Edwards, *A Nation at War*, pp. 311–12.
23 Ekins with McNeill, *Fighting to the Finish*, chs 16–18.
24 Ekins with McNeill, *Fighting to the Finish*, pp. 598–601.
25 Ekins with McNeill, *Fighting to the Finish*, pp. 515ff, 521–23.
26 Ekins with McNeill, *Fighting to the Finish*, p. 626.
27 Ekins with McNeill, *Fighting to the Finish*, pp. 586–88, 638–51.
28 Ekins with McNeill, *Fighting to the Finish*, pp. 506–11.
29 Ekins with McNeill, *Fighting to the Finish*, p. 511.
30 Ekins with McNeill, *Fighting to the Finish*, pp. 654–55.
31 Grey, *Up Top*, pp. 261–79.
32 Grey, *Up Top*, pp. 314–19.
33 Grey, *Up Top*, pp. 216–35.
34 Chris Coulthard-Clark, *The RAAF in Vietnam: Australian Air Involvement in the Vietnam War 1962–1975*, Allen & Unwin in association with the Australian War Memorial, Sydney, 1995, ch. 9, esp. pp. 201, 205–13.
35 Coulthard-Clark, *RAAF in Vietnam*, pp. 126–29.

10 THE WHITLAM GOVERNMENT AND THE END OF THE VIETNAM WAR 1972–75

1 Peter Edwards, *A Nation at War: Australian Politics, Society and Diplomacy during the Vietnam War 1965–1975*, Allen & Unwin in association with the Australian War Memorial, Sydney, 1997, pp. 319–20;

Ian McNeill and Ashley Ekins, *On the Offensive: The Australian Army in the Vietnam War 1967–1968*, Allen & Unwin in association with the Australian War Memorial, Sydney, 2003, pp. 655–58.
2 Brigadier Ian Geddes, quoted in Edwards, *A Nation at War*, p. 320.
3 Ekins with McNeill, *Fighting to the Finish*, pp. 657, 787.
4 Edwards, *A Nation at War*, pp. 320–25.
5 Edwards, *A Nation at War*, p. 321.
6 James Curran, 'Whitlam v Nixon', *The Australian*, 1 August 2012 (an excerpt from *The Monthly*, August 2012).
7 Edwards, *A Nation at War*, p. 328.
8 Edwards, *A Nation at War*, pp. 325–28.
9 Edwards, *Arthur Tange*, pp. 201–16.
10 Edwards, *A Nation at War*, pp. 329–99.
11 *Sydney Morning Herald*, 30 April 1975.

11 LESSONS, LEGACIES AND LEGENDS

1 Kim Beazley, 'A National Asset', in Brendan Taylor, Nicholas Farrelly and Sheryn Lee eds, *Insurgent Intellectual: Essays in Honour of Professor Desmond Ball*, ISEAS Publishing, Singapore, 2012, p. 167.
2 Peter Edwards, *Permanent Friends? Historical Reflections on the Australian-American Alliance*, Lowy Institute Paper 08, Longueville Media for the Lowy Institute, Sydney, 2005, ch. 3, 'The Challenges of the 1970s and 1980s'.
3 Garry Woodard, *Asian Alternatives: Australia's Vietnam Decision and Lessons on Going to War*, Melbourne University Publishing, Melbourne, 2004, pp. 348–50.
4 David Goldsworthy, David Dutton, Peter Gifford and Roderic Pitty, in David Goldsworthy ed., *Facing North: A Century of Engagement with Asia*, Melbourne University Press, Melbourne, 2001, p. 314.
5 D Goldsworthy, D Dutton, P Gifford and R Pitty, 'Reorientation', ch. 8 in D Goldsworthy, *Facing North*, pp. 310–71.
6 D Goldsworthy, D Dutton, P Gifford and R Pitty, 'Reorientation', ch. 8 in D Goldsworthy, *Facing North*, p. 312.
7 A useful summary of these themes is given in Ashley Ekins with Ian McNeill, *Fighting to the Finish: The Australian Army and the Vietnam War, 1968–1975*, Allen & Unwin in association with the Australian War Memorial, Sydney, 2012, pp. 697–705. The principal reference in the *Official History of Australia's Involvement in Southeast Asian Conflicts 1948–1975* is FB Smith, 'Agent Orange: The Australian Aftermath', in Brendan G. O'Keefe with FB Smith, *Medicine at War: Medical Aspects of Australia's Involvement in Southeast Asia 1950–1972*, Allen & Unwin in association with the Australian War Memorial, Sydney, 1994, pp. 281–363.
8 Ekins, *Fighting to the Finish*, p. 701.
9 Smith, 'Agent Orange: The Australian Aftermath', pp. 281–363.
10 Professor John Mathews, quoted in Robin Hill, 'Old Wounds Re-opened', *The Bulletin*, 15 March 1994, pp. 40–41.
11 Graham Walker, 'The Official History's Agent Orange Account: The Veterans' Perspective', ch. 10 in Ashley Ekins and Elizabeth Stewart eds, *War Wounds: Medicine and the Trauma of Conflict*, Exisle Publishing,

Wollombi NSW, 2011, pp. 148–61. See also Peter Edwards, 'Australia's Agent Orange Story: A Historian's Perspective', ch. 11 in Ekins and Stewart, *War Wounds*, pp. 162–82.

12 Department of Veterans' Affairs information cited in Ekins, *Fighting to the Finish*, p. 701.

13 *A Fair Go: Report on Compensation for Veterans and War Widows*, Australian Government Publishing Service, Canberra, March 1994, p. vii.

14 See, for example, the article by Graham Walker cited in note 11, and VVFA publications such as the *Vietnam Veterans Peacekeepers and Peacemakers Journal*.

15 Woodard, *Asian Alternatives*, ch. 16.

FURTHER READING

As indicated in the Preface, this book relies heavily on the research and analysis of the nine volumes of the *Official History of Australia's Involvement in Southeast Asian Conflicts 1948–1975*. Those volumes, like those of the Australian official histories of the 1914–18, 1939–45 and Korean wars, were based on unrestricted access to all relevant Australian government records. The only two caveats placed on the use of this material were to protect the security of material provided to the Australian government in confidence by foreign governments, and to ensure the security of material relating to the intelligence-gathering process. The books were not subject to official or political censorship: the selection of material and the judgements expressed were those of the authors.

Each volume of the *Official History* includes an extensive bibliography of primary and secondary sources relevant to that volume.

The nine volumes of the *Official History of Australia's Involvement in Southeast Asian Conflicts 1948–1975* are, in order of appearance:
- Edwards, Peter, with Pemberton, Gregory, *Crises and Commitments:*

- *The Politics and Diplomacy of Australia's Involvement in Southeast Asian Conflicts 1948–1965*, Allen & Unwin in association with the Australian War Memorial, Sydney, 1992.
- McNeill, Ian, *To Long Tan: The Australian Army and the Vietnam War 1950–1965*, Allen & Unwin in association with the Australian War Memorial, Sydney, 1993.
- O'Keefe, Brendan, *Medicine at War: Medical Aspects of Australia's Involvement in Southeast Asian Conflicts 1950–1972*, with 'Agent Orange: the Australian aftermath' by FB Smith, Allen & Unwin in association with the Australian War Memorial, Sydney, 1994.
- Coulthard-Clark, Chris, *The RAAF in Vietnam: Australian Air Involvement in the Vietnam War 1962–1975*, Allen & Unwin in association with the Australian War Memorial, Sydney, 1995.
- Dennis, Peter and Grey, Jeffrey, *Emergency and Confrontation: Australian Military Operations in Malaya and Borneo 1950–1966*, Allen & Unwin in association with the Australian War Memorial, Sydney, 1996.
- Edwards, Peter, *A Nation at War: Australian Politics, Society and Diplomacy during the Vietnam War 1965–1975*, Allen & Unwin in association with the Australian War Memorial, Sydney, 1997.
- Grey, Jeffrey, *Up Top: The Royal Australian Navy and Southeast Asian Conflicts 1955–1972*, Allen & Unwin in association with the Australian War Memorial, Sydney, 1998.
- McNeill, Ian, and Ekins, Ashley, *On the Offensive: The Australian Army in the Vietnam War 1967–1968*, Allen & Unwin in association with the Australian War Memorial, Sydney, 2003.
- Ekins, Ashley, with McNeill, Ian, *Fighting to the Finish: The Australian Army and the Vietnam War 1968–1975*, Allen & Unwin in association with the Australian War Memorial, Sydney, 2012.

Australia's commitments to the Malayan Emergency of 1948–60, the Indonesian Confrontation of 1963–66, and the Vietnam War (or Second

Indochina War) to which Australian service personnel were committed between 1962 and 1973 all arose from decisions made by those responsible for the nation's foreign and defence policies. While separate conflicts, they shared the context of the turbulent period in Southeast Asia when decolonisation of the European empires intersected with the global Cold War. *Crises and Commitments* discusses the individuals and the domestic and international political forces that shaped Australian strategic policies in this period. It relates and analyses Australian policy towards Southeast Asia from the end of the 1939–45 war to the commitment of the first infantry battalion to Vietnam in 1965. It places the commitment of Australian forces to Malaya, Malaysia and Vietnam in the context of Australian concerns for the security of all of Southeast Asia, including both the Indochinese peninsula and the archipelagic region stretching from Sumatra in the west to the eastern end of the island of New Guinea. *Crises and Commitments* discusses the complex relationship of Australian policy towards these two parts of Southeast Asia, culminating in the commitment of an infantry battalion and other forces to each of two simultaneous conflicts, in Borneo and Vietnam. The book also discusses the establishment of a selective system of conscription which, although introduced with possible commitments to Malaysia and Papua New Guinea as well as Indochina in mind, came to be associated exclusively with Vietnam.

The political, social and diplomatic history of the commitment to Vietnam is continued in *A Nation at War*. This book discusses the handling by the Menzies, Holt, Gorton, McMahon and Whitlam governments of the international pressures and domestic politics of a war that initially had considerable public support but that became increasingly divisive and controversial. The book, which received the Colin Roderick Award for the best book of its year on any Australian topic, provides detailed analysis of not only the political and diplomatic milieu but also the changes in Australian society that created a vigorous and often contentious protest movement. An appendix by Sue Langford describes the operation of the national service scheme introduced in 1964, including all the birthdates drawn in ballots between 1965 and 1972.

As the present book has emphasised, the three Australian commitments were conducted predominantly by the army. The army's role in the Vietnam War is discussed in authoritative detail in the three volumes by Ian McNeill and Ashley Ekins. The first, *To Long Tan*, discusses the development of the army during the 1950s and the first years of the commitment to Vietnam, concluding with the immediate aftermath of the battle of Long Tan in 1966. *To Long Tan* was awarded the Templer Medal for the best book on an army in Britain or the Commonwealth. McNeill died in 1998 and his work was completed in *On the Offensive* and *Fighting to the Finish* by Ashley Ekins, who had been his principal assistant and designated co-author.

All three volumes contain important, detailed and nuanced discussions of many of the military themes summarised in the present work. These include the differences of opinion, both among Australian officers and between Australian and American commanders, as to the relative emphasis on pacification and main force operations, and related issues such as the 'body count' and 'kill ratio', as well as policies on individual versus unit replacement. McNeill and Ekins discuss the Australian soldiers' relationships with the South Vietnamese forces and with the New Zealand infantry and artillery units who worked closely with the Australian task force. They also analyse contentious issues such as the decision to base the task force at Nui Dat and the logistics unit at Vung Tau; the costs of the Dat Do minefield and the reasons for its failure; and the tensions between the army and the RAAF over helicopter support for the task force.

An immense amount of information about the army's involvement in Vietnam is included in the appendices to the three volumes, especially in *Fighting to the Finish*. Each of the three contains a summary of every operation conducted within the period discussed in the volume. The central focus of all three volumes is the perspective of the successive commanders of the task force, but they all analyse the changing and demanding nature of the war as it was experienced by all ranks, from the Chairman of the Chiefs of Staff Committee and Chief of the General Staff (the positions now known as Chief of the Defence Force and Chief of Army) through to the private soldiers, both regulars and national servicemen. These volumes, in both narrative and appendices, provide the information that is essential for an understanding of the individual and collective experience of the tens of thousands of Australians who served in army units in Phuoc Tuy province and elsewhere in Vietnam south of the 17th parallel.

One theme of the present book is the way that Australian military doctrine and training were directed towards counter-insurgency in Southeast Asia, based on experience in the Malayan Emergency and Confrontation. The nature of that experience is related in *Emergency and Confrontation* by Peter Dennis (on the Malayan Emergency) and Jeffrey Grey (on Confrontation). Like the Vietnam War, albeit far smaller conflicts, these were fought largely by the infantry battalions of the Royal Australian Regiment, together with squadrons of the Special Air Service and other units. An understanding of Australian operational experience in these two conflicts is important in its own right and in explaining the strengths and weaknesses of the operational approaches used in the Vietnam War. Counter-terrorist operations in the Malayan Emergency were officially only the secondary role of the forces committed to the British Commonwealth Far East Strategic Reserve, but the experience gained in the Emergency did much to shape Australian views on operations in Southeast Asia. The tactics employed by British and Commonwealth forces in Malaya have long been discussed, often in comparison with Vietnam and other more recent conflicts, as an example of successful counter-insurgency. Confrontation is surely Australia's forgotten war: highly successful but conducted amid much secrecy, overshadowed by the controversies surrounding the Vietnam War, and neglected ever since.

While the Vietnam War was predominantly a ground war, the Royal Australian Air Force made a significant contribution to the Australian commitment, principally through the Iroquois helicopters of No. 9 Squadron, the Canberra bombers of No. 2 Squadron, and the Caribou transports of the RAAF Transport Flight Vietnam, later No. 35 Squadron (or 'Wallaby Airlines'). Chris Coulthard-Clark relates the work of these and other RAAF units, such as the airfield construction squadrons, in *The RAAF in Vietnam.* The RAAF service began with the commitment of Sabre jet fighters to Ubon in Thailand in 1962 and lasted until the service of Hercules transport aircraft during the turbulent days preceding the fall of Saigon.

Australia was the only 'third country' – that is, ally of the United States and the Republic of Vietnam – that committed elements from all three armed services to Vietnam. The Royal Australian Navy's contribution was less prominent than those of the army or the RAAF, but should not be overlooked. *Up Top*, by Jeffrey Grey, discusses the RAN's commitments to all three Southeast Asian conflicts, placing them in the context of the navy's changing roles and mission in this period. In addition to operations in the waters around Malaysia, Indonesia and Vietnam, the book also discusses such related matters as the contribution of senior RAN officers to the Royal Malaysian Navy.

The official histories of the 1914–18 and 1939–45 wars included separate volumes on medical matters. *Medicine at War* continues that tradition, containing important information and analysis in both narrative and statistical tables. In earlier conflicts tropical diseases caused as many casualties as enemy action. Brendan O'Keefe notes that countering a malaria outbreak in the task force in 1968 was one important element in the undramatic, but vitally important, story of minimising losses. He refers also to the improvements in medical evacuation (medevac) and the treatment of battlefield casualties which led to many lives being saved. A considerable amount of statistical and other information is included in appendices. *Medicine at War* also includes the essay by FB Smith, 'Agent Orange: The Australian aftermath', cited in Chapter 11 of this book.

The relationship of the Australians with their American and South Vietnamese allies in the field, an important theme in many of these works, is also prominent in the history of the Australian Army Training Team Vietnam (AATTV):

- McNeill, Ian, *The Team: Australian Army Advisers in Vietnam 1962–1972*, University of Queensland Press in association with the Australian War Memorial, Brisbane, 1984.

Although not part of the *Official History* series, this book might well be seen as complementary. The prior publication of *The Team* allowed McNeill and Ekins to focus on the service of the RAR battalions, beginning with 1RAR in 1965–66 and then the 15 battalion tours of the nine battalions of RAR in the task force from 1966 to 1971.

NEW ZEALAND OFFICIAL HISTORIES

The relationship between the Australian and New Zealand forces in Vietnam, including the ANZAC battalions, is analysed not only in the relevant volumes of the Australian official history but also in two volumes of official New Zealand war history:

- McGibbon, Ian, *New Zealand's Vietnam War: A History of Combat, Commitment and Controversy*, Exisle Publishing, Auckland, 2010.
- Rabel, Roberto, *New Zealand and the Vietnam War: Politics and Diplomacy*, Auckland University Press, Auckland, 2005.

On New Zealand's role in the two earlier conflicts, see:

- Pugsley, Christopher, *From Emergency to Confrontation: The New*

Zealand Armed Forces in Malaya and Borneo 1948–66, Oxford University Press, Melbourne, 2003.

OTHER ACCOUNTS OF AUSTRALIA'S VIETNAM WAR

The single-volume accounts of Australia's Vietnam War vary considerably in style and scope. The most noteworthy recent examples are listed here:

- Caulfield, Michael, *The Vietnam Years: From the Jungle to the Australian Suburbs*, Hachette Australia, Sydney, 2007.

This is an under-rated account of Australians' experience of the Vietnam War, in Vietnam and in Australia, based on the thousands of hours of interviews conducted for the ABC television series *Australians at War*, of which Caulfield was producer, and collected in the Australians at War Film Archive. Caulfield has skilfully blended the oral testimony of veterans, protesters and others with the work of historians, especially in the *Official History* volumes listed above.

- Davies, Bruce, with McKay, Gary, *Vietnam: The Complete Story of the Australian War*, Allen & Unwin, Sydney, 2012.

Bruce Davies served in Vietnam with both the Training Team and an infantry battalion. His account, while claiming to be 'the complete story of the Australian war', is focused largely on the experience of Australian soldiers. Much of the information, source material and analysis will be familiar to readers of *To Long Tan*, *On the Offensive* and *Fighting to the Finish*, often presented here from the perspective of junior army officers.

- Ham, Paul, *Vietnam: The Australian War*, HarperCollins, Sydney, 2007.

Paul Ham's *Vietnam* is a best-selling account by a skilled journalist. Many of its 49 chapters read like feature articles in a quality newspaper, introducing readers to a broad range of aspects and themes of Australia's Vietnam war, especially as experienced by the soldiers in the field. Based substantially on a large number of interviews with veterans, the book is a highly readable and evocative account, but several writers have questioned its accuracy on points of factual detail and some of its broader judgements.

- McKay, Gary and Stewart, Elizabeth, *Viet Nam Shots: A Photographic Account of Australians at War*, Allen & Unwin, Sydney, 2002.

In *Viet Nam Shots* Elizabeth Stewart, who worked on the *Official History*, and Gary McKay, a Vietnam veteran and prolific author, present a reliable, concise and richly illustrated account of the Australian experience of the Vietnam War told through photographs, most of which were chosen from the Australian War Memorial's extensive collection, and a succinct and informative text.

- Palazzo, Albert, *Australian Military Operations in Vietnam*, 2nd edition, Army History Unit, Canberra, 2011.

This is part of the *Australian Army Campaigns Series*, written principally for members of the Australian Army.

THE AUSTRALIAN SOLDIER'S EXPERIENCE

Of the unit histories relevant to this book, some of the more noteworthy are:
- Breen, Bob, *First to Fight: Australian Diggers, N.Z. Kiwis and U.S. Paratroopers in Vietnam, 1965–66*, Allen & Unwin, Sydney, 1988.
- Hall, Robert, *Combat Battalion: The Eighth Battalion in Vietnam*, Allen & Unwin, Sydney, 2000.
- Horner, David, *The Gunners: A History of Australian Artillery*, Allen & Unwin, Sydney, 1995.
- ——, *SAS: Phantoms of War: A History of the Australian Special Air Service*, Allen & Unwin, Sydney, 2002.
- Horner, David, and Bou, Jean (eds), *Duty First: A History of the Royal*

- *Australian Regiment*, Allen & Unwin, Sydney, 2008.
- O'Brien, Michael, *Conscripts and Regulars with the Seventh Battalion in Vietnam*, Allen & Unwin, Sydney, 1995.
- O'Neill, Robert, *Vietnam Task: The 5th Battalion, the Royal Australian Regiment 1966–67*, Cassell, Melbourne, 1968.

A distinguished novelist has written an account of one often overlooked encounter, which illustrates many of the broader themes of the Australian soldier's experience:

- Windsor, Gerard, *All Day Long the Noise of Battle: An Australian Attack in Vietnam*, Pier 9, Sydney, 2011.

A detailed and provocative study of the Dat Do minefield is:

- Lockhart, Greg, *The Minefield: An Australian Tragedy in Vietnam*, Allen & Unwin, Sydney, 2007.

Gary McKay, a decorated Vietnam veteran, is the author or editor of a number of books on the experience of those who served. They include:

- McKay, Gary, *In Good Company: One Man's War in Vietnam*, Allen & Unwin, Sydney, 1987.
- ——, Gary, *Bullets, Beans and Bandages: Australians at War in Viet Nam*, Allen & Unwin, Sydney, 1999.
- ——, Gary, *On Patrol with the SAS: Sleeping with Your Ears Open*, Allen & Unwin, Sydney, 2007.

On a related topic, see also:

- McKay, Gary and Stewart, Elizabeth, *With Healing Hands: The Untold Story of Australian Civilian Surgical Teams in Vietnam*, Allen & Unwin, Sydney, 2009.

BIOGRAPHIES

Several biographies have been published in recent years of major figures in the political and military decisions discussed in this book. They include:

- Blair, Anne, *Ted Serong: The Life of an Australian Counter-Insurgency Expert*, Oxford University Press, Melbourne, 2002.
- Edwards, Peter, *Arthur Tange: Last of the Mandarins*, Allen & Unwin, Sydney, 2006.
- Frame, Tom, *The Life and Death of Harold Holt*, Allen & Unwin in association with the National Archives of Australia, Sydney, 2005.
- Grey, Jeffrey, *A Soldier's Soldier: A Biography of Lieutenant-General Sir Thomas Daly*, Cambridge University Press, Melbourne, 2013.
- Hancock, Ian, *John Gorton: He Did it His Way*, Hodder, Sydney, 2002.
- Horner, David, *Strategic Command: General Sir John Wilton and Australia's Asian Wars*, Oxford University Press, Melbourne, 2005.
- Lowe, David, *Australian Between Empires: The Life of Percy Spender*, Pickering & Chatto, London, 2010.

THE AUSTRALIAN CONTEXT

To place the Southeast Asian commitments in the context of Australian military history since European settlement, see:

- Grey, Jeffrey, *A Military History of Australia*, 3rd edition, Cambridge University Press, Melbourne, 2008.

To place the Southeast Asian conflicts in the context of Australia's relations with Southeast Asia in the 20th century, see:

- Edwards, Peter, and Goldsworthy, David, eds, *Facing North: A Century of Australian Engagement with Asia*, vol. 2, 1970s to 2000, Melbourne University Press and the Department of Foreign Affairs and Trade, Melbourne, 2003.

- Goldsworthy, David, ed., Facing *North: A Century of Australian Engagement with Asia*, vol. 1, 1901 to the 1970s, Melbourne University Press and the Department of Foreign Affairs and Trade, Melbourne, 2001

A thoroughly researched account of the role of the Department of External (later Foreign) Affairs in Australian decision-making on the Vietnam commitment is:
- Woodard, Garry, *Asian Alternatives: Australia's Vietnam Decision and Lessons on Going to War*, Melbourne University Publishing, Melbourne, 2004.

THE SOUTHEAST ASIAN CONTEXT

In recent years historians have published several important works on the international history of Southeast Asia between 1945 and 1975, placing the controversies of the Vietnam War into a wider regional context. Among those of particular relevance to this book are:
- Bayly, Christopher, and Harper, Tim, *Forgotten Wars: The End of Britain's Asian Empire*, Allen Lane, London, 2007; also published as *Forgotten Wars: Freedom and Revolution in Southeast Asia*, Harvard University Press, Cambridge MA, 2007.
- Fenton, Damien, *To Cage the Red Dragon: SEATO and the Defence of Southeast Asia 1955–1965*, NUS Press, Singapore, 2012.
- Hack, Karl, *Defence and Decolonisation in Southeast Asia: Britain, Malaya and Singapore 1941–68*, Curzon, London, 2001.
- Osborne, Milton, *Southeast Asia: An Introductory History*, 10th edition, Allen & Unwin, Sydney, 2010.
- Stubbs, Richard, *Hearts and Minds in Guerrilla Warfare: The Malayan Emergency 1948–1960*, Oxford University Press, Singapore, 1989.
- Subritzky, John, *Confronting Sukarno: British, American, Australian and New Zealand Diplomacy in the Malaysian-Indonesian Confrontation, 1961–5*, Macmillan, London, 2000.

THE AMERICAN CONTEXT

Books on the American war in Vietnam continue to be published in considerable numbers.

A best-selling account by a well-informed journalist is:
- Karnow, Stanley, *Vietnam: A History*, 2nd revised and updated edition, New York, Penguin, 1997.

An excellent account by a distinguished political and diplomatic historian is:
- Herring, George C., *America's Longest War: The United States and Vietnam, 1950–1975*, 3rd revised and updated edition, McGraw-Hill, New York, 1996.

A recent account of the international context of the American war is:
- Lawrence, Mark Atwood, *The Vietnam War: A Concise International History*, Oxford University Press, New York, 2008.

One widely regarded as a standard guide is:
- Anderson, David L, *The Vietnam War*, Palgrave, Basingstoke UK, 2005.

A controversial account that challenges many of the generally held views of the war is:
- Moyar, Mark, *Triumph Forsaken: The Vietnam War, 1954–1965*, Cambridge University Press, Cambridge, 2006.

A study of the military lessons of the Malayan and Vietnam conflicts is:
- Nagl, John A., *Learning to Eat Soup with a Knife: Counterinsurgency Lessons from Malaya and Vietnam*, University of Chicago Press, Chicago, 2005.

INDEX

1ALSG *see* Australian Army. 1st Australian Logistics Support Group
1ATF *see* Australian Task Force
1RAR *see* Australian Army. 1st Battalion, Royal Australian Regiment
2RAR *see* Australian Army. 2nd Battalion, Royal Australian Regiment
3RAR *see* Australian Army. 3rd Battalion, Royal Australian Regiment
4RAR *see* Australian Army. 4th Battalion, Royal Australian Regiment
5RAR *see* Australian Army. 5th Battalion, Royal Australian Regiment
6RAR *see* Australian Army. 6th Battalion, Royal Australian Regiment
7RAR *see* Australian Army. 7th Battalion, Royal Australian Regiment
8RAR *see* Australian Army. 8th Battalion, Royal Australian Regiment

AATTV *see* Australian Army Training Team Vietnam
abbreviations xvii–xviii
Abdul Rahman Putra, Tunku 57, 81–82, 121, 130, 291, *figure*
Abrams, General Creighton 210, 211, 291
Aceh 5, 7
Acheson, Dean 33
ACP (Australian Communist Party) 20, 29, 99
advisory role, Australian 74, 85, 106–7, 240–41
A Fair Go 283
Afghanistan 262, 267, 276, 284
Agent Orange 277, 280–82
AIF (Australian Imperial Force) 24, 26
aircraft, transport *see* Caribou transport aircraft
All Day Long the Noise of Battle 204–5
ALP *see* Australian Labor Party

American alliance 77, 94–95, 97, 115, 120, 136, 144, 158, 179, 233, 263, 265, 266, 267–68
Andersen Fire Support Base 204
Anderson, David 115, 291
Anglo–Malaysian Defence Agreement 87
Anglo–New Zealand–Australia–Malaya 52
Annam 8, 11
anti-colonial movements 3, 9, 18
anti-war movement
 Australia 99, 123–24, 140–44, 157–58, 164–66, 199–202, 222–24, 232, 237
 United States 123, 164, 222
 worldwide 188, 199
ANZAC in Vietnam 160, 180–81, 238–39
ANZAM 52
ANZUS Council *figure*
ANZUS treaty 32, 75, 79, 87, 96, 197–98, 251, 266
armoured personnel carriers 150, 151, 205, 206, 212
Army of the Republic of Vietnam
 Battle of Binh Ba 212
 cemeteries erased by communists 270
 creation of 62
 Easter offensive 243
 losses to Viet Cong 91
 numerical advantage 167
 Operation Pinnaroo 206
 RAN and RAAF support 242
 strengths and weaknesses 101, 226
 Tet offensive 189
 training of 221, 226, 240–41, 247
ARVN *see* Army of the Republic of Vietnam
ASEAN (Association of Southeast Asian Nations) 191, 273
ASIO (Australian Security Intelligence Organisation) 24
Askin, Sir Robert 157–58
Association of Southeast Asian Nations (ASEAN) 191, 273
atrocity claims 200–201, 212

Australia
 1949 election 29
 1955 election 55
 1966 election 140–44, 159
 1969 election 214–17
 1972 election 243–44, 246
 aid program to Indonesia 111
 alliance with Britain 25, 47, 249, 263
 commitment to Vietnam *see* commitment of troops to Vietnam (Australia)
 conservatism 29–31
 defence expenditure 40, 79–80, 85, 170
 defence policy 21–26, 41, 65–66, 71–72, 79–80, 104, 249, 263–68, 271
 defence reforms 253–55
 defence review 84–86
 foreign policy 21–26, 31–32, 41, 104, 248–51, 257, 268, 271
 immigration, post-war 30, 257, 258
 post-1945 commitments 39
 relations with Asia xii, 20–44, 45–66, 268–69, 270–71
 relations with US 32, 71, 72, 133, 248–51, 263 *see also* American alliance
 reliance on allies for security 40–41, 65, 287
 SEATO member 51
 support for British in Malaya 29
 support for French in Indochina 44
 support for US policy on Vietnam 93, 97, 105, 115, 117–18, 120, 133, 135, 156–57, 285
 and Vietnam, 1956-60 59–63
Australian–American alliance *see* American alliance
Australian Army
 1st Australian Logistics Support Group (1ALSG) 148, 183
 1st Battalion, Royal Australian Regiment (1RAR) 24, 56, 127–29, 131, 138, 142, 147, 153, 183, 203, 208, 275
 2nd Battalion, Royal Australian

Regiment (2RAR) 24, 56, 180, 203
3rd Battalion, Royal Australian
   Regiment (3RAR) 24, 56, 89, 98,
   109, 110, 125, 126, 138, 139, 182,
   205, 208, 238, *figure*
4th Battalion, Royal Australian
   Regiment (4RAR) 138, 139, 180,
   238–39
4th Battalion, Royal Australian
   Regiment (4RAR/NZ) 180, 238,
   239
5th Battalion, Royal Australian
   Regiment (5RAR) 149, 172, 180,
   211
6th Battalion, Royal Australian
   Regiment (6RAR) 149, 172, 180
   A Company 150
   B Company 150
   D Company 150–51, 154, 181
7th Battalion, Royal Australian
   Regiment (7RAR) 178, 180, 203,
   204, *figure*
   C Company 204
8th Battalion, Royal Australian
   Regiment (8RAR) 221, 227
3 Cavalry Regiment 205
deployment 1962–73 289–90
establishment of regular army 24
Pacific Islands Regiment 86, 219–20
relations with RAAF 153–54
size 85
voluntary recruits 24, 26, 277
Australian Army Training Team Vietnam
   76, 77–79, 97, 106, 240–41, 246–48
Australian commanders, relations with
   US commanders 128, 154–55,
   210–11
Australian Communist Party 20, 29, 99
Australian Defence Force Academy 254,
   255
Australia–New Zealand–United States
   security treaty *see* ANZUS treaty
Australian Imperial Force 24, 26
Australian Labor Party 54, 94, 112, 120,
   140, 153, 164
Australian Peace Council 25, 30, 99

Australian Security Intelligence
   Organisation (ASIO) 24
Australian Task Force
   alcohol consumption 228
   command arrangement 176
   commanders 154, 171, 181–82, 211,
      225, 227, 238
   creation of 137–38
   deployment outside Phuoc Tuy 203–5
   morale 228–29
   operations 172, 182, 202–13, 225–29,
      238–39
   Phuoc Tuy province 144–49, 238–39
   relations with local population 155
Australian Vietnam Forces National
   Memorial 283
Australian War Memorial xv

B-52 bombers 206
Bali 5
Ball, Macmahon 123
Balmoral Fire Support Base 209
Bao Dai 32–34, 43, 50, 59–62, 291
Ba Ria 146, 155, 205
Barnard, Lance 163, 246, 253, 291
Barrie, Admiral Chris 276
Barwick, Sir Garfield 291, *figure*
   Acting Minister for External Affairs
      69
   attitude towards Indonesia 72, 80, 83,
      84
   Chief Justice of High Court
      appointment 97
   Indonesian Confrontation against
      Malaysia 88, 96
   military commitment to Vietnam 76
   US defence of South Vietnam 75
Battle of Ap Bac 91
Battle of Binh Ba 212–13
Battle of Coral–Balmoral 205–9
Battle of Long Tan 150–52, 274
battle of Nui Le 239
battle of Suoi Chau Pha 178
battle of the bunkers 204
Baume, Professor Peter 282
Beazley, Kim C 265, 266, 291

Bevin, Ernest 34, 291
Bien Hoa 127–29, 143, 189, 203, 204, 207
Binh Ba 212–13
Binh Gia 146, 155
body count 169, 210, 225
bombers 36, 37, 38, 55, 86, 153, 160, 184, 214, 230, 242
Boonaroo (ship) 183
Borneo
  Australian commitment of troops 89–90, 125–26
  British territory 12, 81
  guerilla activity 89
  operations in 125–26, 138–40
Bowen, Nigel 236
Brisbane, HMAS 184, 242
Britain
  Asian colonies 12–15, 18
  attacks US bombing campaign 156
  engagement in Southeast Asia 18, 40, 51, 52–53, 71, 130
  European Common Market bid 69
  grants independence to South Asian empire 14
  Malayan emergency 15, 28, 35–36, 59
  Malaysia, support for xi, 81–84, 109–10
  opposition to military intervention in Indochina 46
  opposition to Soviet communism 23
  relations with US 121
  SEATO member 51
  seeks diplomatic solution to Indochina crisis 69
  seeks diplomatic solution to Vietnam crisis 104, 116, 121
  Thailand, air presence in 77
  withdrawal of forces east of Suez 170, 192, 196, 263
British Chiefs of Staff 52
British Commonwealth 23
British Empire 2, 25, 31
Brookes family 13
Brunei 13–14, 81
Buddhist monks, suicide 92, *figure*

Bundy, William 106
Bunting, Sir John 117, 195, 291
Burgmann, Dr EH 47
Burma 2, 5, 14, 17, 18, 42
Burton, Dr JW 22, 23, 24, 28, 32, 35, 291
Bury, Leslie 231, 236
Bush, President George HW 266

cables affair, Whitlam government 259
Cairns, Dr JF 'Jim' 120, 123, 140, 223, 224, 250, 251, 257, 291, *figure*
Calcutta conference 17, 28
Calwell, Arthur 26, 72, 83, 86, 119–20, 140, 143, 144, 158, 160, 163, 291, *figure*
Cambodia
  communist government 263, 268, 270
  communist party 11
  French protectorate 8
  genocidal regime 270
  incursion by US and South Vietnamese 223
  independence 32
  settlement 271
  Sihanouk deposed 223
  supply lines for Vietnamese communists 70, 168
Cameron, Clyde 250, 257, 292
Canberra bombers 20, 55, 160, 184, 214, 230, 242
Caribou transport aircraft 86, 97, 137, 184, 213, 230, 242
Carrington, Lord *figure*
Carter, Jimmy 263
Casey, Richard 41–44, 49, 64, 292, *figure*
casualties
  American 265
  Australian 151, 172–73, 175, 181, 206, 208, 209, 210, 212, 225, 228, 239, 258
  national servicemen 142–43, 151, 239
  Vietnamese 151, 189, 208, 209, 212, 223
Catholics, support for Diem 59, 61

Central Intelligence Agency (US) 11, 93, 264
Ceylon 5, 14, 18
chain of command 147, 148, 290
Chamberlain, FE 163
Che Guevara 188
Chiang Kai-shek *see* Jiang Jieshi
Chifley, JB 'Ben' 292, *figure*
Chifley government
　defence policies 22–26
　foreign policies 21–26
　Indonesian revolution 26–29
　Malayan Emergency 26–29
China
　civil war 5
　communist victory 42
　invades Vietnam 270
　military strength 79
　military threat 119–20
　recognised by the west 234–35, 252
　recognises Democratic Republic of Vietnam 33
　relations with Vietnam 271–72
　support for Vietnamese communists 42, 45, 167, 168
　support for wars of national liberation 68
Chinese Communist Party 13, 28
Chin Peng 15, 292
Chou En-lai *see* Zhou Enlai (Chou En-lai)
Christmas bombing 249–50
chronology xxi–xxvi
Churchill, Sir Winston 18, 41, 46, 292
civic action projects, South Vietnam 205, 219, 226, 231
Claret operations 110–11, 126, 139
Clark, Manning 47
clearance diving teams 160, 184, 213, 230, 242
Clifford, Clark 171, 179–80, 190, 232, 292
Cochinchina 8, 11
Cold War 1, 16–19, 37, 68, 266
colonialism in Asia 2–4, 8–9

Commander Australian Force Vietnam 147–48
command structures 147–48
commitment of troops to Afghanistan (Australia) 267–68
commitment of troops to Borneo (Australia) 109–10
commitment of troops to Indonesia (Australia) 88–90, 110–11, 285
commitment of troops to Iraq (Australia) 267
commitment of troops to Korea (Australia) 38–39
commitment of troops to Malaya (Australia) xi, 36, 53–59
commitment of troops to Vietnam (Australia) xi–xii
　first commitment 76, 107, 112–16, 118
　to a battalion group 129, 131
　two-battalions 136
　three-battalions 159, 178–79, 194
　three services 182–85
　different from US xii
　exit strategy 192, 273
　international reaction to 121–22
　motivation 133
　opposition to 109, 116–18
　parliamentary reaction to 118–20
　pressure from US 169, 170–71, 178–79, 198, 264
　public opinion *see* Vietnam War – public opinion
　troop numbers 129, 137–38, 152–53, 159–60, 179, 182–83, 194, 202, 211, 230
commitment of troops to Vietnam (NZ) 114, 121, 160, 180–81, 213
commitment of troops to Vietnam (United States) 130, 214
Committee in Defiance of the National Service Act 201–2
Commonwealth Brigade, 27th 39
communism
　Asia 17
　Australia 20, 21, 25, 125
　Cambodia 270

Europe 16, 20
global war against 74
Indochina 10–12, 272
Southeast Asia 33
Vietnam 10–12, 256, 269–70
Western opposition to 25
Condon, Private Gordon *figure*
Confrontation, Indonesian 80–84
   Australian commitment to 88–90, 110–11, 285
   end 132, 139, 140
   escalation 99, 103
   operations in 125–27
   tension between Australia and US 96
conscientious objectors 143–44, 201, 276
conscription 275–77 *see also* national service
   call for 85
   First and Second World Wars 26
   introduced, 1964 100
   opposition to 124, 201, 222
   public attitudes to 275–76
continental defence policy 195, 236, 249, 255
Coral Fire Support Base 208–9
Cosgrove, Major General Peter 283
Coulthard-Clark, Chris xiii, 242
counter-insurgency tactics 38, 56, 58, 78, 95, 113, 129, 147, 176, 209, 275
Critchley, TK 84, 292
Cuba 69
Curtin, John 26, 266
Cutler, Sir Roden 237

Dakotas 36, 37
Daly, Lieutenant General Sir Thomas 198, 205–6, 219, 220, 225, 292, *figure*
Darul Islam 7
Dat Do minefield 173–76, 201, 212, 226, 228, 278 *see also* mines
Davidson, JW 47
deaths *see* casualties
decolonisation, Southeast Asia 1–15
Dedman, JJ 23, 292
Defence Committee (Australia) 65, 79, 85, 99, 107, 112, 129, 234

Defence Review, 1963 84–86, 99
Defence White Paper 265
De Gaulle, Charles 69, 95, 292
Democratic Labor Party 54–55, 220
Democratic Republic of Vietnam *see* North Vietnam (Democratic Republic of Vietnam)
demonstrations, anti-war *see* anti-war movement
Dennis, Peter xiii
Department of Veterans' Affairs 277, 278
destroyer escorts 90, 110
destroyers 53, 55, 90, 110, 159, 160, 184, 213, 242
Dibb, Paul 265
Diem *see* Ngo Dinh Diem
Dien Bien Phu 48, 67
dissent 123, 124, 125, 137, 162–66, 201, 224
DLP (Democratic Labor Party) 54–55, 220
domino theory 42–43, 77, 268–73, 288
DRV *see* North Vietnam (Democratic Republic of Vietnam)
Dulles, John Foster 46, 68, 292, *figure*
Dunstan, Colonel Donald 208–9, 239, 292
Dutch colonies 5–6, 12–13, 26–27
Dutch East India Company 5

Easter offensive 242–43
Eden, Sir Anthony 46, 292
Eisenhower, Dwight D 19, 46, 68, 292
Ekins, Ashley xiii, xv, xvi, 176
Ellsberg, Daniel 232
engineers, army 90, 206
Europe, post Second World War 16–17
Evans, Gareth 271, 292
Evatt, Dr HV 22, 28, 32, 61, 292
Evatt, Justice Phillip 281–82
Ewell, Lieutenant General Julian 210, 225, 292
exit strategy 192, 273

F-111 aircraft 86, 179, 198
Facing North 268

FAD Committee *see* Foreign Affairs and Defence Committee
Fairbairn, David 236
Fairbairn, Geoffrey 124
Fairhall, Allen 134, 195, 214, 292
FANK (Forces Armées Nationales Khmers) 241, 243
Far East Strategic Reserve 52–53, 55, 87–88
Faulkner, Senator John 282
Federation of Malaya 14
fighters 55, 76, 77, 86, 153
fire support bases 204, 205, 209, *figure*
fire support vehicles 238
Fischer, Tim 283
Fitzgerald, CP 47, 123
Five Power Defence Agreement 196, 237, 253
Five Power Staff Agency 44
Forces Armées Nationales Khmers (FANK) 241, 243
Ford, Gerald 251, 255, 263
Foreign Affairs and Defence Committee 80, 89, 108, 109, 112, 114–15, 117, 131, 135, 234
forward defence policy 83, 93, 115, 130, 170, 193, 195, 216, 236, 249, 253, 254, 263, 265, 284
fragging 229
France
  colonial interests 2, 8–9, 18, 19, 43–44
  Indochina War 45–46, 48–49, 50
  post Second World War 18
  recognises independence of Vietnam, Laos and Cambodia 32, 33
  SEATO member 51, 121
Fraser, Malcolm 293, *figure*
  Minister for Defence 218–19, 230
  Minister for Education and Science 236
  Minister for the Army 134, 143, 203, 219
  relations with Asia 269
  relations with Gorton 219–20
  resigns from Cabinet 231

  support for refugees 258–59
  withdrawal of troops 220
Freeth, Gordon 196, 216, 293
friendly fire incidents 142, 181, 214
frigates 53, 55

Geneva Accords 49, 50, 51, 68
Geneva Agreement 70
Geneva Conference 46, 48–50
Germany 16, 17, 42, 69
Gia Long, Emperor 8
Giap, General *see* Vo Nguyen Giap
Gorton, John 293, *figure*
  1969 election 214–15
  Assistant Minister for External Affairs 194
  defence policy 236
  deputy leader, Liberal Party 231
  endorses Vietnam War 225
  foreign and defence policies 195–96
  Minister for Defence 231, 236
  Minister for the Navy 193
  party dissatisfaction with 220
  Prime Minister 193–94
  vacates leadership 231
  views on foreign affairs 193–94
  visits US 195, 197–98
  vote of confidence 231
Gotto, Ainsley 195, 293
Gould, Bob 165
Gower, Steve xv
Graham, Brigadier Stuart 154, 171, 173, 176, 177, 181–82, 293
Grey, Jeffrey xiii, 126
Guam doctrine 197, 214, 264
Gulf of Tonkin 98, 184

Hanoi 8, 12, 95–96, 98, 189, 235, 249, 252, 255, 269–70
Harkins, General Paul 78
Harries, Owen 124
Harrison, Eric 35, 293
Harrison Fire Support Base 204
Hasluck, Paul 293, *figure*
  advises Holt on foreign affairs 136
  Governor-General 195

inept defence of government policies 124
Minister for External Affairs 97, 134, 195
proclaims cessation of hostilities 248
views South Vietnam as threat to Australia 98
welcomes US bombing of North Vietnam 112
Hatta, Mohammad 6
Hawke, Bob 251, 265, 266, 293
Hayden, Bill 265, 271
Healey, Denis 121
helicopters 86, 89, 149, 151, 153, 154, 184, 212, 213, 242
Henderson, Brigadier WG 227, 238, 293
herbicides 277, 280, 281
Hewitt, Sir Lenox 195, 293
Hobart, HMAS 160, 184, 214
Ho Chi Minh 293
  appeals to US for support 11
  background 9–12
  communist training 33
  death 226
  figurehead 167
  leader of Viet Minh 11
  success against French 42
  Vietnamese support for 33
Ho Chi Minh campaign 255
Ho Chi Minh trail 70, 96, 168
Holt, Harold 293, *figure*
  'all the way with LBJ' 156–58
  anti-communist commitment in Southeast Asia 135
  death 185–86
  electoral triumph 158–59
  parliamentary experience 135, 136
  prime ministership 134–38, 162–63, 185–86
  visits Asia 135, 160
  visits Britain 135, 157
  visits US 156
Holyoake, Keith 160, 180, 293
Home, Lord *figure*
Honolulu talks 112–13, 127
Horne, Donald 141–42

Howard, John 266, 267, 276, 287–88
Hue 8, 12, 189, 190, 204
Hughes, Brigadier RL 182, 205–6, 208, 293
Hughes, TEF 124
Hughes, Wilfred Kent 193
Hughes, WM 26
Hyde, Michael 165

India 5, 14, 17, 18, 131
Indochina
  Australian aid 44
  communism 10–12, 272
  French sovereignty 8–9, 11–12
  internationalisation of military operations in 46–48
  and Menzies government 32–35
  national and regional rivalries 1, 271
  'United Action' crisis 46–48
  US aid 34
Indochina War, First
  and Australia 41–44
  beginning 11
  end 50
  French public opinion 45
  Phuoc Tuy province 144–45
  US aid 43
Indochina War, Second xii, 67–72, 173, 271 *see also* Vietnam War
Indochina War, Third 270, 271
Indochinese Communist Party 10, 11
Indonesia
  anti-communist forces 132
  and Australia 26–27, 63–66, 192
  Confrontation *see* Confrontation, Indonesian
  coup, 1965 131–32, 272–73
  Dutch colonial government 26–27
  independence 6–7, 27
  'New Order' regime 191, 272–73
  relations with China 103, 104
  threat to Australia's security 99, 100
  withdraws from United Nations 99, 104
Indonesian Air Force 86
Indonesian Army 79, 132

Indonesian Revolution 5–7, 26–29
insurance policy 76–77, 268, 273, 288
insurgencies, communist-led 17
intelligence agencies 24, 264
Iran 263
Iraq 262, 267, 276, 284, 287
Irian Jaya 7
Iroquois helicopters 86, 153, 213, 314
Islamic movements 7

Jackson, Brigadier OD 154, 293
Japan 3, 4, 10, 11, 42, 121
Java 6, 7
Jeffery, Major General Mike 283
Jeparit (ship) 183
Jiang Jieshi 5
Jockel, Gordon 84
Johnson, Lyndon Baines 293
  does not stand for re-election 190
  ends bombing of North Vietnam 190
  failing policy in South Vietnam 101
  foreign policies 94–95
  hopes to prevent defeat in Vietnam 95
  mission to Asia 73–74
  pressure from 'hawks' and 'doves' 102, 105
  Vietnam policies questioned 233
  visits Australia 157
joint facilities, Australia and US 72, 251, 264, 266
Jones, Mike 165
jungle warfare 36, 56, 89, 139, 240
Jungle Warfare Training Centre 56, 78, 240

Kashmir dispute 131
Kennedy, John Fitzgerald 68, 70, 74, 87, 93, 233, 294
Kennedy, Robert 188
Kerry, John 228
Khan, Lieutenant Colonel Colin 211
Khe Sanh 189
Khmer Rouge 11, 270
Killen, James 236
kill ratio 169, 210, 312
King, Martin Luther 188

Kirby, Warrant Officer 2 Jack 181
Kissinger, Henry 235, 249, 294
Konfrontasi *see* Confrontation, Indonesian
Korean War 36, 38–41

Lai Tek 15, 294
Laking, George 106
Langer, Albert 165
Laos
  communist government 263, 268
  communist party 11
  crises 1959–61 68–72
  French protectorate 8
  independence 32
  neutrality 68, 70
  strategic importance 67, 68
  US aid 69
Laver, Brian 165
Le Duan 62, 167, 226, 294
Lee Kuan Yew 81, 99, 121, 130, 253, 272, 294
Legge, JD 123
Letourneau, Jean 44, 294
Lewis, Graham 258
Lincoln bombers 36, 37, 38, 55
Living with Asia 140
Lloyd, Lieutenant Colonel RDF 241
Lockhart, Greg 176
Lodge, Henry Cabot 93
Lombok 5
Long Binh 189, 203, 204
Long Phuoc 145, 149, 155
Long Tan 145, 149, 150–52, 155, 274
Lon Nol, General 223
Lynch, Phillip 200, 294

MacArthur, General Douglas 39
McDonald, Brigadier Bruce 238, 239, 294
MacDonald, Major General AL 207, 211, 294
MacDonald, Malcolm 34, 294
McEwen, John 115, 163, 192, 231, 294
Mackay, Major General Ken 152, 159, 294

McMahon, William 294
  denounces Whitlam's visit to China 235
  FAD Committee 114–15, 218
  feud with McEwen 163
  Minister for External Affairs 218–19
  party lack of confidence in 192
  Prime Minister 231
  reputation for incompetence 236
  Treasurer 170
  visits US 171, 236
  withdrawal of troops 235–36
McNamara, Robert S 171, 179, 190, 232, 294
McNeill, Ian xiii
Malacca 13, 14
Malaya
  British rule 12–15
  communist-led insurgency 17, 28
  independence 57
  navy 56
  population 13
Malayan Communist Party 14–15, 57
Malayan Emergency 12–15, 26–29
  Australian commitment to 52–59, 284
  and Menzies government 35–37
  Royal Australian Air Force in 37–38
  Royal Australian Navy role 55–56
  success of coalition operations 58
Malayan Races Liberation Army 14, 38, 57, 58
Malayan Union 14
Malaysia
  Australian commitment to 87–91, 179, 196, 253
  British support 81–84
  creation of 81–84
  Indonesian hostility towards 82–84, 90
  split with Singapore 130–31
Manila Treaty 51, 53, 75
Mao Zedong (Mao Tse-tung) 5, 68, 188, 294
Menzies, Dame Pattie *figure*
Menzies, Sir Robert 29–31, 294, *figure*
  accused of deception over request for troops 118, 233

anti-communist stance 30
Australian conservatism 29–31
confidence in US supremacy 72, 106, 285
cooperation with US 65, 72, 94–95
defence policy 284
denounces calls for negotiated settlement 117
focus on global issues 69
and Indochina 32–35
and Malayan Emergency 35–37, 108
and Malaysia 83, 87–88
pro-Britain 29, 31, 83
relations with Indonesia 83
retires 134
support for commitment to Vietnam 107, 108, 285, 287
mines 173–76, 243
  casualties 175, 201, 206, 212, 225–26, 228, 278
  clearing 206, 212–13
minesweepers 89, 90, 110
Minh Dam Secret Zone 145, 173, 206, 226, *figure*
Mirage fighters 86
Mobile Advisory and Training Teams 240–41
monks, suicide 92, *figure*
Moratorium 222–25, 232, *figure*
Mountbatten, Admiral Lord Louis 18, 294
Moyes, Bishop 123
Murdoch, Air Marshal Alister 153
Murdoch, Sir Keith 35, 295
My Lai massacre 223

Nam Viet 8
napalm 164, 200
Nasution, Abdul Haris 7, 65, 132, 295
nationalist movements 3, 23, 30
National Liberation Front 62, 164, 165–66, 270
National Service Act 100, 124, 201–2, 237, 247, 275
national servicemen
  casualties 142–43, 151, 239

discharge 279
draft resisters 237
numbers in battalions 137
repatriation 279, 280
national service scheme 275–77 *see also* conscription
  end 246–47
  first intakes 124
  length of service 100, 237
  operation 100
  opposition to 137, 275–76
  volunteers 237
NATO (North Atlantic Treaty Organization) 16
Netherlands East Indies 2, 5–6, 7, 17, 19, 27
New Guinea 6, 7 *see also* West New Guinea
New Zealand
  air presence in Thailand 77
  Battle of Long Tan 151
  commitment of troops 114, 121, 160, 180–81, 213
  SEATO member 51
Ngo Dinh Diem 295, *figure*
  assassination 81, 93, 101
  creates Republic of Vietnam 59–60
  end of regime 91–95
  favouritism towards Catholics 61, 62, 73, 91
  Prime Minister 59–62
  replaced by generals 92–93
  visits US and Australia 61
Ngo Dinh Nhu 91, 92, 93, 295
Ngo Dinh Nhu, Madame 91–92, 295
Nguyen Cao Ky 102, 160, 295
Nguyen family 8
Nguyen Khanh 101, 295
Nguyen Van Thieu 102, 295
Nixon, Richard M 295
  resignation 251, 263
  support for Republic of Vietnam 255
  tension with Whitlam government 251
  visits China 235

wins election 190, 249
withdrawal of troops 197, 214, 221
Nixon doctrine 197, 264
Noack, Private Errol 142
North Atlantic Treaty Organization (NATO) 16
North Borneo 81
North Vietnam (Democratic Republic of Vietnam)
  bombing by US 106, 112, 156, 164, 168, 190, 249–50
  goal of uniting Vietnam 166, 269–70
  independence 11, 12
  land reform 60
  postwar regime 269–70
  recognition of 33, 252–53
  strategic advantage 167
  support from Soviet Union and China 167
North-West Cape station, Western Australia 72
nuclear deterrents 39, 72, 79, 193, 266
Nui Dat 148–49, 151, 152, 155, 171–72, 176, 182, 203, 205, 207, 208, 211, 228, 229, 240, 241, 312
Nui Le 239

Office of Strategic Services (US) 11
Official History of Australia's Involvement in Southeast Asian Conflicts 1948–1975 xiii, xiv, xv, 277
O'Keefe, Brendan xiii
O'Neill, Captain Robert 172, *figure*
O'Neill, Lieutenant Colonel Kevin 227
Operation Ainslie 176
operational methods 152, 154–55, 274–75
Operation Bribie 172
Operation Coburg 203–5
Operation Ivanhoe 239
Operation Paddington 177
Operation Pinnaroo 206
Operation Renmark 172
Operation Rolling Thunder 112, 168, 190
Operation Toan Thang 206–7

orphans 257, 258

pacification operations 116, 147, 152, 169, 171, 177, 202, 207, 210–11, 275
Pakistan 5, 14, 51, 121, 131
Paltridge, Senator Shane 115, 295
Papua 7
Papua New Guinea 86, 100, 110, 137, 220
Paris peace negotiations 207, 247, 249, 250, 255
Partai Kommunis Indonesia 7, 63, 64, 79, 82, 104, 131–32
Pathet Lao 67, 68, 69
PAVN *see* People's Army of Vietnam
peace negotiations 207, 247, 249, 250, 255
Peacock, Andrew 219, 295
Pearson, Brigadier CMI 'Sandy' 211, 295
Penang 13, 14, 54
Pentagon Papers 190, 232–37
People's Action Party 81, 130
People's Army of Vietnam
  beginnings 10
  Binh Ba 212
  Chinese sanctuaries 42–43
  Coral–Balmoral assault 208, 209
  headquarters 208
  Indochina War 44, 45, 48, 49
  infiltrate PLAF 101
  involved in Laos 69
  reinforce Viet Cong 96, 127, 207
  remain in South Vietnam 255–56
  Saigon offensive 207
  sign ceasefire agreements 49
  strength 58, 189, 226, 243
  supply routes 45, 67, 77, 168, 226
  Tet offensive 189
People's Liberation Armed Forces
  achievements 101
  formation 62–63
  ready to drive wedge through South Vietnam 127
  Saigon offensive 190, 207
  strength 73, 101, 189
Perak 54

Perth, HMAS 184
Petrov, Vladimir 48, 118, 295
Pham Van Dong 10
Phan Huy Quat 115
Phan Rang 185
Philippines 5, 17, 51, 82, 121
Phipps, Rear Admiral Sir Peter 112, 113, 295
Phuoc Tuy province 144–49, 152, 155, 162, 168–69, 171, 177, 182, 200–208, 210–12, 219, 224, 226–27, 236, 238–39, 240–43
PKI *see* Partai Kommunis Indonesia
PLAF *see* People's Liberation Armed Forces
Plimsoll, Sir James 117, 119, 295
Pollard, Sir Reginald 78
Portugal 2, 5
post-traumatic stress disorder 277, 279–80
Price, Geoffrey 256, 258, 295
protest movement *see* anti-war movement
Provisional Revolutionary Government (of South Vietnam) 252–53, 255, 270

RAAF *see* Royal Australian Air Force (RAAF)
Radford, Admiral Arthur 46, 295
RAN *see* Royal Australian Navy (RAN)
Rangoon 43
RAR *see* Australian Army
Reagan, Ronald 265
refugees 256–57, 258–59
Reid, Alan 218, 236, 295
relations between Australian and US commanders 154–55, 210–11
Repatriation Medical Authority 283
Republic of China, Taiwan 136
Republic of Vietnam *see* South Vietnam (Republic of Vietnam)
Returned Service League (RSL) 30, 278, 280
revolutions of 1968 187–88
Richardson, Warrant Officer Jock *figure*

Ridgway, General Matthew 46
Roosevelt, Franklin D 18, 296
Rostow, Walt 74
rotation by units 155
Royal Australian Air Force (RAAF)
  1 (Bomber) Squadron 38, 55
  2 Squadron 55, 160, 185, 214, 242
  3 Squadron 55
  9 Squadron 149, 150, 154, 183, 184, 213
  35 Squadron 184, 213, 242
  38 (Transport) Squadron 37
  77 Fighter Squadron 38, 55
  79 Squadron 77
  acquisition program 86
  commitments 182
  component of Australian Force Vietnam 147
  in Malaya 36–38, 53
  relations with army 153–54
  in Thailand 77, 79
  transport aircraft 36, 37, 82, 86, 89, 97, 137
  Transport Flight Vietnam 97, 184
  withdrawal 241–42
Royal Australian Navy (RAN)
  commitments 56, 183, 213–14
  Helicopter Flight Vietnam 184, 213
  Indonesian Confrontation 110
  Korean War 38
  withdrawal 241–42
Royal Australian Regiment *see* Australian Army
Royal Commission into exposure to chemicals 281–82
Royal New Zealand Air Force 213
RTFV *see* Royal Australian Air Force Transport Flight Vietnam
Rusk, Dean 72, 75, 76, 85, 96, 296, *figure*
RVN *see* South Vietnam (Republic of Vietnam)

Sabah 13–14, 81, 90, 196
Sabre fighters 55, 76, 77
Saigon 12, 43, 61, 189, 190, 207, 255–60
Samuels, Peter 124

Sanderson, Lieutenant General John 271
Santamaria, Bartholomew Augustine 21, 78, 296
Sarawak 13–14, 81, 139
SAS *see* Special Air Service
Save Our Sons 124, 199
Scherger, Sir Frederick 37, 89, 107, 112–15, 127, 296, *figure*
SEAC (Southeast Asia Command) 18
SEATO *see* South-East Asia Treaty Organization
self-reliance in defence 254, 265
Serong, Colonel FP 'Ted' 78–79, 296
Shann, Keith 'Mick' 84, 296
Sharkey, Lawrence 'Lance' 21, 28, 296
Sharp, Admiral USG 112, 113, 296
Shedden, Sir Frederick 23, 24, 296
ships 183–84
Sihanouk, Prince Norodom 121, 223, 296
Sihanouk trail 168
Singapore
  Australian commitment to 179, 196, 253
  British territory 13
  fall of 3
  separation from Malaysia 81, 130–31
Slope 30 176–77
Smith, FB xiii, 315
Snedden, Billy 296
SOS (Save Our Sons) 124
South Africa 69
Southeast Asia
  and Australia 20–44, 45–66, 269, 270–71
  British territories 12–15, 18
  communist-led insurgencies 17
  decolonisation 2–15
  diplomacy, Australian 271
  European domination 2–4
  independence 5
  nationalist movements 3, 23, 30
  post 1965 191
Southeast Asia Command 18

334 AUSTRALIA AND THE VIETNAM WAR

South-East Asia Treaty Organization (SEATO) 50–52, 53, 65, 66, 68, 74–77, 79, 88, 121, 197, *figure*
South Vietnam (Republic of Vietnam) 1954–1975 *map (pictorial section)*
  Australian Army advisers 74, 75, 76–79, 85
  communist infiltration 62
  coups 93, 101
  creation of 59
  crisis, 1965 101–4
  domino in Cold War 73
  factional strife 101
  land reforms 73
  revolutionary forces 73
  struggle against insurgency 91
  tactical zones 146
  threat to Australia 119
  training of forces 221, 226, 240–41, 247
  US advisors 74, 76, 85
  US aid 62, 74
Souvannouphong, Prince 67
Soviet Union
  control across Europe 16, 42, 188
  espionage 24, 48
  global ambitions 34
  schism with China 68
  support for communists in Asia 17–18, 45, 61, 167, 168
  Western opposition to 25
Special Air Service (SAS) 89, 109, 111, 112, 126, 127, 139, 154, 227, 275, 313
Spender, Sir Percy 31–32, 34, 41, 296, *figure*
Stalin, Joseph 4, 12, 21, 25, 296
Straits Settlements 13
strategic hamlets program 91, 176–77
Students for a Democratic Society 165
Subandrio, Dr 64, 296, *figure*
Suharto, President 132, 138, 296
Sukarno, President 296, *figure*
  ambition to control West New Guinea 63–65, 90
  anti-Western, pro-Chinese 64, 99
  Australia's commitment to Vietnam 121
  Australia's relations with 72, 84
  Confrontation 99
  Indonesian independence 6–7
  links with Chinese 103–4
  opposition to formation of Malaysia 82
  removed from power 132
  threat to Australia 90
Sydney, HMAS 127, 183, 279

Taiwan 136
Tange, Sir Arthur 65, 84, 85, 219, 254, 297, *figure*
tanks 152, 159, 173, 178, 179, 206, 208–9, 212, 238, *figure*
task force *see* Australian Task Force
Tate, Michael 276
Taylor, General Maxwell 74, 102, 115, 171, 297
teach-ins 123–24
Tet offensive 189–91, 203, 216
Thailand
  able to resist insurgencies 272
  commitment of troops to 73–77
  domino in Cold War 73, 74
  independence 2
  SEATO member 51
  support for Australian commitment to Vietnam 121
  US forces in 75
The Lucky Country 141
Thieu, General 121, 248
Tonkin 8, 11 *see also* Gulf of Tonkin
Townley, Athol 76, 86, 134, 297
Townsend, Lieutenant Colonel Colin 150
Townsend, Simon 201
transport aircraft *see* Caribou transport aircraft
Trinh family 8
Truman, Harry S 11, 19, 297
Truong Chinh 10

UMNO *see* United Malays National Organisation

INDEX **335**

unions, trade 20–21, 122, 142, 250, 251
United Kingdom *see* Britain
United Malays National Organisation 14, 53
United Nations 22, 27, 39
United States
  accused of misleading public 233
  bombing of North Vietnam 106, 112, 156, 164, 168, 190, 249–50
  constraints in warfare 168
  foreign policy 197
  governed the Philippines 2
  military strategies 113, 114, 168–69, 210–11
  opposition to communism 19, 50, 93
  opposition to European colonialism 18, 19
  policy of containment of Soviet Union 16
  policy towards Southeast Asia 51, 71, 75, 191, 197, 214
  post Second World War 18
  rapprochement with Vietnam 272
  relations with China 235
  relations with Indonesia 84
  reluctance to share military plans with allies 104–5, 220–21
  requests allies for support in Vietnam 96, 106–7, 130, 159, 169, 287
  SEATO member 51
  support for French Indochina 12, 19, 34, 43
United States Air Force 184–85, 206
United States Army
  135th Assault Helicopter Company 184, 213
  173rd Airborne Brigade 128
United States Field Force Commands, II Field Force Vietnam 147, 210
United States Navy, 7th Fleet 184
unit rotation 155
universities, protest movement 164–66, 188
Uren, Tom 250, 297

Van Kiep 241
Vendetta, HMAS 184
veterans 277–84
  counselling service 279, 280–81
  disability pensions 282
  health disorders 279–82, 284
  repatriation 277–79
  welfare 284
Veterans' Compensation Review Committee 282
Viet Cong
  5th Division 145–46, 204
  274 Regiment 145–46, 177, 178, 204
  275 Regiment 145–46, 150, 204
  assassinations by 182
  Battle of Long Tan 150–52
  cadre executed by Saigon police chief 194, *figure*
  D445 Provincial Battalion 145, 150, 172, 205
  guerrilla warfare 226
  infiltration by PAVN soldiers 96
  mine tactics 175
  name 60
  strategies 178
  strength 73
  Tet offensive 189
Viet Minh 10, 11, 32, 34–35, 42, 44, 45, 47, 50, 60, 67
Vietnam
  17th parallel 49
  1956–1960 59
  communism 10–12, 256, 269–70
  French rule 8, 10
  history 8
  independence 32
  international acceptance of two Vietnams 61
  map 145, 174
  partition 49–50
  post-war 269–70
  recognition, international 33, 34
Vietnam: Seen from East and West 141, 142
'Vietnam era' xii, xiii, xiv, 140, 187, 248, 261, 262, 268, 275, 276

Vietnamese Revolution 8–12
Vietnam Independence League *see* Viet Minh
'Vietnamisation' policy 190, 197, 203, 222, 226, 227, 240
Vietnam National Army 43
Vietnam Veterans Against the War 228
Vietnam Veterans Association of Australia 279, 280
Vietnam Veterans Counselling Service 280–81
Vietnam Veterans' Day 151
Vietnam Veterans Federation of Australia 283
Vietnam War
  calls for negotiated settlement 116
  ceasefire 49, 189, 247, 248, 249
  cessation of hostilities 248
  evalutions of 262
  exit strategy 192, 273
  gains 272, 286, 288
  international reactions to 116
  lessons and legacies xii, 261–67, 284–88
  media reports 156, 190
  opposition to *see* anti-war movement
  portrayed as a failure 262
  public opinion 116–17, 122–25, 140–42, 189–90, 191, 201, 230, 250, 262
  turning point 187–217
  'victory' 286
  war of attrition 166–69
Vietnam Workers' Party 11
Vincent, Major General D 'Tim' 154, 211, 297
Vo Nguyen Giap 10, 45, 48, 243, 297
Vung Tau 97, 144, 148–49, 228, *figure*

Walker, Alan 123
Waller, (John) Keith 84, 106, 297, *figure*
war histories, official xiii, xv *see also Official History of Australia's Involvement in Southeast Asian Conflicts 1948–1975*

Warner, Denis Ashton 35, 76–77, 103, 124, 297
war on terror 266–67
Warr, Lieutenant Colonel John 172, 211, *figure*
Weir, Brigadier Stuart 225–26, 297
welcome-home marches 142, 278, 283
Wentworth, WC 47, 193
Westmoreland, General William 116, 128, 154–55, 169, 210, 297
West New Guinea 6, 27, 63–66, 72, 82, 83
West Papua 7
White, Bruce 143
White, William 143, 297
Whitlam, Edward Gough 297
  1969 election 216
  attitude towards refugees 258
  Labor Party Leader 163, 215
  opposition to Vietnam War 215–16
  views on Vietnam War 143–44
  visits China 234
  visits US 251
Whitlam government 245–60
  defence policy 253–54
  dismissal 245, 259, 264
  economic policy 245–46
  flaws 245–46
  foreign policy 248–51, 257, 268
  reforms 246–47
  relations with Asia 269
Willesee, Senator Donald 249, 297
Wilson, Harold 104, 156, 297
Wilton, John Gordon Noel 52, 107–8, 128, 129, 144, 147–48, 153, 198, 220, 298
Windsor, Gerard 204
withdrawal of troops
  American 180, 190, 197, 198, 214, 215, 221, 263
  Australian 198, 215, 216, 220–22, 227, 228, 229–32, 234, 235, 238–39, 246–48
  British 170, 192, 196
Woodard, Garry 97, 267
Woolcott, Richard 160

World War, Second
   postwar period 1, 2, 6, 10, 20

Youth Campaign Against Conscription
   124

Zarb, John 201
Zhou Enlai (Chou En-lai) 49, 234, 298